T0260745

Artificial Intelligent Techniques for Electric and Hybrid Electric Vehicles

Scrivener Publishing
100 Cummings Center, Suite 541J
Beverly, MA 01915-6106

Publishers at Scrivener
Martin Scrivener (martin@scrivenerpublishing.com)
Phillip Carmical (pcarmical@scrivenerpublishing.com)

Artificial Intelligent Techniques for Electric and Hybrid Electric Vehicles

Edited by

Chitra A.,

Department of Energy and Power Electronics, Vellore Institute of Technology,

Vellore, India

P. Sanjeevikumar, Jens Bo Holm-Nielsen

Center for Bioenergy and Green Engineering, Aalborg University, Denmark

and

S. Himavathi

Department of Electrical and Electronics Engineering, Pondicherry Engineering

College, Puducherry, India

Scrivener
Publishing

WILEY

This edition first published 2020 by John Wiley & Sons, Inc., 111 River Street, Hoboken, NJ 07030, USA and Scrivener Publishing LLC, 100 Cummings Center, Suite 541J, Beverly, MA 01915, USA
© 2020 Scrivener Publishing LLC
For more information about Scrivener publications please visit www.scrivenerpublishing.com.

Wiley Global Headquarters
111 River Street, Hoboken, NJ 07030, USA

For details of our global editorial offices, customer services, and more information about Wiley products visit us at www.wiley.com.

Limit of Liability/Disclaimer of Warranty
While the publisher and authors have used their best efforts in preparing this work, they make no representations or warranties with respect to the accuracy or completeness of the contents of this work and specifically disclaim all warranties, including without limitation any implied warranties of merchantability or fitness for a particular purpose. No warranty may be created or extended by sales representatives, written sales materials, or promotional statements for this work. The fact that an organization, website, or product is referred to in this work as a citation and/or potential source of further information does not mean that the publisher and authors endorse the information or services the organization, website, or product may provide or recommendations it may make. This work is sold with the understanding that the publisher is not engaged in rendering professional services. The advice and strategies contained herein may not be suitable for your situation. You should consult with a specialist where appropriate. Neither the publisher nor authors shall be liable for any loss of profit or any other commercial damages, including but not limited to special, incidental, consequential, or other damages. Further, readers should be aware that websites listed in this work may have changed or disappeared between when this work was written and when it is read.

Library of Congress Cataloging-in-Publication Data

ISBN 978-1-119-68190-8

Cover image: Pixabay.Com
Cover design by Russell Richardson

Set in size of 11pt and Minion Pro by Manila Typesetting Company, Makati, Philippines

Printed in the USA

10 9 8 7 6 5 4 3 2 1

Contents

Preface

An emission-free mobility system is the only way to save the world from the greenhouse effect and other ecological issues. This belief has led to a tremendous growth in the demand for electric vehicles (EV) and hybrid electric vehicles (HEV), which are predicted to have a promising future based on the goals fixed by the European Commission's Horizon 2020 program. Consequently, progress can be seen as a result of the huge amount of ongoing research currently being conducted in the emerging EV/HEV sector. Hence, the technology needs to be supported by bringing an academic perspective to industrial demands in order to aid the development of proper documentation to direct this progress.

With this goal in mind, this book brings together the research that has been carried out in the EV/HEV sector and the leading role of advanced optimization techniques with artificial intelligence (AI). This is achieved by compiling the findings of various studies in the electrical, electronics, computer, and mechanical domains for the EV/HEV system. In addition to acting as a hub for information on these research findings, this book also addresses the challenges in the EV/HEV sector and provides proven solutions that involve the most promising AI techniques.

Since the commercialization of EVs/HEVs still remains a challenge in industries in terms of performance and cost, these are the two tradeoffs which need to be researched in order to arrive at an optimal solution. Therefore, this book focuses on the convergence of various technologies involved in EVs/HEVs. Since all countries will gradually shift from conventional internal combustion (IC) engine-based vehicles to EVs/HEVs in the near future, it also serves as a useful reliable resource for multidisciplinary researchers and industry teams.

Among the contributors to this book are those from various esteemed national and international institutions; namely, Tanta University, Egypt; NIT Mizoram, NIT Meghalaya and NIT Pondicherry, India; Anna University Chennai, India; Thiagarajar College of Engineering, Madurai, India; and Vellore Institute of Technology, Vellore, India. I would like to thank all the contributors for their valuable research contributions and time. My sincere thanks to Vellore Institute of Technology for providing all the support necessary to make this book a reality. I would also like to extend my heartfelt gratitude to the Scrivener Publishing team for providing endless support over the course of the compilation of this book.

The Editors
May 2020

IoT-Based Battery Management System for Hybrid Electric Vehicle

P. Sivaraman[1]* and C. Sharmeela[2]

[1]Leading Engineering Organisation, Chennai, India
[2]CEG, Anna University, Chennai, India

Abstract

The basic function of the BMS are to monitoring and control the battery process such as charging and discharging cycle, ensure the healthy condition of the battery, minimizing the risk of battery damaging by ensuring optimized energy is being delivered from the battery to power the vehicle. The use of monitoring circuit in BMS will monitor the key parameters of the battery like voltage, current, temperature during both charging and discharging situation. It estimates the power, State of Charge (SoC), State of Health (SoH) and ensures the healthiness based on the measurement. Balancing the cell is one of the important features of the BMS system. It will monitor the individual cells/group of cells connected in parallel and balancing the cells online. It also conducts the diagnostics of the battery to ensure the safe operation. If, BMS identified any one cell is weak, it will give intimation or alarm for cell replacement. It also provides the protection against overcharging, undercharging, overcurrent, under voltage, short circuit and temperature variations (low and high temperature). In recent years, Internet of Things (IoT) plays a major role in monitoring and control, also it enables the remote data logging facility for battery parameters, conditions, etc.

Keywords: Electric vehicles, hybrid electric vehicles, batteries, internet of things, battery management system, Li-ion batteries, SoC, SoH

1.1 Introduction

Lithium-Ion batteries are widely used in Electric Vehicle (EV) and Hybrid Electric Vehicle (HEV) due to its various advantages over other types of

---

Corresponding author: psivapse@gmail.com

Chitra A, P. Sanjeevikumar, Jens Bo Holm-Nielsen and S. Himavathi (eds.) Artificial Intelligent Techniques for Electric and Hybrid Electric Vehicles, (1–16) © 2020 Scrivener Publishing LLC

batteries. It has the unique feature which requires a Battery Management System (BMS) to actively monitor its parameters and also to ensure the reliable, control and safe operation of battery during their charging/discharging cycle [1, 16].

The basic function of the BMS is to monitor and control the battery process such as charging and discharging cycles, ensure the health condition of the battery, minimizing the risk of battery damaging by ensuring optimized energy is being delivered from the battery to power the vehicle. The monitoring circuit in BMS is used to monitor the key parameters of the battery like voltage, current, temperature at both charging and discharging situations in order to ensure the safe operation. It estimates the power, SoC, SoH and ensures the healthiness based on the measurement [17]. The typical two-wheeler battery SoC status indication is shown in Figure 1.1.

It also monitors the EV and HEV ancillary systems like charger operations, protection and safety devices (fuses and circuit breakers), thermal management, etc. Balancing the cell is one of the important features of the BMS system. It will monitor the individual cells and/or group of cells connected in parallel and balancing the cells online. The diagnostics of the battery is conducted to ensure the safe operation. If BMS identified any one cell is weak, then it will give intimation or alarm for cell replacement. It will also provide the protection against overcharging, undercharging, overcurrent, under voltage, short circuit and tempera\ture variations (both low and high temperatures) [20, 21], i.e. it will provide the signals to protection devices if any

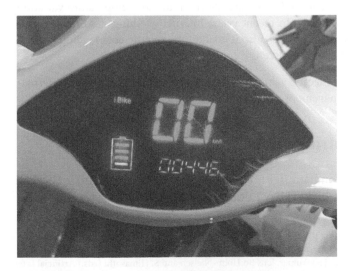

Figure 1.1 Typical-two wheeler SoC status indication.

parameter monitoring value exceeds the pre-set value or threshold value and will give the notification alarm [3, 4, 15]. It will control the charging, power down, power up and it communicates all the parameters to the vehicle [2].

The BMS acts as the interface with other systems of the vehicle like vehicle controller, motor controller, safety system, communication system and climate controller [5, 6]. The two or more numbers of battery strings are connected in parallel to a common DC bus. The BMS shall aggregate the string monitored data and communicate it with the main host system (vehicle master control system) [7, 8]. In recent years, Internet of Things (IoT) plays a major role in monitoring and control of the equipment for reliable and safe operation. IoT also enables the remote data logging facility for battery parameters, battery conditions, etc. [10, 16, 17].

This chapter explains the concept of IoT-based battery management system for EV and HEV.

1.2   Battery Configurations

The battery packs are designed to deliver the higher voltage, higher current or both. The number of cells to be connected in series and number of cells to be connected in parallel is based on the voltage and current requirements to powering the electric motor in the vehicle [13]. The multiple individual cells are connected in series for higher voltage requirement. The battery pack voltage is the product of number of cells connected in series and cell voltage. The typical name plate details of Li-Ion cell are listed in Table 1.1.

Table 1.1 Typical name plate details of Li-Ion cell.

S. No.	Specifications	Value
1	Nominal voltage (V)	3.7
2	Maximum charge voltage (V)	4.2
3	Nominal capacity (mAh)	3,200
4	Maximum charge current (mA)	3,100
5	Maximum charge current C rating	1
6	Standard discharge current (mA)	620
7	Standard discharge current C rating	0.2
8	Maximum discharge current (A)	10

The expression for voltage of the battery pack is given in Equation 1.1.

$$V_{\text{battery pack}} = N_s \times V_{\text{cell}}$$

(1.1)

Where

$V_{\text{battery pack}}$ is voltage of the battery pack
N_s is number of cell connected in series
V_{cell} is cell voltage

Example 1: Calculate the battery pack voltage for 3.7 V, 3,100 mAh, 40 numbers of series connected cells.
The cell voltage is 3.7 V.
No. of cells is 40.
Applying the number of cells and cell voltage in Equation 1.1, the battery pack voltage is 148 V.
The series connection of individual cells is called as Series Cell Modules (SCM) and is shown in Figure 1.2.
For higher current requirement multiple individual cells are connected in parallel. The battery pack current is the product of number of cells connected in parallel and cell current. The expression for current of the battery pack is given in Equation 1.2.

$$I_{\text{battery pack}} = N_p \times I_{\text{cell}}$$

(1.2)

Where

$I_{\text{battery pack}}$ is current of the battery pack
N_p is number of cell connected in parallel
I_{cell} is cell current

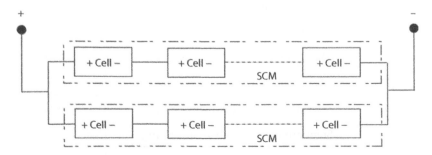

Figure 1.2 Series cell connection.

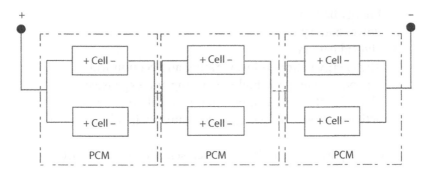

Figure 1.3 Parallel cell connection.

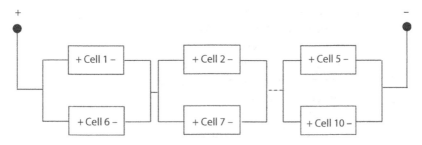

Figure 1.4 Series and parallel cell connection of 2P5S.

Example 2: Calculate the battery pack voltage for 3.7 V, 3,100 mA, 10 numbers of parallel connected cells.

The cell current is 3,100 mA.

No. of cells is 10.

Applying the number of cells and cell current in Equation 1.2, the battery pack current is 31,000 mA or 31 A.

The parallel connection of individual cells is called as Parallel Cell Modules (PCM) is shown in Figure 1.3.

The series and parallel connection of multiple number of cells is used to achieve the desired voltage and/or current. For an example, 2P5S module has the total number of 10 cells with 2 cells in parallel and 5 cells in series. Figure 1.4 shows the series and parallel configuration of 2P5S module.

1.3   Types of Batteries for HEV and EV

The types of battery has to be chosen by considering technical requirements such as power and energy requirements, commercials involved in it [18, 19]. The different types of batteries for HEV and EV are listed below

1. Energy battery
2. Power battery
3. Hybrid battery
   - The energy battery is low C rating and economical.
   - The power battery is higher C rating and expensive.
   - Hybrid battery is a combination of small power battery with active or passive coupling, energy battery with ultra-capacitor.

The important parameters of battery pack selection for HEV are

1. Energy (kWh)
2. Continuous discharge power (kW)
3. Peak discharge power (kW)
4. Continuous charge power (kW)
5. Peak charge power (kW)
6. Storage and ambient temperature
7. No. of charging and discharging cycle
8. Cooling requirements
9. Weight (kg) Safety
10. Disposal/Recycling procedures
11. Mounting direction
12. Dimensions

1.4   Functional Blocks of BMS

The basic function of the BMS is to monitor and control the battery process such as charging and discharging, ensure the health condition of the battery and minimizing the risk of battery from damage. BMS also ensure the optimized energy from the battery is being delivered to power the vehicle.

The monitoring circuit in BMS is used to monitor the key parameters of the battery during both charging and discharging conditions such as

- Voltage
- Current
- Power
- Cell temperature
- Ambient temperature

It estimates the State of Charge (SoC) and Depth of Discharge (DoD) of the battery based on the measurements.

1.4.1   Components of BMS System

The following components are minimum essential for BMS system:

1. Voltage sensor
2. Current sensor
3. Cell temperature sensor
4. Ambient temperature sensor
5. Interface circuits to communicate with vehicle controller
6. Interface circuit to communicate with remote device

A. Voltage Sensor

The battery State of Charge (SoC) and State of Health (SoH) depends on cell voltage. The accuracy of cell voltage measurement plays a major role in estimation of battery SoC and SoH in travel. Inaccurate measurement of every milli voltage has an impact in battery SoC and SoH in travel. The selected/used voltage sensor shall have the better accuracy in cell voltage measurements during charging and discharging time period.

B. Current Sensor

The current sensors are used to measure the current flowing in the circuit i.e., current flow from the charger to battery during the battery charging and current flow from the battery to vehicle electric motor during the discharging. Current measurement of the battery pack is required to ensure the safety during the operation, to log abuse conditions and estimate SoC and SoH. The product of voltage and current is used to find the charging and discharging power in and out to the battery.

The measurement of current by using current sensors is done by two methods which are discussed below:

1. Shunt method
2. Hall effect sensor.

In shunt method, a shunt sensor (high precision resistor) of lower value in milli Ohm is connected in series with battery pack to measure the current flow. The current flow in the circuit is calculated as per Ohms law and given in Equation 1.3.

$$I = \frac{V_{shunt}}{R_{shunt}} \tag{1.3}$$

Where

> I is current flow in A
> V_{shunt} is voltage drop (V) in shunt
> R_{shunt} is shunt resistance in Ω

The typical block diagram showing the measurement of current using shunt is represented in Figure 1.5.

The disadvantages of using shunt sensor for current measurement introduced losses and it generates heat during their entire operation. Heat has to be dissipated properly without affecting the other equipment's performance. The resistance of shunt sensor changing with respect to temperature changes. Shunt resistance has to be calibrated with temperature.

Hall effect sensors or Hall sensors are used to measure the current flow in the circuit by measuring the magnetic field generated by current flowing in a circuit or wire.

The typical block diagram of measurement of current by using hall sensor is shown in Figure 1.6.

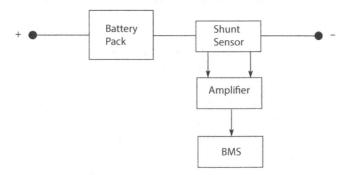

Figure 1.5 Measurement of current by using shunt sensor.

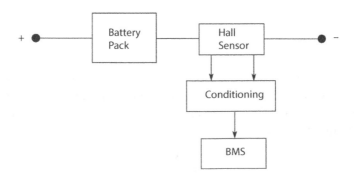

Figure 1.6 Measurement of current by using hall sensor.

C. Cell Temperature Sensor

The battery pack characteristics and degradations during operation are affected by temperature. Sometimes changes in temperature is leading to cell failure. The cell temperature is measured by cell temperature sensor installed in top of the cell. The BMS is measuring the actual temperature on the cell during the charging and discharging time through this cell temperature sensor. The accuracy of the measurement is important in order to find the healthiness of the battery.

D. Ambient Temperature Sensor

The BMS is measuring the actual ambient temperature during the charging and discharging through ambient temperature sensor installed in the battery stack.

E. Interface Circuits to Communicate With Vehicle Controller

All the measured and estimated parameters by BMS like SoC, SoH, power, temperature, etc., are communicated to vehicle controller for user information. Interface circuits are used between the BMS and vehicle controller to transfer the data. From the vehicle display the users understand the SoC, SoH, expected km of driving, nearest charging station through GPS, problems like over temperature in cell, battery under voltage, etc.

F. Interface Circuits to Communicate With Remote Device

This interface circuit enables the monitoring of vehicle parameters such as SoC, SoH, power, battery voltage, cell temperature, etc., from remote location. Various advantages are there for monitoring these parameters in remote devices like storing the history of the vehicle performance, tracking of vehicle location, etc.

G. State of Charge

This State of Charge (SoC) is expressed as the ratio of amount of battery left at measurement time to amount of energy of the battery when it was new. The expression for SoC is given in Equation 1.4.

$$
\begin{aligned}
SoC &= \frac{\text{Amount of energy left at measurement time in the battery}}{\text{Amount of energy of the battery when it was new}} \\
&= \frac{\text{Battery residual AH}}{\text{Battery nominal AH capacity}}
\end{aligned}
\tag{1.4}
$$

The SoC of the battery is estimated based on voltage and Coulomb counting. The SoC, determines the usable capacity that is available for the usage and estimate the vehicle mileage.

H. Depth of Discharge

The Depth of Discharge (DoD) of the battery is defined on the amount of capacity that is discharged from its overall capacity [23, 24]. It also indirectly says the SoC of the battery after the discharge. The DoD is the ratio of discharged energy from the battery to overall energy capacity of the battery. The expression for DoD is given in Equation 1.5.

$$DoD = \frac{\text{Discharged energy from the battery (kWh)}}{\text{Overall energy capacity of the battery (kWh)}} \quad (1.5)$$

Example 1: The battery pack overall capacity is 25 kWh of electric energy and 20 kWh energy is discharged. The DoD is 80%. It means, 80% of 25 kWh energy is discharged and 20% of 25kWh energy is available in the battery.

Example 2: The battery pack overall capacity is 50 AH and battery manufacturer recommending 80% of DoD. What capacity of energy is available to discharge while considering the 80% DoD.

Answer: The energy availability for discharge by considering 80% DoD is calculated from Equation 1.6.

$$\left(\begin{array}{c} \text{Energy availability} \\ \text{from the battery (AH)} \end{array} \right) = \left(\begin{array}{c} \text{Overall energy capacity} \\ \text{of the battery (AH)} \end{array} \right) \times DoD$$

$$= 50 \times 80\% \quad (1.6)$$

Energy availability from the battery (Ah) = 40

The life of the battery depends on charging and discharging cycle of the battery and battery discharge capacity.

I. Cell Diagnostics

During the vehicle operation, any of following things can go wrong and shall lead to performance degradation or failure of equipment:

- Cell over temperature
- Higher current leakage
- Under voltage or over voltage.

The individual cell temperature may exceed the pre-set value during the vehicle operation. In series configurations, voltage variations are widely encountered and in parallel configurations, the leakage current problems are widely encountered. Sometimes these will lead to catastrophic failure of the equipment.

J. Cell Balancing
Li-Ion batteries should not be overcharged for safe operation because overcharging the Li-Ion batteries affects its internal materials. The BMS is monitoring the battery pack voltage actively and cuts off the charger once any one cell reached the threshold value even others cells are not fully charged. Whenever cells are connected in parallel tend to self-balance all the cells that are connected in parallel, i.e., voltage in overcharged cells are balancing the undercharged cells results in self balancing. This cells balancing are classified into two types.

1. Passive cell balancing approach
2. Active cell balancing approach

The passive cell balancing is achieved by depletion of overcharged cells to make the cell Ah capacities to be equal.
The active cell balancing is achieved by diverting the overcharged cells to lesser charged cells to make the cell Ah capacities to be equal.

K. Thermal Management for Battery Pack
The performance of the battery pack is depends on temperature and change in temperature affects the vehicle mileage [22]. The typical operating temperature of the battery pack during on board of the vehicle is 5 to 40°C. If the temperature is high then battery performance is reduced and the temperature is low then battery performance is increased.

1.5 IoT-Based Battery Monitoring System

In general, IoT is a mediator or medium of communication between the various sensors (hardware) and application (software). The important task of IoT is to collect the data from the various hardware using different protocols,

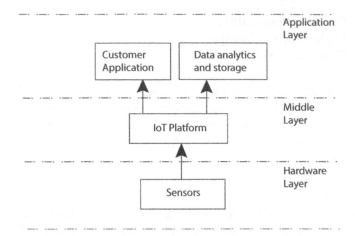

Figure 1.7 General block diagram of IoT based system architecture.

remote location device configuration and its control [9, 11, 12, 14]. The general block diagram of IoT-based system architecture is shown in Figure 1.7.

The voltage sensor, current sensor and temperature sensors are used to measure the battery parameters such as voltage, current, cell temperature and ambient temperature respectively used in the battery management system. The measured parameters are used to estimate the power flow, SoC, SoH, Depth of Discharge (DoD), etc., and communicate to vehicle master controller locally

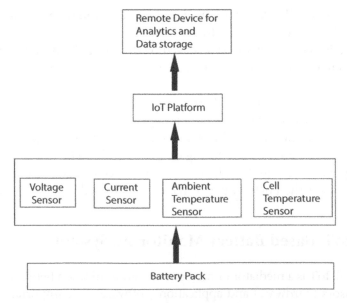

Figure 1.8 Block diagram of IoT based battery monitoring system.

[12, 16, 17]. In an IoT-based system, these measured and estimated parameters are communicated to remote location via wireless communication [27]. The block diagram of IoT-based battery monitoring system is shown in Figure 1.8.

Wireless technology is a broad term. It includes necessary procedures and formats of connection or communication between two or more devices by using wireless signals [26, 27]. In literature, there are different types of wireless technologies that are for monitoring the battery system. They are

1. ZigBee communication
2. Wi-Fi communication
3. GSM communication
4. Bluetooth communication
5. GPRS communication
6. GPS

A. Zigbee Communication
The Zigbee is a wireless communication is based on IEEE standard 802.15.4 and used for connectivity and networking. All the devices available near the vicinity are connected via Zigbee communication. The advantage of Zigbee communications is flexibility in network structure resulting in higher number of devices connectivity. The disadvantage of Zigbee communications are lesser coverage area and not secured network like Wi-Fi.

B. Wi-Fi communication
The Wi-Fi is one of the popular wireless communications used to connect the multiple devices in lesser coverage area [25]. The advantages of Wi-Fi communications are mobility and convenient transfer of data. The disadvantages of Wi-Fi communications are security and connectivity range.

C. Global System for Mobile Communication
Global System for Mobile (GSM) communication is one type of worldwide popular wireless communication [28]. The frequency band for GSM communication is either 900 MHz or 1,800 MHz. The advantages of GSM communication are there are no roaming issues and it can be easy to implement. The disadvantage of GSM communication technology is license to be obtained every time for usage of this technology.

D. Bluetooth Communication
The Bluetooth technology is widely used in mobile phone communication for transferring the data between multiple devices. The main advantage of

Bluetooth technology is that it is interference-free when used to transferring both data and voice for short distance. The disadvantages of Bluetooth technology are they are highly unsecure and have limited connectivity range.

E. General Packet Radio Service Communication

The General Packet Radio Service (GPRS) is one of the wireless communication technologies widely used across the world particularly in mobile phones.

Advantages of GPRS:

- It enables wireless access from any location and anywhere in the network signal coverage
- It enables high-speed data transfer
- It supports various applications
- It provides higher bandwidth and point-to-point services
- The communication via GPRS in cheap as compared with GSM.

Disadvantages of GPRS:

- Limited number of users and also it cannot be used at a time in same location
- Limited in capacity for its users
- Small delay in transfer
- Not possible to use the GPRS outside the network coverage area.

F. Global Positioning System (GPS) Communication

Global Positioning System (GPS) communication technology is satellite-based to transfer the data to GPS receiver across the world [28]. It transfers the signal at speed of light and GPS receiver receives the signal with slightly small difference because of distance between the satellites. The GPS-based system has an accuracy range of ±10 m.

References

1. Basu, A. K. and Bhattacharya, S. (Eds.), *Overview of Electric Vehicles (EVs) and EV Sensors*, Singapore, Springer, 2019.
2. IEEE Standard Technical Specifications of a DC Quick Charger for Use with Electric Vehicles, IEEE 2030.1.1, 2015.

3. Dhameja, S., *Electric Vehicle Battery Systems*, USA, Newnes, 2001.

4. Un-Noor, F., Padmanaban, S., Mihet-Popa, L., Mollah, M.N., Hossain, E., A comprehensive study of key electric vehicle (EV) components, technologies, challenges, impacts, and future direction of development. *Energies*, 10, 1–84, 2017.

5. *Electric Vehicle Conductive Charging system—Part 21: Electric Vehicle Requirements for Conductive Connection to an AC/DC Supply*, IEC 61851-21, 2017.

6. *Electric and Hybrid Vehicle Propulsion Battery System Safety Standard*, SAE J2929-2012.

7. Grunditz, E.A. and Thiringer, T., Performance Analysis of Current BEVs Based on a Comprehensive Review of Specifications. *IEEE Trans. Transp. Electr.*, 2, 270–289, 2016.

8. Chen, H., Su, Z., Hui, Y., Hui, H., Dynamic charging optimization for mobile charging stations in Internet of Things. *IEEE Access*, 6, 53509–53518, 2018.

9. Pattar, S., Buyya, R., Venugopal, K., Iyengar, S.S., Patnaik, L.M., Searching for the IoT resources: Fundamentals, requirements, comprehensive review, and future directions. *IEEE Commun. Surveys Tuts.*, 20, 2101–2132, 2018.

10. Friansa, K., Haq, I. N., Santi, B. M., Kurniadi, D., Leksono, E., Yuliarto, B., Development of Battery Monitoring System in Smart Microgrid Based on Internet of Things (IoT). *Eng. Phys. Int. Conf.*, 170, 484–487, 2016.

11. Atzori, L., Iera, A., Morabito, G., The Internet of Things: A Survey, in: *Comp. Netw.*, 54, 2787–2805, 2010.

12. Gao, D., Zhang, Y., Li, X., The Internet of Things for Electric Vehicles: Wide Area Charging-swap Information Perception, Transmission and Application. *Adv. Mat. Res.*, 1560 -1565, 608–609, 2012.

13. Chon, S. and Beall, J., *Intelligent battery management and charging for electric vehicles*, pp. 1–7, USA, Texas Instruments, 2017.

14. Li, J., Liu, W., Wang, T., Song, H., Li, X., Liu, F., Liu, A., Battery-Friendly Relay Selection Scheme for Prolonging the Lifetimes of Sensor Nodes in the Internet of Things. *IEEE Access*, 7, 33180–33201, 2019.

15. Xing, Y., Ma, E. W. M., Tsui, K. L., Pecht, M., Battery Management Systems in Electric and Hybrid Vehicles. *Energies*, 4, 1840–1857, 2011.

16. Harish, N., Prashal, V., Sivakumar, D., IOT Based Battery Management System. *Int. J. Appl. Eng. Res.*, 13, 5711–5714, 2018.

17. Wahab, M. H. A., Anuar, N. I. M., Ambar, R., Baharum, A., Shanta, S., Sulaiman, M. S., Fauzi, S. S. M., Hanafi, H. F., IoT-Based Battery Monitoring System for Electric Vehicle. *Int. J. of Eng. Technol.*, 7, 505–510, 2018.

18. Piao, C., Liu, Q., Huang, Z., Cho, C., Shu, X., VRLA Battery Management System Based on LIN Bus for Electric Vehicle. *Adv. Technol. Teach.*, 163, 753–763, 2011.

19. Sivaraman, P. and Sharmeela, C., Solar Micro-Inverter, in: *Handbook of research on recent developments in electrical and mechanical engineering*, USA, IGI global publication, Sept 2019.

20. Sivaraman, P. and Sharmeela, C., Existing issues associated with electric distribution system, in: *New solutions and technologies in electrical distribution networks*, USA, IGI global publication, Dec 2019.

21. Sivaraman, P. and Sharmeela, C., Introduction to electric distribution system, in: *New solutions and technologies in electrical distribution networks*, USA, IGI global publication, Dec 2019.

22. Widodo, A., Shim, M.C., Caesarendra, W., Yang, B.-S., Intelligent prognostics for battery health monitoring based on sample entropy. *Expert Syst. Appl.*, 38, 11763–11769, 2011.

23. Zhang, J.L. and Lee, J., A review on prognostics and health monitoring of Li-ion battery. *J. Power Sources*, 19, 6007–6014, 2011.

24. Cheng, K.W.E., Divakar, B.P., Wu, H.J., Ding, K., Ho, H.F., Battery Management System (BMS) and SOC development for electrical vehicles. *IEEE Trans. Veh. Technol.*, 60, 76–88, 2011.

25. Chau, C.K., Qin, F., Sayed, S., Wahab, M., Yang, Y., Harnessing battery recovery effect in wireless sensor networks: Experiments and analysis. *EEE J. Sel. Areas Commun.*, 28, 7, 1222–1232, Sep. 2010.

26. Xiang, X., Liu, W., Xiong, N.N., Song, H., Liu, A., Wang, T., Duty cycle adaptive adjustment based device to device (D2D) communication scheme for WSNs. *IEEE Access*, 6, 76339–76373, 2018.

27. Teng, H., Liu, Y., Liu, A., Xiong, N.N., Cai, Z., Wang, T., Liu, X., A novel code data dissemination scheme for Internet of Things through mobile vehicle of smart cities. *Future Gener. Comput. Syst.*, 94, 351–367, May 2019.

28. Zhou, H., Wang, H., Li, X., Leung, V.C.M., A survey on mobile data offloading technologies. *IEEE Access*, 6, 5101–5111, 2018.

2

A Noble Control Approach for Brushless Direct Current Motor Drive Using Artificial Intelligence for Optimum Operation of the Electric Vehicle

Upama Das[1*], Pabitra Kumar Biswas[1] and Chiranjit Sain[2]

[1]Department of Electrical and Electronics Engineering, National Institute of Technology Mizoram, Chaltlang, Aizawl, India
[2]Department of Electrical Engineering, National Institute of Technology Meghalaya, Bijni Complex, Laitumukhrah, Shillong, Meghalaya, India

Abstract

Different electric motors have been used as electric vehicle propulsion schemes. As conventional sources are scarce, electric vehicles are emerging nowadays as an alternative solution for transportation. These are the most elegant green transport option, that takes very less power, and possesses high-speed operation compared to conventional vehicles. BLDC motors are suggested for use in an electric vehicle for high-speed noiseless operation, and the absence of brushes makes it almost maintenance-free. Vehicles carry the load for a specific distance within a particular time. And so, the speed and torque control are necessary to reach the destination with minimum expenditure. The less cost of semiconductor devices makes the supply section very economical for BLDC motor. Different control techniques, classical and artificial intelligence controllers, are preferred to control the BLDC motor based electric vehicles. Classical controllers have many benefits, but has a drawback of failure in optimizing system efficiency. Advances in artificial intelligence applications like fuzzy-logic control, neural-network, genetic-algorithm, have substantially affected electric motor drives by providing optimal control. These different AI methods for PMBLDC motor drive are discussed in this chapter to provide guidance and fast reference to readers and engineers researching in the field of an electric vehicle.

Corresponding author: upama.eee@nitmz.ac.in

Chitra A, P. Sanjeevikumar, Jens Bo Holm-Nielsen and S. Himavathi (eds.) Artificial Intelligent Techniques for Electric and Hybrid Electric Vehicles, (17–48) © 2020 Scrivener Publishing LLC

Keywords: Electric vehicle, BLDC motor drive, classical controller, artificial intelligence-based controllers, close loop control

2.1   Introduction

Electric vehicles are more competent than internal combustion vehicles. So, we are proposing more electric vehicles than conventional cars. In this system, the idea of retrofitting traditional vehicles to electric vehicles is proposed. A BLDC motor drive and its controller can be implemented as per the weight and torque specifications on existing standard vehicles, which will reduce the cost. BLDC motor has high torque, high efficiency, reduced noise, smooth speed control, and longer lifetime. As the name suggests, the brushless dc motor does not have brushes, and they are commutated electronically. These motors are also known for their high durability due to simplicity in design and high rpm capabilities. They have applications in both small and large industries. The motor is controlled by a controller with the assist of the view of the rotor location. For sensing the rotor location, certain types of controllers employ magnetic sensors or revolving encoders.

In some cases, the sensorless technique is used to detect the position by knowing the back emf of the BLDC motor. It contains three output terminals, and logic circuits operate these. Advanced systems use a microcontroller to manage an increase in velocity and speed.

The lead-acid battery energizes the brushless direct current motor. Accelerator consists of a varistor. The varistor output wills according to the acceleration, and this output is provided to the controller. The signal from the accelerator is the reference signal. The speed sensors placed in the BLDC motor offer the information of the real rpm of the motor. These two signals are compared in the controller, and the power output from the chopper drive is varied. The signal from the chopper is given back to the motor. According to the output from the chopper drive, the motor speed can be controlled.

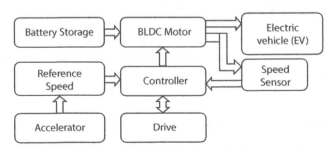

Figure 2.1 The central control block diagram of BLDC Motor Drive.

The central control block diagram of BLDC Motor Drive operated electric vehicle is shown in Figure 2.1.

2.2   Introduction of Electric Vehicle

One or more than one powerful electric motor is placed in an electric vehicle. BLDC motor is a trendy choice for EV impulsion. An electric vehicle can be supplied by a battery, solar panels, or electrical generator [1]. EVs are not limited to road vehicles like trains, cars, and buses, and they also include off-road transport like submarines, and surface vessels, electric aircraft, and spaceship. From the mid-19th century, the EVs first came into existence as electricity was then the most preferred for the impulsion for motor vehicles. These electric cars were also providing a great comfort level, and their operation was also easy compared to the gasoline cars of that time. For so many past decades, internal combustion engines are considered to be the best suited for the transportation system. But electric power-operated vehicles like the train and small vehicles also exist parallelly. In the 21st century, as technology advanced and even the awareness for the non-conventional source of energy increased, the EVs are now a new revolution. The do-it-yourself (DIY) engineers started working on it, and Federal programs are also implemented to increase this EV technology. It is projected that in the near future, EVs will replace most of the IC engine vehicles.

2.2.1   Historical Background of Electric Vehicle

A Hungarian priest, Ányos Jedlik, designed the primary electric vehicle with an electric motor in 1827 [2]. A few years down the line, in 1835, the minor-range EV was built by Dr. Sibrandus Stratingh, and Dr. Robert Anderson invented the electric carriage powered by non-rechargeable primary cells between 1832 and 1839. Early experimental electric cars were moving on rail tracks around the same period. In 1838, an electric locomotive was designed by a Scotsman named Robert Davidson. The first large scale production of the electric vehicle was done in America in the 1900s. After the advancement of cheap IC engine base cars by Ford, the electric vehicles were not used by the collective [3]. Lack of power storage arrangement, i.e., battery at that time, was the limitation of electric vehicles. Still, the electric train was very much accepted. Later in the 20th century, the United Kingdom encouraged the use of electric vehicles, and it was the most significant user at that time. Those days EV was used to do specialist roles such as chassis trucks, ambulances, forklifts, tractors, and domestic food supply. Lack of natural fossil resources forced the rapid growth of electric trains in Switzerland. After the invention of rechargeable batteries by Edison, a massive percentage of cars in the USA were electric. As the road infrastructure improved and the availability of substantial petrochemical reservoirs in different states like Texas, Oklahoma, and California, resulted in the mass growth of cheap affordable internal combustion-driven cars compare to EVs to operate over long distances [4].

2.2.2   Advantages of Electric Vehicle

The advantages of implying electric vehicles are discussed below.

2.2.2.1   *Environmental*

No tailpipe air emissions are emitted at the location where EVs power them. Usually, they also produce less pollution in terms of noise than a vehicle with an IC engine, in standstill or motion. The use of electric vehicles will have an immensely positive effect on the environment, except those countries that depend on coal-based thermal power plants for power generation [5, 6]. In Nepal, a distinct type of electric vehicle is invented, which helps to control the pollution created by other vehicles. A survey by Cambridge Econometrics shows that the EVs can minimize air pollution at such a rate that by 2050, the European countries will reduce 88% of CO_2 emissions from cars. Millions of tons of toxic nitrogen oxides (NOx) will be removed from the environment per year by implementing EV technology.

2.2.2.2   *Mechanical*

They can convert energy back into stored electricity from movement like the regenerative braking systems. These vehicles are effortless, and they can utilize the full energy, which is converted to get the required speed and torque precisely [7]. This can be used to minimize the wear of the brake system and diminish the overall energy demand of a tour. Since BLDC engines are used to operate EVs, they are capable of providing noiseless and smooth and vibration-free operation compare to internal combustion engines [8].

2.2.2.3   *Energy Efficiency*

The tank to wheel efficiency of an electric vehicle is better than ICE vehicles, and electric vehicles do not consume fuel while stationary compare to internal combustion engines. However, considering the well-to-wheel efficiency, which is less but still, the total emission of EVs is lesser compared to conventional gasoline or diesel-based cars [9–12].

Well-to-wheel ability mainly depends on the method of electricity production. In the total lifecycle of EVs and diesel vehicles, EVs produce lesser greenhouse gases [13].

2.2.2.4 Cost of Charging Electric Vehicles

In different places, the cost of running an EV is different, as it mostly depends on the availability of fuel in that place. In some countries, the cost of fuel is so high that people prefer electric vehicles in comparison to conventional vehicles. In the USA, the fuel cost of an electric vehicle is more than the gas-powered vehicles because of their block rate tariff of electricity. A survey on electricity consumption was conducted by Purdue University, where it was found that the majority of users in California are already paying in the third price tier for electricity each month. And so, merging electric vehicles will increase energy consumption, which will lead them to the fourth tier of power. Due to this increment, they have to pay $0.45 per kWh extra to give supply to their vehicles. A block rate tariff system aims to minimize the consumption or to save electricity. According to the author, Tyner, these electric vehicles are not feasible under this block rate tariff system [14].

2.2.2.5 The Grid Stabilization

As EVs can be attached to the electrical grid when not being used, lead acid-powered vehicles have the ability to even bring down the requirement for electricity by injecting power from their storage into the network through times of high usage thereby carrying out most of their loading at night when the generating capacity is not used [15]. Our present power generating system may need to mix-up through the variable non-conventional power sources such as wind and solar photovoltaic. These will require massive processing and loading capacity that could be exploited to change charging speeds and production energy during times of scarcity.

2.2.2.6 Range

The traveling distance range is shorter in the case of the electric vehicle compared to internal combustion engines. Though the running cost of EVs is decreasing still, it needs to charge or re-fuel very often. It is not convenient to charge the vehicle repeatedly when traveling, and so, many consumers prefer to charge their vehicle at home as it has a longer charging period.

2.2.2.7   Heating of EVs

In the winter season, EVs need much more energy to increase the temperature inside the vehicle and also to defrost the car windows. In the IC engines, due to the combustion process, the interior of the vehicle already remains heated. The EVs are using batteries to provide energy to all the sections of the car, so, to give this much heat, it needs a high rating of cells. Otherwise, in the case of ordinary rating batteries, there will be extra pressure for this energy requirement for heating. The electric vehicles can be preheated or cooled, with little or no need for battery energy while taking power from the grid, especially for short trips.

In newly approved designs, the passenger's body heat is used with the super-insulated cabins that can warm the car. The most economical and feasible way is to implement a heat pump system to solve the EV's thermal management. The system is capable of reducing the heat inside the vehicle during the summer and increase the heat during the winter. Ricardo Arboix (2008) established a new theory of using a heat pump system combining with EV-battery and cabin thermal management. To implement this theory in EV models, a heat exchanger is thermally connected with the traditional air conditioning module, which is supplied by the battery. The system has extended the battery life and overall performance of electric vehicles [16].

2.2.3   Artificial Intelligence

The ability to execute tasks usually related to intelligent beings by computer-based logical operations is called artificial intelligence. The word is often functional to the development assignment of systems capable of human characteristic consistent processes like the talent to realize the sense, simplify, or be trained from prior knowledge. The progress of digital computers enhances the power of computers, which can be carried out to derive different types of mathematical models or playing brain games like an expert. But still, there is no comparison of the human brain as no computer program can do a task over broader provinces or in responsibilities requiring common familiarity.

The British logician and computer pioneer Alan Mathison Turing carried out the first significant effort in the area of AI in the middle of the 20th century. In 1935 Turing described a conceptual computer machine composed of an infinite memory and a scanner moving back and forward in the course of memories, character by character, interpreting what it gets, and writing additional symbols. The scanner's actions are instructed by an instruction program that is also stored as symbols in the memory. This is the stored-program principle of Turing, and it means the ability for the computer to work on its data and thus modify or enhance it [17].

2.2.4   Basics of Artificial Intelligence

AI is the ability of a control process to suitably understand peripheral values, do proper training and study of the past statistics, and utilizes this in implementing precise goals and tasks through flexible alteration. In an AI control, the working condition or the environment is analyzed, and proper action is taken to enhance its rate of success. The utility function intended for an AI can be simple or complex. Objectives can be described or induced directly. If the AI is designed to "reinforce training," goals can be directly triggered by encouraging some behavioral styles or punishing others. Alternatively, by determining a "fitness function" to transform and favorably imitate better effective AI systems. An evolution-based AI system can encourage goals, similar to how animals evolved to innately desire specific purposes, such as finding food [18].

AI has provided an enormous opportunity and scope for electrical automation and is bringing a grand change in the economic point of view as well as in organizational security and practical power. Ever since the advancement of AI, it has achieved a remarkable effect on the field of automotive electrical control and all other areas of life. Its appearance has even shown out the direction for many fields to develop. AI in engineering has dramatically advanced the practice of physical, electrical automation, and it should be given complete consideration by related companies and staff [19, 20].

In the electrical field, electric vehicle control plays a crucial role. When monitoring is obtained, output performance can be efficiently enhanced, increasing fabrication expenses and other resources. The purpose of AI is mainly focused on a fuzzy and neural network-based controller in electric vehicle control. Artificial intelligence in automation development can promote innovations and overall progress in electrical vehicle control. In contrast, power system malfunction will be omitted, encouraging the relentless advancement of artificial intelligence software, forming a new path in electric vehicle control, through the concept of all facets of smart engineering implementation, allowing common existing conditions to start to improve [21].

2.2.5   Advantages of Artificial Intelligence in Electric Vehicle

The idea of design AI control is not complicated. The typical conventional controller requires to consider the control gains according to the process plant. Still, there are typically other unpredictable variables in the system creation, such as adjusting parameters and numerical form, to make the system more complicated. AI management is not involved, so the object design not required to be controlled by the AI feature approximator. Results can be improved rapidly by properly adjusting related parameters. The fuzzy logic controller, for example, responds more quickly, and the percentage overshoot becomes very less. It's easier to employ. The controller of AI is more accessible to fiddle with the standard controller and is flexible to the adaptation of new parameters or new sequences. The conventional control system is designed for a definite object, so the control action is perfect only for a distinct purpose. Still, it is not consistent with the effect of other control objects. The artificial intelligence control algorithm can obtain a reasonable estimate of consistency, whether for the particular or unfamiliar contribution of data.

2.3   Brushless DC Motor

A brushless DC electric motor is an electronically switched synchronous DC motors, which are supplied by direct current via an inverter which produces a sequential electrical current to drive the motor through a control-loop. The controller maintains the required output of the motor by giving an exact energizing pulse to the stator winding. The BLDC motor and PMSM has an almost identical construction. Comparing to conventional brushed motors brushless motor have electronic control which provides high torque-to-weight ratio, high speed, increased proficiency, improved performance, condensed noise, longer service life (no brush and switch erosion) which means and the maintenance cost is very less, elimination of switching ionizing sparks, an overall reduction of electromagnetic interference (EMI). Instead of brushes, switching to electronics allows greater flexibility and non-existent capabilities. These motors are used in the cd drive, printer, hand-operated power tools, and aircraft, spaceship. The conventional brushed motor came into existence during the early 19th century. Whereas BLDC motor was possible to develop after the availability of solid-state devices in the 1960s [22, 23].

The semi-conductor electronics development in the 1970s enabled the elimination of the switch and brushes in DC motors [25–27]. Their working life is very long as there is no friction loss due to the absence of brushes and only need to take care of the bearing arrangement. Though BLDC motors can solve certain drawbacks of brushed motors, it still has some disadvantages of less robust, more complex, and costly electronic console. A conventional brushless motor has a rotating magnetic field that spins around a static armature. An electrical regulator replaces the brushed DC motor's brush/commutator unit, which periodically changes the stage to the windings to maintain the motor spinning by using electronic power elements [28].

Higher temperature weakens the permanent magnets and the isolation of the winding of BLDC motor, and so the performance and efficiency of a brushless motor are limited by heat. Still, these motors are more efficient than conventional motors when converting electricity into mechanical power because of the speed at which the input from the position sensor decides the energy transformation. The enhanced efficiency is most exceptional in the performance curve of the engine's no-load and low-load region. When applied to a high mechanical load, both the BLDC motor and the high-quality brushed motors are equal. A stepper and a BLDC motor have almost the same construction. But the differences are in operation as BLDC motor does not produce rotation in step, and stepper motors do not need a position sensor for detecting rotor location. It is also possible to hold a well-designed brushless motor system at zero rpm and finite torque. Brushless motors are superior to the brushed motors but still because of the complexity of control arrangement, and the overall expenditure avoids the BLDC motors from completely substituting conventional motors in several zones. Yet, many applications have been dominated by brushless motors, especially CD/DVD and hard drives, fans for cooling in electronic appliances, and in cordless power tools. BLDC motors of Low speed, low power configuration are used for gramophone recording in direct drive turntables. For electric vehicles, hybrid vehicles, and private transporters, brushless motors can be used. Many electric bicycles and RC models use brushless motors like the same principle of self-balancing scooter wheels, which are sometimes mounted in the wheel hub and the stator connected to the axle and the magnets placed on the revolving wheel [29].

2.4   Mathematical Representation Brushless DC Motor

Before proceeding the control part, it is vital to find the governing equations of the system and then establish the mathematical model of the system. The three-phase synchronous machine and the BLDC motor has the same mathematical model supplied by Voltage Source Inverter as shown in Figure 2.2. Though the presence of a permanent magnet rotor in the BLDC motor makes the dynamic characteristics different. The permanent magnet cylindrical rotor is used to makes the air gap uniform. The dynamic equations of phase voltages of three-phase star connected stator are mentioned below:

$$V_{an} = r_s + L_s \frac{dI_a}{dt} + M_s \frac{dI_b}{dt} + M_s \frac{dI_c}{dt} + E_a \qquad (2.1)$$

$$V_{bn} = r_s + L_s \frac{dI_b}{dt} + M_s \frac{dI_c}{dt} + M_s \frac{dI_a}{dt} + E_b \qquad (2.2)$$

$$V_{cn} = r_s + L_s \frac{dI_c}{dt} + M_s \frac{dI_b}{dt} + M_s \frac{dI_a}{dt} + E_c \qquad (2.3)$$

Where, L_s = armature self-inductance.
   M_s = armature mutual inductance.
   r_s = armature resistance.
   V_{an}, V_{bn}, and V_{cn} and are the phase voltages at the terminal.
   I_a, I_b and I_c are motor input currents.
   E_a, E_b, E_c are motor back-EMF.

The nature of flux distribution is trapezoidal in BLDC motor; due to this, the applicability of the d-q reference model prepared for PMSM becomes invalid. As the delivery of flux is trapezoidal, i.e., non-sinusoidal, it is wise to develop a phase variables model for PMBLDCM. The development of this phase variables model requires certain assumptions which are as follows:

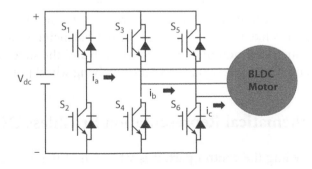

Figure 2.2 VSI fed BLDC Motor.

i.   Iron and stray losses are not taken into account.
ii. The currents induced in rotor because harmonic fields of the stator are dismissed.
iii. Inverter Control gives proper damping to the machine.

The BLDC motor model can be utilized for three phases. Still, based on the procedure of derivation, it is acceptable for the desired multiple phases. The stator's voltage equations are depicted below:

$$
\begin{bmatrix} V_{an} \\ V_{bn} \\ V_{cn} \end{bmatrix} = \begin{bmatrix} r_s & 0 & 0 \\ 0 & r_s & 0 \\ 0 & 0 & r_s \end{bmatrix} \begin{bmatrix} I_{an} \\ I_{bn} \\ I_{cn} \end{bmatrix} + \frac{d}{dt} \begin{bmatrix} l_{aas} & l_{abs} & l_{acs} \\ l_{bas} & l_{bbs} & l_{bcs} \\ l_{cas} & l_{cbs} & l_{ccs} \end{bmatrix} \begin{bmatrix} I_a \\ I_b \\ I_c \end{bmatrix} + \begin{bmatrix} E_{as} \\ E_{bs} \\ E_{cs} \end{bmatrix}
$$

$$(2.4)$$

Here r_s are the per phase stator resistance and identical for all phases.

$$ E_p = (B1V) N = N(B1r\omega) = N\phi_a \omega = \lambda_p \omega \qquad (2.5) $$

In equation (2.5), N = Number of conductors arranged in series per phase, V = velocity, 1 = Conductor length, r = Rotor bore radius, ω = Angular velocity, B = Flux density.

The multiplication of (BLr) depicts ϕ_a which consists of dimensions similar to the flux, and it has direct proportionality with the air-gap flux, ϕ_g which is expressed below.

$$ \phi_a = Blr = \frac{1}{\pi} B\pi lr = \frac{1}{\pi}\phi_g $$

$$(2.6)$$

For the balanced condition, the summation of phase currents of the stator is considered to be zero, which provides simplified inductance matrix as follows:

$$
\begin{bmatrix} V_{an} \\ V_{bn} \\ V_{cn} \end{bmatrix} = \begin{bmatrix} r_s & 0 & 0 \\ 0 & r_s & 0 \\ 0 & 0 & r_s \end{bmatrix} \begin{bmatrix} I_{an} \\ I_{bn} \\ I_{cn} \end{bmatrix} + \begin{bmatrix} (L_s - M_s) & 0 & 0 \\ 0 & (L_s - M_s) & 0 \\ 0 & 0 & (L_s - M_s) \end{bmatrix} \frac{d}{dt} \begin{bmatrix} I_a \\ I_b \\ I_c \end{bmatrix} + \begin{bmatrix} E_{as} \\ E_{bs} \\ E_{cs} \end{bmatrix}
$$

$$(2.7)$$

The electromagnetic torque of the machine is

$$T_e = [E_{as} I_{as} + E_{bs} I_{bs} + E_{cs} I_{cs}] \frac{1}{\omega_m} \left(\text{N} - \text{m} \right) \tag{2.8}$$

The spontaneously incited emfs are composed as follows.

$$e_{as} = f_{as} (\theta_r) \lambda_p \omega \tag{2.9}$$

$$e_{bs} = f_{bs} (\theta_r) \lambda_p \omega \tag{2.10}$$

$$e_{cs} = f_{cs} (\theta_r) \lambda_p \omega \tag{2.11}$$

The functions $f_{as} (\theta_r), f_{bs} (\theta_r)$ and $f_{cs} (\theta_r)$ shown in Equations (2.9), (2.10) and (2.11) have an identical shape as of $e_{as}\ e_{bs}\ e_{cs}$, with the positive peak as +1 and negative peak as −1. The electromagnetic torque, after incorporating the above functions, is

$$T_e = \lambda_p [f_{as} (\theta_r)\ i_{as} + f_{bs} (\theta_r),\ i_{bs} + f_{cs} (\theta_r),\ i_{cs}] \text{(N–m)} \tag{2.12}$$

The reason for naming this machine as a DC machine is that the phase voltage equation of the BLDC motor and armature voltage equation of the DC machine is identical. The motion equation is as follows:

$$J \frac{d\omega}{dt} + B\omega = (T_e - T_l) \tag{2.13}$$

Where, J = Inertia, B = Friction co-efficient and T_l = Load Torque. The relationship between speed and position of the rotor is depicted by

$$\frac{d\theta_r}{dt} = \frac{P}{2} \omega \tag{2.14}$$

Joining all the pertinent conditions the framework in state equation structure is

$$\dot{x} = Ax + Bu \tag{2.15}$$

Where,

$$x = [I_{as}\ I_{bs}\ I_{cs}\ \omega\ \theta_r]^t \tag{2.16}$$

$$A = \begin{bmatrix} \dfrac{-r_s}{L_{1s}} & 0 & 0 & -\dfrac{\lambda_p}{L_{1s}}f_{as}(\theta_r) & 0 \\[3mm] 0 & \dfrac{-r_s}{L_{1s}} & 0 & -\dfrac{\lambda_p}{L_{1s}}f_{bs}(\theta_r) & 0 \\[3mm] 0 & 0 & \dfrac{-r_s}{L_{1s}} & -\dfrac{\lambda_p}{L_{1s}}f_{cs}(\theta_r) & 0 \\[3mm] \dfrac{\lambda_p}{J}f_{as}(\theta_r) & \dfrac{\lambda_p}{J}f_{bs}(\theta_r) & \dfrac{\lambda_p}{J}f_{cs}(\theta_r) & \dfrac{-B}{J} & 0 \\[3mm] 0 & 0 & 0 & \dfrac{P}{2} & 0 \end{bmatrix} \tag{2.17}$$

$$B = \begin{bmatrix} \dfrac{1}{L_{1s}} & 0 & 0 & 0 \\[3mm] 0 & \dfrac{1}{L_{1s}} & 0 & 0 \\[3mm] 0 & 0 & \dfrac{1}{L_{1s}} & 0 \\[3mm] 0 & 0 & 0 & -\dfrac{1}{J} \\[3mm] 0 & 0 & 0 & 0 \end{bmatrix} \tag{2.18}$$

Where,
$$L1_s = L_s - M_s \tag{2.19}$$

$$u = [V_{as}\ V_{bs}\ V_{cs}\ T_1]^t \tag{2.20}$$

The variable θ_r, i.e., rotor position, is necessary to get the value of the function as mentioned above.

2.5   Closed-Loop Model of BLDC Motor Drive

As the open-loop system is more stable than the closed-loop system hence making the close loop BLDC drive as shown in Figure 2.3 more durable, as per the desired application, the different types of the controller, along with the converter topology, are used. The inner loop of the drive consists magnetic sensor, which is used to provide the information about the rotor position of the BLDC drive, and based on that information; the gate signal generator generates the commutating signals for three-phase VSI. The triggering pulse used for the converter is the back EMF of the motor, which is coming from the particular position of the rotor. Gate signal generator includes the back EMF generator and gate logic decoder, and the combined effect of these two signals along with the reference signal generates the triggering pulses.

The electronic commutation provides the rotor and stator of BLDC motor to run at the same frequency, and that is why it is called one type of synchronous motor. The system is powered with voltage source inverter/switching power supply, which can be a universal bridge [30]. The controller consists of a power converter in which three-phase VSI works as a brush of BLDC motor and to operate the VSI different types of converters like bidirectional converter, CUCK converters, SEPIC converters are used. These converters handle the power and power factor requirement of the drive. Along with the converters, the system consists of the BLDC motor, magnetic sensor, and different types of control algorithms [48–50]. There are different command signals like torque, voltage, speed, the current, which are used to generate the control signal for the system. The two main types of more popular drives are voltage source and current source based BLDC motor drive [31–33].

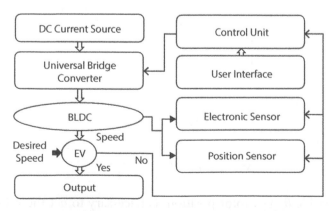

Figure 2.3 The overall model of BLDC motor for EV.

2.5.1   P-I Controller & I-P Controller

Both the controllers, P-I and I-P, as shown in Figures 2.4 and 2.5, respectively, minimizes the steady-state error of a process, but the P-I controller takes less time [24, 32–35].

The closed-loop transfer function of the P-I and I-P controller is given by Equations (2.21) and (2.22) respectively,

$$\frac{C(s)}{R(s)} = \frac{K_m\left(sK_p + K_i\right)}{T_m s^2 + \left(1 + K_m K_p\right)s + K_m K_i} \qquad (2.21)$$

$$\frac{C(s)}{R(s)} = \frac{K_i K_m}{T_m s^2 + \left(1 + K_m K_p\right)s + K_i K_m} \qquad (2.22)$$

Where the output and the input signal are represented by C(S) and R(S) respectively, K_i and K_p are the integral and proportional gains, K_m and T_m is the mechanical gain and time constant of the motor drive. The transfer function considering the load torque is represented by Equation (2.23).

$$\frac{C(s)}{T_l(s)} = \frac{s\left(1 + sT_m\right)}{T_m K_p s^2 + \left(K_m + T_m K_i + K_p\right)s + K_i} \qquad (2.23)$$

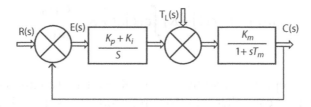

Figure 2.4 Transfer function representation of P-I controller.

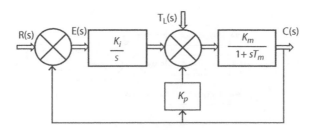

Figure 2.5 Transfer function representation of I-P controller.

It is seen from the above transfer functions that both the controllers have the same characteristic equations. Still, zero is added in the case of the IP controller. Therefore, for a step input, the over-shoot is less for the I-P controller.

2.6   PID Controller

The fast development of science and technology requires a system which has higher response speed higher control accuracy and higher stability, and PID controller is one of the latest control strategies in which traditional PID controller is used to controlling all the model of linear processes. The general representation of the PID controller is shown below in Figure 2.6. However, most of the industrial processes are not linear; some procedures are complex or unable to establish an arithmetical representation at the same time, so the common control of PID cannot accurately run such processes [36]. For its simplicity and robustness, the Classic PID control technique is used. The theory of PID control is to define additive, integrative, and differential controls.

$$e\ (t) = x(t) - y(t) \tag{2.24}$$

The PID controller is represented by the Equation (2.25), given below:

$$u(t) = K_p e(t) + K_I \int_0^t e(t)dt + K_D \frac{de(t)}{dt} \tag{2.25}$$

Where, K_p = Proportional controller gain, K_I = Integral controller gain, and K_D = Differential controller gain. The proportional link in the PID controller is used to replicate the deviated signal. If a deviation is present, then it can reduce the deviation of the signal from the original one. The integral

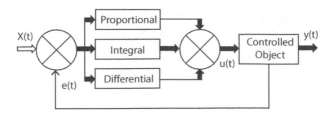

Figure 2.6 Schematic of a PID controller.

part minimizes or removes the steady-state error, and the differential part may reveal the changing tendency of the deviation signal. Before the increment of the deviation, the derivative controller introduces a sufficient correction factor, speeds up the system's action, reduces the adjustment time. The problem with the classical controller is the appropriate selection of these gain parameters for the process plant. Different types of PID gain tuning methods are there, such as trial and error, Ziegler–Nichols methods, genetic algorithm techniques.

2.7   Fuzzy Control

BLDC drive operation is controlled in two ways; torque is the first, and speed is the second. These two parameters are controlled simultaneously by the fuzzy logic controllers. The first loop contains two loops with current control, and the second loop contains or adjusts the BLDC drive speed [37–44]. Fuzzy linguistic logic is expressed in the form of rules of If and Then. These laws specify the set of values known as the fuzzy membership function. Figure 2.7 demonstrates various types of blurry membership apps.

For fuzzy logic control system models, the most important things are the selection of membership functions for inputs and outputs and based on these the design of if–then law, i.e., the fuzzy rule base. A membership function represents the degree of each input's involvement in a graphical way. Every input and output response may have separate membership functions. Instead of mathematical equations, Fuzzy logic presents functional linguistic laws [45–49]. Most processes are too complicated for effective simulation, even with advanced approaches in this process being unfeasible. However, the linguistic term of fuzzy logic provides a feasible method to define such a system's operational characteristics. The overall fuzzy logic system is shown in Figure 2.8. Fuzzyfier, inference, and de-fuzzyfier become the three traits of abstract controllers. The number of membership functions determines the superiority of control by using a fuzzy controller, and the control quality depends on the number of membership functions.

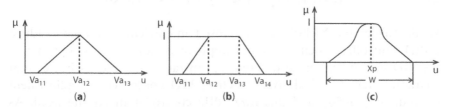

Figure 2.7 (a) Triangle, (b) trapezoid, and (c) bell membership functions.

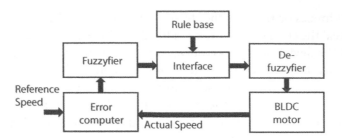

Figure 2.8 General Fuzzy logic controller.

Table 2.1 Rule base of fuzzy logic controller.

P1/P2	NB	NM	NS	Z	PS	PM	PB
NB	PB	PB	PM	PM	PS	PS	Z
NM	PB	PM	PM	PS	PS	Z	NS
NS	PM	PM	PS	PS	Z	NS	NS
Z	PM	PS	PS	Z	NS	NS	NM
PS	PS	PS	Z	NS	NS	NM	NM
PM	PS	Z	NS	NS	NM	NM	NB
PB	Z	NS	NS	NM	NM	NB	MB

Therefore, to choose the number of functions, an adjustment must be considered between the quality and the computational time of control for the evaluation of the closed-loop control of BLDC motor drive. To describe the functions, seven linguistic variables are used for both input and output variables. Table 2.1 displays the membership function logic rule base. From this table, it can be found that the combinations of two inputs, p1 and p2, provides different outputs like NB, PB, NM, NS, Z, PM, PS, MB. These outputs decide the different control actions of the system.

2.8 Auto-Tuning Type Fuzzy PID Controller

While Ziegler and Nichols have proposed an efficient technique to adjust a PID controller's coefficients and improve performance by optimizing the PID parameters using different optimization techniques but cannot guarantee that it will always be active, PID controller self-adjustment is required [50–56], and this fuzzy-PID controller meets the need. As shown in Figure 2.9, the controller consists of two parts: the traditional

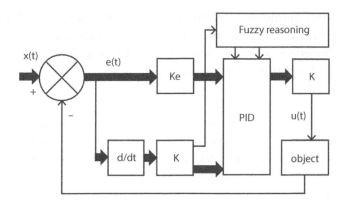

Figure 2.9 Block representation of the Auto-tuning type Fuzzy PID control system.

PID controller and the self-tuning Fuzzy Logic Control (FLC) part. Now the PID controller's control operation after self-tuning can be defined as a self-tuning Fuzzy PID controller. Using the fuzzy rules to modify the online PID parameters where we are a blurred self-tuning PID controller [57–61]. Here the error and the error shift frequency are denoted by e and ec, respectively. The terms Ke and kec are quantitative variables, ku is the ranking factor from all dimensions of the system, i.e., the stability, response rate, over-shoot, and stable system failure and the function of PID controller gains are as follows [62].

The proportional gain K_p was designed to speed up the system reaction time and increase the system's regulatory accuracy. However, the harder it is to overshoot the more extensive system by K_p, or even volatile the system. The price of K_p is too small. It reduces the accuracy of the regulation so that the response is slowed down, thereby extending the system's regulatory time, static and dynamic characteristics. So, the derivative controller K_d is designed to improve these dynamic characteristics, mainly reduces the change in error in any direction in response to the process before the error occurs. K_d advances the brake response process and so the regulatory time extends, which reduces the system's anti-jamming performance.

2.9   Genetic Algorithm

A genetic algorithm is an optimization tool, which means its job is to search for the ultimate solution(s) to a specific control problem by maximizing or minimizing some control variables. It works on the basis of the evolutionary computation by imitating the biological processes of reproducing fittest solution by the natural selection process [63, 64]. As evolution is random in nature, this optimization technique allows the level of randomization and the control to be set for a method [65]. These algorithms are much better and more effective than random search or trial and error-based search [66] but need no further data on the issue.

i. Encoding
As in PID controller, there are three control gain need to be controlled so, in this step first three separate binary strings are considered to represent the gain parameters K_p, K_i, and K_d to ensure the independence of the variables [67].

ii. Initialization
Next, the random population is chosen within the boundaries. The limits for the controller gains have been selected in such a way that it should not lead to an unstable system.

iii. Objective Function
Now to determine the fitness level of the population, the objective function selection is essential. The integral of the squared error (ISE) is used to model a GA-PID controller.

iv. Fitness Function
The function of fitness is the function to be improved by the algorithm [68]. The chromosome refers to the control solution to the process attempted by the genetic algorithm [69, 70].

v. Selection
Roulette wheels have been applied to select individuals from a population. The offspring is produced based on the selected variable. The preference variable depends on the individual's health level, and the fitness value is higher than the individual's offspring.

2.10   Artificial Neural Network-Based Controller

An artificial neural network act as a controller by monitoring and altering the working condition of a dynamic system by using different types of signal. Neural Nets are correctly applied when the control problems are non-linear. The neural network can be implemented as a nonlinear controller if the neural nets are successfully used. Along with it, the ANN controller needs to know about the process plant and its parameters. There are several methodologies to train the ANN controller. A neural network consists of different layers, as shown in Figure 2.10 [70], where input layer nodes represent linguistic input variables. These nodes serve as identity roles in the membership network.

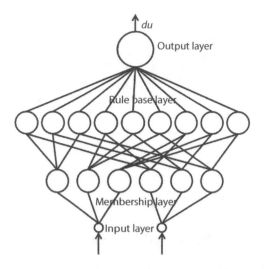

Figure 2.10 Neural Network Layers.

2.11 BLDC Motor Speed Controller With ANN-Based PID Controller

The overview of BLDC motor drives with a conventional and the ANN-PID speed controller is shown in Figure 2.11. We know that the traditional feedback controller has many applications in industrial as well as commercial applications. Earlier classical controller, i.e., PID, was used in controlling the speed of BLDC motor, and it proves its effectiveness in different forms. In spite of the number of advantages, there are some disadvantages related to the PID controller. This controller works on the optimal setting of the plant. If any of the parameters of the plant are removed, or a new parameter is added, the controller action is disturbed because it is a fixed gain feedback controller. Therefore, the controller needs to be calculated repeatedly to get a new ideal setting. The system which is operated under variable time delay, large nonlinearity, and disturbance, the classical PID controller is not able to provide ultimate control action for that system. For these types of highly complex and nonlinear systems, only the PID controller is not enough to give the sustainable or desired result because of their limitations. For that purpose, many researchers are working on a PID controller combining with an artificial neural network (ANN). This approach is called a Neuro-PID intelligent controller. ANN controller is involved with any conventional controller like PI, IP, Fuzzy, to obtain the desired result in process or control industries.

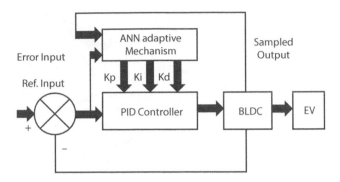

Figure 2.11 ANN-based PID controller.

2.11.1   PID Controller-Based on Neuro Action

ANN adaptive mechanism is used to measure the disturbance from the output and tunes the various parameter of the PID controller according to it. With the help of tuning the setting, it can diminish the noise and thus progresses the operation of the controller. Feedforward adaptive control does not include the inner closed-loop, and so its response is swift. But it has a disadvantage of the effect of unmeasured disturbances. These can be eliminated by proper tuning of PID gains by using neural networks.

The PID gains were balanced to achieve quick conjunction and the best control action for a simple process-based system. The neural network can be equipped by indenting the forward modal to act as a controller by proper training of reverse process design or as a simulator. The backpropagation algorithm is mostly considered in different types of applications among many neural network learning approaches.

2.11.2   ANN-Based on PID Controller

The implementation of the flowchart of the ANN-PID controller is shown in Figure 2.12. Among the various control techniques, PID control is a significant method as it is not affected by noise and constant to change parameters [71]. The purpose of backpropagation is used in different types of neuro-controllers to train them to achieve as much as possible desired plant output. The PID speed controller is adopted with the ANN algorithm in the process industries because there are different types of non-linearity and Gaussian noise during the process.

The control action of the neural system and the values of different PID parameters are selected suitably according to the specific problem. Neuro controllers are classified in three ways. The first one is a series type second one is a

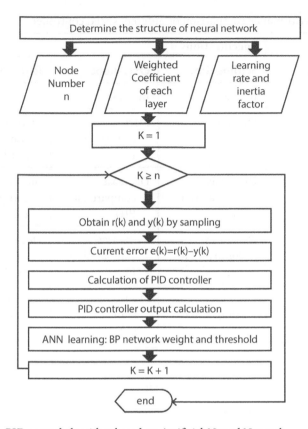

Figure 2.12 PID control algorithm based on Artificial-Neural Network.

parallel type, and the third one is the self-tuning type. The series type plays an essential role as a part of the neural network, and it shows the reverse dynamics of the system. A parallel model adjusts the controller gain of a classical controller. Apart from that, the self-tuning neural controller tunes the various control parameter, including series, parallel, and conventional controller.

2.12 Analysis of Different Speed Controllers

The performance analysis of the BLDC motor based on various parameters like rising and settling time, peak overshoot with a different type of speed controllers on electric vehicle is specified in Table 2.2 below. This comparative analysis is validated, which is shown in Figure 2.13, the versatility in responses of speed controller as P, PI, and PID of the closed-loop BLDC Drive for Electric Vehicle. The idea can be established that the addition of

Table 2.2 Performance comparison of different speed controllers.

Controller	Specifications		
	Settling time	Overshoot	Rise time
PI	Increase	Increase	Decrease
PID	Decrease	Decrease as compared to PI	Increase as compared to PI
FUZZY	Decreases compared to PID	Decrease as compared to PID	Increase as compared to PID
GA	Decreases compared to FUZZY	Decreases compared to FUZZY	Decreases compared to FUZZY
ANN	Decreases compared to GA	Decreases compared to GA	Decreases compared to GA

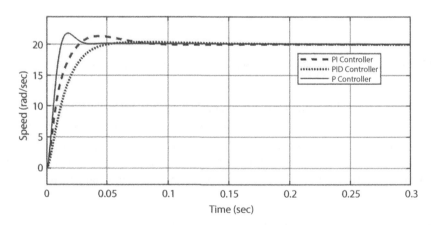

Figure 2.13 Comparative Step response of the closed-loop BLDC Drive for Electric Vehicle with P, PI and PID speed controller.

each of the gain factors with the P controller decreases the overshoot of the system, which is best at the time of PID, but it also makes the system slow. Figure 2.14 clearly shows that the best-optimized output is achieved by implementing an artificial neural network on this closed-loop control of BLDC motor electrical vehicle drive. Here the optimized output has

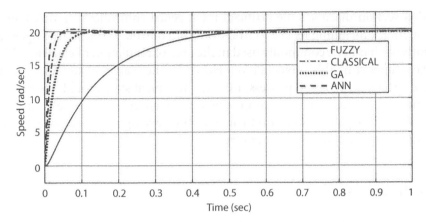

Figure 2.14 Comparative Step response of the closed-loop BLDC Drive for Electric Vehicle with Fuzzy, classical controller, GA, and ANN.

zero overshoot and steady-state error, and also, the time response analysis has shown tremendous improvement. For any industrial application, the reliable output of a motor is needed. The modern method of calculating indexes of product efficiency is quite time-consuming. An artificial intelligent controller can be used in Electric vehicles where there is inadequate machine awareness or great difficulty. For operators such as crossover and mutation, genetic algorithms may also be located to find optimal solutions in the search space as it has also shown a good response. But ANN is more important tools to find a reasonable solution to a complex issue fast. They're not fast, but they can do a decent quest. With the help of these parameters, we can conclude the relative stability or performance of BLDC motor the parameters which are mentioned here vary due to different type of loading like step loading continuous loading periodic loading, when applied for an optimum operation on an electric vehicle. These parameters are also rating dependent means if the rating of motor and reference speed is changed; these parameters are changed.

2.13   Conclusion

Electric vehicles are also facing new challenges with economic development. It was challenging to adapt the traditional manual control to the current situation of society. The advent of AI technologies has fostered BLDC motor invention for the optimum operation of electric vehicle control, which is of great importance for electrical automation development.

This section discusses the artificial intelligence controller's modules and functions, including its use to BLDC motor control. Artificial intelligence software has been commonly used in the area of regulation of electric vehicles, supporting this subject's level. However, there are still some issues in the specific application process. Relevant technical staff should, therefore, continue to study and evolve in terms of encouraging the rate of use of artificial intelligence software to achieve the development and progress of BLDC electric vehicle motor control.

References

1. Faiz, A., Weaver, C. S., Walsh, M. P., *Air Pollution from Motor Vehicles: Standards and Technologies for Controlling Emissions*, p. 227, World Bank Publications, Washington, D.C, 1996.
2. Guarnieri, M., Looking back to electric cars. *Proc. HISTELCON 2012 – 3rd Region-8 IEEE HISTory of Electro – Technology Conference: The Origins of Electrotechnologies*, pp. 1–6, 2012.
3. Hendry, M. M., *Studebaker: One can do much remembering in South Bend*, vol. X, 3rd Q, pp. 228–275, Automobile Quarterly, New Albany, Indiana, 1972.
4. Loeb, A.P., Steam versus Electric versus Internal Combustion: Choosing the Vehicle Technology at the Start of the Automotive Age. *Transportation Research Record, Journal of the Transportation Research Board of the National Academies, No. 1885*, 2004. https://doi.org/10.3141/1885-01
5. Gribben, C., Debunking the Myth of EVs and Smokestacks, Electric Vehicle Association of Greater Washington, D.C., 1996. www.evdl.org/docs/power-plant.pdf
6. Buekers, J., Van Holderbeke, M., Bierkens, J., Int Panis, L., Health and environmental benefits related to electric vehicle introduction in EU countries. *Transport. Res. D-Tr. E.*, 33, 26–38, 2014.
7. Patil, D.S., Pawar, V.S., Mahajan, N.S., Effectiveness of fuzzy logic controller on the performance of unified power flow controller. *International Conference on Global Trends in Signal Processing, Information Computing and Communication (ICGTSPICC)*, pp. 476–479, 2016.
8. Holdway, A. R., Williams, A. R., Inderwildi, O. R., King, D. A., Indirect emissions from electric vehicles: emissions from electricity generation. *Energy Environ. Sci.*, 3, 12, pp. 1825–1832, 2010.
9. Nealer, R., Reichmuth, D., Anair, D., *Cleaner Cars from Cradle to Grave: How Electric Cars Beat Gasoline Cars on Lifetime Global Warming Emissions*, (PDF). Union of Concerned Scientists (UCS), Cambridge, England, 2014.

10. Blanco, S., *UCS: Well-to-wheel, EVs cleaner than pretty much all gas cars*, 17 November 2015, Autoblog (website). Union Of Concerned Scientists, Cambridge, England, Retrieved 22 November 2015.

11. Lepetit, Y., *Electric vehicle life cycle analysis and raw material availability*, October 2017, (PDF). Transport & Environment. Transport and environment- 2nd floor, 18 Square de Meeûs, Brussels, 1050, Belgium, Retrieved 22 February 2018.

12. Tyner, W., *Electricity pricing policies may make or break plug-in hybrid buys*, Purdue University. Purdue Technology Center Aerospace, Purdue News Service, West Lafayette, 2011.

13. Liasi, S. G. and Golkar, M. A., Electric vehicles connection to microgrid effects on peak demand with and without demand response. *In Electrical Engineering (ICEE), 2017 Iranian Conference on*, pp. 1272–1277, 2017, IEEE.

14. "Behr." Behr.de. 20 May 2009. Archived from the original on 13 October 2009. Retrieved 26 December 2010.

15. Tsai, P.F., Chu, J.Z., Jang, S.S., Shieh, S.S., Developing a robust model predictive control architecture through regional knowledge analysis of artificial neural networks. *J. Process Control*, 13, 5, 423–435, 2003.

16. Power, Y. and Bahri, P.A., Integration techniques in intelligent operational management: A review. *J. Knowledge-Based Systems*, 18, 2, 89–97, 2005.

17. Lecun, Y., Bengio, Y., Hinton, G., Deep learning. *Nature*, 521, (7553), 436–444, 2015.

18. Ji, W.G., Application of artificial intelligence technology in the analysis of automatic electrical control. *J. Electron. Test*, 3, 137–138, 2014.

19. Xiao, S.Q. and Peng, J.C., The application of artificial intelligence technology in electrical automation control. *J. Autom. Instrum.*, 530, 1049–1052, 2013.

20. Wilson, T.G. and Trickey, P.H., "D-C machine with solid-state commutation," in *Electrical Engineering*, vol. 81, no. 11, pp. 879–884, Nov. 1962.

21. De Silva, C. W., *Modeling and Control of Engineering Systems*, pp. 632–633, CRC Press, Boca Raton, London New York, 2009.

22. Moczala, H., *Small Electric Motors*, pp. 165–166, Institution of Electrical Engineers, London, 1998.

23. Xia, C-L, *Permanent Magnet Brushless DC Motor Drives and Controls*, pp. 18–19, John Wiley and Sons, New York, United States, 2012.

24. Gopal, M., *Control systems: principles and design. 2nd ed*, Page 165, Tata McGraw-Hill, New Delhi, 2002.

25. Niasar, A. H., Vahedi, A., Moghbelli, H., Analysis of commutation torque ripple in three-phase, four- switch brushless DC (BLDC) motor drives. *37th IEEE Power Electronics Specialists Conference*, pp. 1–6, 2006.

26. Vanjani, H., Choudhury, U.K., Sharma, M., Vanjani, B., Takagi-Sugeno (TS)-type fuzzy logic controller for three-phase four-wire shunt active power filter for an unbalanced load. *IEEE 7th Power India International Conference (PIICON)*, pp. 1–4, 2016.

27. Sarabakha, A., Fu, C., Kayacan, E., Double- input interval type-2 fuzzy logic controllers: Analysis and design. *IEEE International Conference on Fuzzy Systems (FUZZ-IEEE)*, pp. 1–6, 2017.
28. Chuang, C-Y, Chen, P-S, Hsu, C-C, Li, J-Y, Chen, J-F, Lin, C-L, Novel maximum power point tracker for PV systems using interval type-2 fuzzy logic controller. *IEEE 3rd International Future Energy Electronics Conference and ECCE Asia (IFEEC 2017 - ECCE Asia)*, pp. 1505–1507, 2017.
29. Laoufi, C., Abbou, A., Akherraz, M., Improvement of direct torque control performance of induction machine by using a self-tuning fuzzy logic controller for the elimination of stator resistance variation effect. *International Renewable and Sustainable Energy Conference (IRSEC)*, pp. 1028–1034, 2016.
30. Tabatabaei, H., Fathi, S. H., Jedari, M., A comparative study between conventional and fuzzy logic control for APFs by applying adaptive hysteresis current controller. *Iranian Conference on Electrical Engineering (ICEE)*, pp. 1313–1318, 2017.
31. Iqbal, T., Amjadullah, Zeb, K., Performance of grid interfaced doubly-fed induction generator-wind turbine using fuzzy logic controller based on Gauss Newton algorithm under symmetrical and asymmetrical faults. *International Conference on Electrical Engineering (ICEE)*, pp. 1–6, 2017.
32. Viswanathan, V. and Jeevanathan, S., Approach for torque ripple reduction for brushless DC motor based on three-level neutral- point-clamped inverter with DC-DC converter. *IET Power Electron.*, 8, (1), pp. 47–55, 2015.
33. Park, D-H, Nguyen, A. T., Lee, D-C, Lee, H-G, Compensation of misalignment effect of hall sensors for BLDC motor drives. *IEEE 3rd International Future Energy Electronics Conference and ECCE Asia (IFEEC 2017 - ECCE Asia)*, pp. 1659–1664, 2017.
34. Kim N,, Toliyat, H. A., Panahi, I. M., Kim, M., "BLDC Motor Control Algorithm for Low-Cost Industrial Applications," in *APEC 07 - Twenty-Second Annual IEEE Applied Power Electronics Conference and Exposition*, pp. 1400–1405, Anaheim, CA, USA, 2007.
35. Esfahlani, S. S., Cirstea, S., Sanaei, A., Wilson, G., An adaptive self-organizing fuzzy logic controller in a serious game for motor impairment rehabilitation. *IEEE 26th International Symposium on Industrial Electronics (ISIE)*, pp. 1311–1318, 2017.
36. Bhosale, R. and Agarwal, V., Enhanced the transient response and voltage stability by controlling ultra-capacitor power in DC micro-grid using fuzzy logic controller. *IEEE International Conference on Power Electronics, Drives and Energy Systems (PEDES)*, pp. 1–6, 2016.
37. Charan, C. R., Sujatha, K. N., Satsangi, K. P., Fuzzy logic controller-based model for rooftop/grid-connected solar photovoltaic system. *IEEE Region 10 Humanitarian Technology Conference (R10-HTC)*, pp. 1–6, 2016.
38. Fahassa, C., Zahraoui, Y., Akherraz, M., Bennassar, A., Improvement of induction motor performance at low speeds using fuzzy logic adaptation

mechanism based sensorless direct field-oriented control and fuzzy logic controllers (FDFOC). *5th International Conference on Multimedia Computing and Systems (ICMCS)*, pp. 777–782, 2016.

39. Carrasquilla-Batista, A. and Chacon-Rodrıguez, A., Proposal of a fuzzy logic controller for the improvement of irrigation scheduling decision-making in greenhouse horticulture. *1st Conference on Ph.D. Research in Microelectronics and Electronics Latin America (PRIME-LA)*, pp. 1–4, 2017.

40. Kumar, D., Gupta, R.A., Gupta, N., Minimization of current ripple and over-shoot in four switches three-phase inverter fed BLDC motor using tracking anti-windup PI controller. *IEEE International Conference on Signal Processing, Informatics, Communication, and Energy Systems (SPICES)*, pp. 1–6, 2017.

41. Jayachandran, S. and Vinatha, P. U., One cycle control bridge-less SEPIC Converter Fed BLDC Motor Drive. *IEEE International Conference on Signal Processing, Informatics, Communication, and Energy Systems (SPICES)*, pp. 1–6, 2017.

42. Sridivya, K. C. N. and Kiran, T. V., Space Vector PWM Control of BLDC Motor Drive. *International Conference on Power and Embedded Drive Control (ICPEDC)*, pp. 71–78, 2017.

43. Poovizhi, M., Kumaran, M. S., Ragul, P., Priyadarshini, L. I., Logambal, R., Investigation of mathematical modeling of brushless dc motor (BLDC) drives by using MATLAB-SIMULINK. *International Conference on Power and Embedded Drive Control (ICPEDC)*, pp. 178–183, 2017.

44. Bae, J., Jo, Y., Kwak, Y., Lee, D-H, A design and control of rail mover with a hall sensor-based BLDC motor. *IEEE Transportation Electrification Conference and Expo, Asia-Pacific (ITEC Asia-Pacific)*, pp. 1–6, 2017.

45. Kumar, R. and Singh, B., Grid interactive solar PV based water pumping using BLDC motor drive. *IEEE 7th Power India International Conference (PIICON)*, pp. 1–6, 2016.

46. Seol, H-S, Lim, J., Kang, D-W, Park, J. S., Lee, J., Optimal Design Strategy for Improved Operation of IPM BLDC MotorsWith Low-Resolution Hall Sensors. *IEEE T. Ind. Electron.*, Volume: 64, Issue: 12, Pages: 9758–9766, Year: 2017.

47. Seol, H-S, Kang, D-W, Jun, H-W, Lim, J., Lee, J., Design of Winding Changeable BLDC Motor Considering Demagnetization in Winding Change Section. *IEEE Trans Magn.*, vol. 53, issue: 11, pp. 1–5, 2017.

48. Heins, G., Ionel, D.M., Patterson, D. *et al.*, Combined experimental and numerical method for loss separation in permanent magnet brushless machines. *IEEE Trans. Ind. Appl.*, 52, (2), pp. 1405–1412, 2016.

49. Skóra, M., Operation of PM BLDC motor drives with a faulty rotor position sensor. *International Symposium on Electrical Machines (SME)*, pp. 1–6, 2017.

50. Babadi, A. N., Pour, A. H., Amjadifard, R., Improved source-end current Power Quality performance of a BLDCmotor drive using a novel DC-DC converter. *Iranian Conference on Electrical Engineering (ICEE)*, pp. 1360–1365, 2017.

51. Nair, U., An intelligent fuzzy sliding mode controller for a BLDC motor. *International Conference on Innovative Mechanisms for Industry Applications (ICIMIA)*, pp. 274–278, Arun Prasad, 2017.

52. Pahlavani, M. R. A., Ayat, Y. S., Vahedi, A., Minimisation of torque ripple in slotless axial flux BLDC motors in terms of design considerations. *IET Electr. Power App.*, Volume: 11, Issue: 6, Pages: 1124–1130, Year: 2017.

53. Bharathiar, S.S., Yanamshetti, R., Chatterjee, D. *et al.*, Dual-mode switching technique for reduction of commutation torque ripple of brushless dc motor. *IET Electr. Power Appl.*, 5, (1), pp. 193–202, 2011.

54. Sharma, P. K. and Sindelar, A.S., Performance analysis and comparison of BLDC motor drive using PI and FOC. *International Conference on Global Trends in Signal Processing, Information Computing and Communication (ICGTSPICC)*, pp. 485–492, 2016.

55. Sathyan, A., Milivojevic, N., Lee, Y-J, Krishnamurthy, M., Emadi, A., An FPGA-Based Novel Digital PWM Control Scheme for BLDC Motor Drives. *IEEE T. Ind. Electron.*, Vol. 56, No. 8, pp. 3040–3049, August 2009.

56. Ma, X-J, Liu, Y., Li, L., Research and Simulation on PID Control Method for Brushless DC Motor Based on Genetic Algorithm and BP Neural Network. *IEEE Vehicle Power and Propulsion Conference (VPPC)*, September 3-5, 2008.

57. Guifang, C., Kun, Q., Bangyuan, L., Xiangping, P., Robust PID Controller in Brushless DC Motor Application. *2007 IEEE International Conference on Control and Automation*, Guangzhou, China - May 30 to June 1, 2007.

58. Ansari, U., Aalam, S., Jafri, M. U. N., Ansari, S., Alam, U., Modeling and Control of Three-Phase BLDC Motor using PID with Genetic Algorithm. in proc. Of the *IEEE International conference on computer modeling and simulation, UK*, pp. 189–194, March 2011.

59. Kim, M-K, Bae, H-S, Suh, B-S, Comparison of IGBT and MOSFET inverters in low-power BLDC motor drives. *37th IEEE Power Electronics Specialists Conference*, pp. 1–4, 2006.

60. Ananthababu, B., Ganesh, C., Pavithra, C.V., Fuzzy based speed control of BLDC motor with bidirectional DC-DC converter. *Online International Conference on Green Engineering and Technologies (IC-GET)*, pp. 1–6, 2016.

61. Haerani, E., Wardhani, L. K., Putri, D. K., Sukmana, H. T., Optimization of multiple depot vehicle routing problem (MDVRP) on perishable product distribution by using genetic algorithm and fuzzy logic controller (FLC). *5th International Conference on Cyber and IT Service Management (CITSM)*, pp. 1–5, 2017.

62. Chuang, C-Y, Chen, P-S, Hsu, C-C, Li, J-Y, Chen, J-F, Lin, C-L, Novel maximum power point tracker for PV systems using interval type-2 fuzzy logic controller. *IEEE 3rd International Future Energy Electronics Conference and ECCE Asia (IFEEC 2017 - ECCE Asia)*, pp. 1505–1507, 2017.

63. Viswanathan, V. and Jeevananthan, S., Hybrid converter topology for reducing torque ripple of BLDC motor. *IET Power Electron.*, Volume: 10, Issue: 12, Pages: 1572–1587, Year: 2017.

64. Hajiaghasi, S., Salemnia, A., Motabarian, F., Four switches direct power control of BLDC motor with trapezoidal back-EMF. *8th Power Electronics, Drive Systems & Technologies Conference (PEDSTC)*, pp. 513–518, 2017.
65. Chen, S., Liu, G., Zhu, L., Sensorless Control Strategy of a 315 kW High-Speed BLDC Motor Based on a Speed-Independent Flux Linkage Function. *IEEE T. Ind. Electron.*, Volume: 64, Issue: 11, Pages: 8607–8617, Year: 2017.
66. Viswanathan, V. and Seenithangom, J., Commutation Torque Ripple Reduction in the BLDC Motor Using Modified SEPIC and Three-Level NPC Inverter. *IEEE T. Power Electr.*, Volume: 33, Issue: 1, Page: 535–546, Year: 2018.
67. Bae, J., Jo, Y., Ahn, J-W, Lee, D-H, A novel speed-power control scheme of a high-speed BLDC motor for a blender machine. *20th International Conference on Electrical Machines and Systems (ICEMS)*, pp. 1–7, 2017.
68. Singh, P. K., Singh, B., Bist, V., Al-Haddad, K., Chandra, A., BLDC Motor Drive Based on Bridgeless Landsman PFC Converter With Single Sensor and Reduced Stress on Power Devices. *IEEE Trans. Ind. Appl.*, Volume: 54, pp. 625–635, Issue: 99, Year: 2017.
69. Chen, C., Du, H., Lin, S., Mobile robot wall-following control by improved artificial bee colony algorithm to design a compensatory fuzzy logic controller. *14th International Conference on Electrical Engineering/Electronics, Computer, Telecommunications and Information Technology (ECTI-CON)*, pp. 856–859, 2017.
70. Benkercha, R., Moulahoum, S., Kabache, N., Combination of artificial neural network and flower pollination algorithm to model fuzzy logic MPPT controller for photovoltaic systems. *18th International Symposium on Electromagnetic Fields in Mechatronics, Electrical and Electronic Engineering (ISEF)*, pp. 1–2, 2017.
71. Haerani, E., Wardhani, L. K., Putri, D. K., Sukmana, H. T., Optimization of multiple depot vehicle routing problem (MDVRP) on perishable product distribution by using genetic algorithm and fuzzy logic controller (FLC). *5th International Conference on Cyber and IT Service Management (CITSM)*, pp. 1–5, 2017.

3

Optimization Techniques Used in Active Magnetic Bearing System for Electric Vehicles

Suraj Gupta*, Pabitra Kumar Biswas†, Sukanta Debnath
and Jonathan Laldingliana

*Department of Electrical and Electronics Engineering, National Institute of
Technology Mizoram, Chaltlang, Aizawl, Mizoram, India*

Abstract

Today pollution is a preeminent threat to the environment. The primary sources of pollution are combustion of liquid fuels in industries or, in transportation in which percentage of pollution is more from transportation. The harmful gases which emit from vehicles by combustion of liquid fuels can only be controlled if the type of the fuel is changed from petroleum produced fuels to electricity. The brilliant and efficient option for controlling pollution is use of electric vehicles (EVs) in place of the conventional one. In electric vehicles, Active magnetic bearing (AMB) is widely used, using which high speed with efficient performance, can be achieved. The major issue is from the control perspective as AMBs are highly nonlinear and unstable; the classical control approach alone cannot give efficient results. So, the artificial intelligence (AI) based control approaches like artificial neural network (ANN) based control, fuzzy logic control (FLC), particle swarm optimization (PSO) control, etc. along with the classical controller can increase the reliability and performance of the overall system. As the AMBs are used in most of the electric vehicle applications, their control like speed control and torque control can be smoothly achieved by the use of AI-based control techniques.

*Corresponding author: suraj.eee.mtech@nitmz.ac.in
†Corresponding author: pabitra.eee@nitmz.ac.in

Chitra A, P. Sanjeevikumar, Jens Bo Holm-Nielsen and S. Himavathi (eds.) *Artificial Intelligent Techniques for Electric and Hybrid Electric Vehicles*, (49–76) © 2020 Scrivener Publishing LLC

Keywords: Active magnetic bearing (AMB), artificial intelligence (AI) control, electric vehicles (EVs), artificial neural network (ANN), fuzzy logic control (FLC), particle swarm optimization (PSO) technique, speed and torque control

3.1   Introduction

In this era of technological advancement as the research in almost every area is on the boom. The young minds are on work under the guidance and acquaintance of the experienced one. Only through continuous research and practice, the idea for actively controlled electromagnetic bearing has been developed, and nowadays, research in this field is going on because of their various advantages and applications, which will be a boon to the current pollution problems of the world.

After the invention of petroleum and diesel engine, its consumption has been increased rapidly not only for transportation but in industries, aircraft, etc. Although the invention of diesel engine brings a revolution, nowadays the pollution scenario of the world itself tells the dark side of the excessive use of these inventions. If the consumption of petroleum-product fuels remains the same, pollution will be increased and in the future, the earth will be uninhabitable.

To control pollution, first, the major sources of pollution i.e. pollution from transportation vehicles, should be controlled and for this, the fuels which they are using to accelerate must be changed because using fuels originated from petroleum products like diesel, petrol, etc. after combustion produces harmful gases. So much researches have been done on the fuels so that after their combustion less or no harmful gases will be emitted. But changing the type of fuel is a broad area of research mostly when

Table 3.1 Classification of various EVs.

Vehicle Types	Propulsion Devices	Energy Carriers	Energy Sources
Micro Hybrid			
Mild Hybrid	Engine	Liquid Fuel	Liquid Fuel
Full Hybrid			
PHEV			
REV			
BEV	Motor	Electricity	Battery

the used source is electricity. The vehicles in which electricity is used as a fuel source is simply stated as Electric vehicles (EVs).

There are many types of Electric vehicles classified on the basis of their source and propulsion system. Table 3.1 shows classification of various EVs. Advancement in research took the Electric vehicle to a new level where, not one but two or more sources are used to make the propulsion. These types of EVs are defined as hybrid electric vehicles (HEVs). Those different sources must have one electric source combined with either hydrogen fuel cells or supercapacitor cells or any other advanced fuel cells [6].

Conventional vehicle which is powered by petroleum-based fuel and electric vehicles have their advantages and disadvantages:

- Pollution from conventional vehicles is too much as compared to EVs as they are mostly powered from renewable energy sources.
- Reduction in carbon emission and nitrogen oxide gas with the use of EVs
- The requirement of initial torque is more for any kind of vehicle and conventional vehicles are good in this.
- For heavy industrial purpose, conventional vehicles are still in use as they are more efficient as compared to EVs.
- For EVs, (in the case of battery-powered electric vehicles, BEV) installation of charging stations is required as they are powered from battery that made them costly. By increasing the battery capacity this problem may resolve.
- Due to being powered from battery EVs have limited driving range with a high initial cost. The engine life is greater than the battery life because continuous charging and discharging of battery result in small battery life.
- Heavy vehicles such as cranes, trucks, lifter etc. still use conventional engines as they need more power and high initial torque.
- The overall efficiency of any kind EVs is less as compared to the conventional vehicle engines.

Further research is still going on in this field to improve the performances of the EVs. Different approaches have been implemented and one of them is the use of magnetic bearing in the place of a conventional bearing [5].

A magnetic bearing is one in which there is no contact between the stationary part and the moving part with the use of magnetic levitation [1]. Depending upon the excitation used magnetic bearing is classified into two types—(i) Active magnetic bearing (AMB) and (ii) Passive magnetic bearing (PMB).

As their names say, active magnetic bearing is one in which the required magnetic field is generated by supplying current in the coil of magnet and in passive magnetic bearing the required magnetic force is generated by a permanent magnet. A comparison will explain advantages and disadvantages of active and passive magnetic bearing:

- Continuous use of passive magnetic bearing will degrade the performance of magnetic properties and overall performance of the system but using active magnet in bearing will maintain the performance of the system.
- Supply is always required for active magnetic bearing for proper bearing action but in passive magnetic bearing permanent magnet will generate the required force.
- Heat, temperature, moist and other atmospheric factors affect the performance of the passive magnetic bearing but active magnetic bearing magnetic force totally depends on the current in the coils.
- Magnetic properties observed in passive magnetic bearing depend on the material used to make it and is limited but in active magnetic bearing that depends on the material and the supply current intensity.
- In bearing operation, the speed observed using PMB is less as compared to AMB. Using AMB highest possible speed can be reached allowed by the wear and tear resistance of the material of the coil.
- As controlling of these magnetic bearing is a major task, using PMB controlling will always be a problem as a closed control loop cannot be formed. But with AMB, a closed control loop can be formed and controlling techniques can be applied.

Due to the above-stated advantages, AMB is preferred over PMB for bearing operations. As to design the electric vehicles should follow basic requirements:

- High initial torque density and power density
- High efficiency at different torque and speed range
- High robustness in different atmospheric condition
- High reliability on long-range use

- High torque capabilities to climb hills
- Fair and justifiable initial and running cost
- Safe even after long use of engine
- Wide torque and speed range
- Even for constant speed and torque operation, it should be efficient.

To achieve the above-stated requirements of EVs, active magnetic bearing is best suited for bearing operations. Although AMB is an exemplary mechatronics product, and meanings of mechatronics will point to the information base for effectively managing AMB. The historical backdrop of AMB is quickly tended to: first uses of the electromagnetic suspension standard have been in exploratory material science, and proposals to utilize this concept for suspending transportation vehicles for fast prepares return to 1937. There are different methods for structuring attractive suspensions for a contact-free help—the AMB is only one of them [1].

Apart from transportation, AMB is used these days in various practical applications like in flywheel energy storage system, high-speed tools, watt-hour meters, ventricular assist devices, artificial hearts, centrifugal compressors, etc. [2]. Propelled vitality stockpiling frameworks for electric firearms and other pulsed weapons on battle vehicles present huge difficulties for rotor-bearing design. AMB is one available developing bearing alternative with significant points of interest regarding lifetime and rotational speed, and furthermore well coordinate into fast flywheel frameworks [3].

The use of AMB in EVs is a broad area of research and the major problem that arises is to control the levitation and then the bearing action. If the controlling is done properly the performance of AMB will be efficient. For controlling the AMB various classical controls are available but among them which is most efficient, can be observed only after mathematical modelling of the whole system with that controller. In the case of using a modern controller or, Artificial Intelligence controller such that many mathematical calculations are not required even these modern controllers are advance in performance [20].

Although AMBs have some disadvantages i.e. large in size, bulky, the cost is high due to the use of control circuit etc., its advantages overcome their disadvantages.

In the later section, basic components of an AMB is briefly described with the proposed AMB model for electric vehicles after that use of AMB in EVs is discussed and finally, control strategies for AMB are explained thoroughly, in which various modern controllers have been explained and their advantages and performances are discussed.

3.2 Basic Components of an Active Magnetic Bearing (AMB)

To obtain a proper bearing operation the very first and basic step is levitation of the rotor at a particular air gap and to attain that, control techniques are used because open-loop AMB is in itself a nonlinear and highly unstable system. The proposed active magnetic bearing system is shown in Figure 3.1 and all the parts have been briefly explained below.

3.2.1   Electromagnet Actuator

First and foremost is the electromagnet actuator, which is U-shaped, iron cored with a copper winding in it as shown in Figure 3.1. The shape of actuator maybe 'I', 'E', 'U', etc. but for the proposed model a single-axis 'U' shaped electromagnet actuator is considered. Depending upon the requirement single-axis single electromagnet actuator or, single-axis double electromagnet actuator can be used. Iron core is used because it provides low core loss, low hysteresis, and high permeability. For winding, copper is used, which is stronger than aluminum, and lamination of copper windings reduces eddy current losses.

When excitation is given to these windings, the actuator becomes an electromagnet and an increment in excitation increase the magnetically attractive power of this electromagnet. So, depending upon the current in the coils of this electromagnet the attractive power can be controlled.

3.2.2   Rotor

The attractive force of the electromagnet actuator acts on the rotor, by totally compensating the gravity acting on it, that how levitation can be

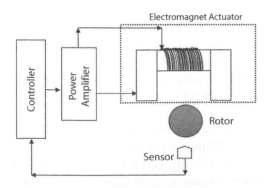

Figure 3.1 Basic block diagram of an AMB with basic components.

attained. For the proposed model of AMB, the rotor is made of ferromagnetic material and shaped like a ball.

Relative permeability (μ_r) of ferromagnetic material is greater than one and relative permeability of diamagnetic materials is less than one.

$$\mu_r < 1, \text{Diamagnetic materials}$$
$$\mu_r > 1, \text{Paramagnetic materials}$$
$$\mu_r \gg 1, \text{Ferromagnetic materials}$$

The magnetic susceptibility (χ_m) can be also be observed to distinguish among the type of magnetic materials. i.e.

$$\chi_m = \mu_r - 1 \qquad (3.1)$$

Therefore, for Diamagnetic materials, $\chi_m < 0$, for paramagnetic materials $\chi_m > 0$ and for ferromagnetic material $\chi_m \gg 0$.

3.2.3   Controller

As stated earlier, since active magnetic bearings are nonlinear and have high instability, a controller is required for smooth and proper operation. Controllers may be classical or modern in nature, but the purpose remains the same i.e. to properly control the position of the rotor. In Figure 3.1 only one controller is shown but according to the proposed model of AMB as shown in Figure 3.2, basically two controllers are required. One to control the position of the rotor which is labeled as a position controller and second is to control the current in the electromagnet actuator and labeled as current controller [25].

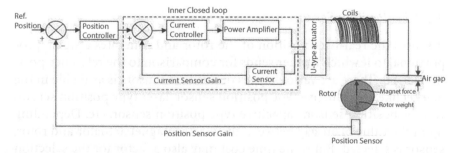

Figure 3.2 Proposed Closed-loop AMB model.

3.2.3.1   Position Controller

Position signal coming from position sensor is compared with the reference position and the error signal is given as input to position controller, depending upon the calibration and setup value of controlling variables, position controller generates an output which is further fed for comparison from current sensor signal.

The position controller can be a classical controller like Proportional-Integral (PI) controller, lead-lag controller, lead controller, Proportional-Integral-Derivative (PID), etc. and in modern controller, they can be Fuzzy logic controller, Genetic Algorithm based PID controller etc. [4, 23, 38].

3.2.3.2   Current Controller

The current in the coil of electromagnet actuator is measured by current sensor and that signal is compared with the output of the position controller, the compared output is given as input to current controller which generates output depending upon is design and controlling variables. Further, the output is fed to the power amplifier.

In the area of classical controller mostly Proportional-Integral (PI) controller is used because of its fast response and better transient state performance. Although modern controller may be used but in the aspect of reliability and performance, PI controller is best [25].

3.2.4   Sensors

Apart from controllers, sensors also play a vital role in controlling of AMB. According to the proposed model of AMB, two controllers are used, so for each controller one sensor is proposed. The very first one sensor is:

3.2.4.1   Position Sensor

It senses the real-time position of the rotor and generates a signal proportional to it which further sends for comparison to the reference position signal. There are various types of position sensors is available in the market like an Inductive type position sensor, laser type position sensor, IR type position sensor, capacitive type position sensor, etc. Depending upon the value of air gap between the electromagnet actuator and rotor, sensor is selected. But some time cost may also a factor for the selection of sensors.

3.2.4.2   Current Sensor

Senses the current in the coil and generates a signal analogous to it that signal is later sent to comparison with the output of position controller. Various current sensors are available in the market like Hall Effect type current sensor, etc.

3.2.5   Power Amplifier

Power amplifiers are used to amplify the input current to the coil. The output of current controller is needed to be amplified in order to make the hovering of rotor that work is done by power amplifier. They are designed in many forms like single switch power amplifier, half-bridge power amplifier, full-bridge power amplifier, symmetrical type, unsymmetrical type, etc. [22].

In power amplifiers, the switching device is used, is mostly MOSFET and IGBT, which are costly. That is why most of the time, a single switch power amplifier is used to make the whole system cost-efficient.

The proposed AMB model is shown in Figure 3.2 here all the blocks and their significance have been briefly described. The working can be explained by dividing this whole block diagram into two closed loops. One is inner closed-loop and second is an outer closed loop.

In inner closed loop, current controller and power amplifier are connected with current sensor in a feedback path. The current sensor senses the current in coil of electromagnet actuator and that signal is compared with the output of position controller, later that error signal is sent to current controller and the output of current controller is amplified by the power amplifier. The inner closed loop tries to make the current in the electromagnetic coil such that the gravitational force acting on the ball is totally compensated by the attraction force of electromagnet at the reference position. i.e.

$$F_g = F_{em} \tag{3.2}$$

Where F_g = gravitational force and F_{em} = attraction force of electromagnet.

In outer closed-loop, position controller, electromagnet actuator, and rotor are connected with position sensors in the feedback path. The position sensor senses the actual position of the rotor and sends a signal which later compared by the reference position value, the error is further fed to position controller for controlling action. Here, the outer closed loop tries to make the position of the rotor at the reference position value.

3.3   Active Magnetic Bearing in Electric Vehicles System

Electric vehicles are boon to the environment and they are going to be basic and mostly preferable transportation systems in the near future for which AMB will become the support on which EVs will run. Various research and prototypes have been developed on the use of AMB in EVs.

Flywheel unit is one of the most significant approaches to capacity and recuperation vitality in electric vehicles. For acknowledging high vitality thickness, the flywheel unit consistently works fast. The active magnetic bearing (AMB) based flywheel unit is frequently utilized [3]. There is no uncertainty that energized vehicles are supplanting internal combustion motor vehicles for road transportation. Among them, electric vehicles (EVs) have been recognized as the greenest road transportation while half breed EVs have been labeled as the too ultra-low discharge vehicles [6].

Most of the vehicular applications required electrical energy sources and storage systems in which rotational operations are performed by the active magnetic bearings. Using active magnetic bearing (AMB) have their advantages over the conventional bearings. Along with this, various research has been performed on the modeling and control prospective of Active magnetic bearing used for EVs [5]. Losses which occur with the use of conventional bearing are one of the reasons for reduced efficiency of EVs, but with the help of AMB, that efficiency will be improved.

Energy stores in a flywheel energy storage system (FESS) is in the form of kinetic energy depends on a turning mass rotating by an electrical machine. As the kinetic energy is directly proportional to the square of rotating speed, more the speed of the rotor will generate more energy. A schematic diagram of a FESS is shown in Figure 3.3 which in EVs, works as a motor during charging and a generator during discharging. The contact between the actuator and rotor is eliminated by the AMB and using which

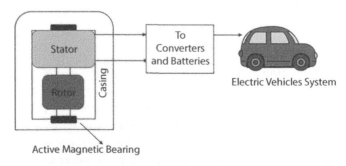

Figure 3.3 Flywheel energy storage using AMB for electric vehicles.

the highest possible speed can be achieved. The casing is provided to create a vacuum, and the output of the energy will be either directly fed to machines or, after converting it into DC its fed to batteries [22].

An important component of FESS is the electric machine, which should be such that, it will fulfill the robust requirements: high efficiency, higher power density, high robustness, and a wide speed range. Existing electric machines in addition to conventional bearing cannot meet those requirements like existing induction motor suffers from high rotor loss along with low power density and low efficiency in harsh and vacuum environment. So, the implementation of AMB in FESS improves overall system performance.

3.4   Control Strategies of Active Magnetic Bearing for Electric Vehicles System

3.4.1   Fuzzy Logic Controller (FLC)

In spite of the fact that the likelihood hypothesis has been a well-established and viable instrument to deal with uncertainty, it tends to be applied uniquely to circumstances whose qualities depend on irregular procedures, that is, forms in which the event of occasions is carefully dictated by some coincidence. In any case, in all actuality, there end up being issues, an enormous class of them whose vulnerability is described by a non-irregular procedure. Here, the vulnerability may emerge because of halfway data about the issue, or because of data which isn't completely dependable, or due inborn imprecision in the language with which the issue is characterized, or because of receipt of data from more than one source about the issue which is clashing [10, 11].

It is in such circumstances that the fuzzy set theory shows massive potential for compelling unraveling of the uncertainty in the issue. Fuzziness means 'vagueness'. Fuzzy set theory is a fantastic numerical concept to deal with the vulnerability emerging because of dubiousness. Understanding human discourse and perceiving written by hand characters are some normal examples where fuzziness shows [12]. It was L.A. Zadeh who propounded the fuzzy set hypothesis in his fundamental paper [28]. From that point forward, a great deal of hypothetical advancements has occurred in this field.

Figure 3.4 shows the working of a fuzzy logic controller (FLC), first, the applied crisp data input is fuzzified in fuzzy subsets by Fuzzification process later depending upon the designed rule-base inference process is applied to the fuzzified input [13]. Later the output of the inference process is converted into crisp or analog type data for better understanding in defuzzification process. Hence, the complete FLC working can be classified as [21, 24]:

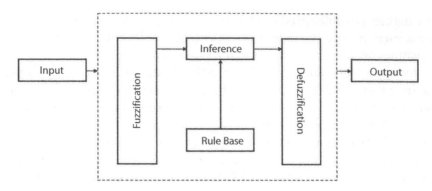

Figure 3.4 Flow diagram of Fuzzy Logic Controller (FLC).

1. Fuzzification
2. Fuzzy inference process
3. Defuzzification

1. Fuzzification—The input data, which is crisp data in nature is converted into fuzzy subsets and sets for fuzzy operations. Input data are either 0 or, 1, yes or, no. But the fuzzified data may take a range of values between 0 and 1.
2. Fuzzy Inference Process—In this step, first the rules are designed using 'if-and-then' method. Depending upon these rules output is generated which is further send to defuzzification. the two very important inferring procedures are:

a) Generalized Modus Ponens (GMP)
b) Generalized Modus Tollens (GMT)

3. Defuzzification—Various methods are available for defuzzification, or simply converting back the fuzzified inference process output in crisp data. The available methods are:

a) Centroids of Sum (COS)
b) Mean of Maxima (MOM)

3.4.1.1   Designing of Fuzzy Logic Controller (FLC) Using MATLAB

MATLAB is a software that is a multi-paradigm numerical computing environment for pacing the research and scientific work [9]. The fuzzy Logic tool is available in MATLAB which can be used for designing the controller for the proposed AMB model. A layout of fuzzy logic tool of MATLAB is shown in Figure 3.5.

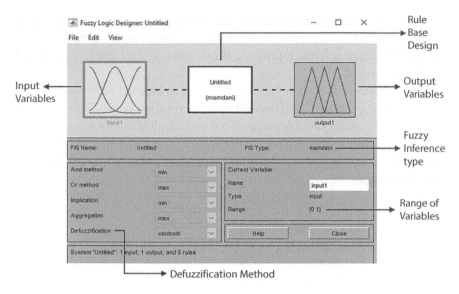

Figure 3.5 Fuzzy logic tool of MATLAB.

Input variables and output variables can be defined from the membership functions and shapes available in MATLAB library, which are triangular, trapezoidal, sigmoidal, etc.

In Figure 3.6, membership function 1 (mf1) is triangular in shape, mf2 is trapezoidal, mf3 is generalized bell-shaped, mf4 is Gaussian mf and mf5 is sigmoidal mf and mf6 is product of two sigmoidal mf. After setting up the input and output variables, rule base can be designed using

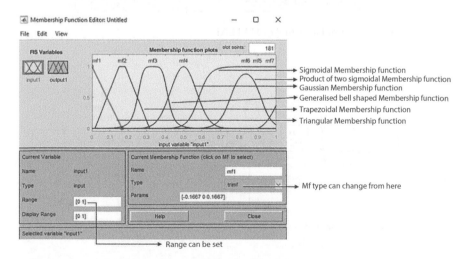

Figure 3.6 Membership function editor of Fuzzy tool of MATLAB.

'if-and-then' logic in rule editor of MATLAB. A simple layout is shown in Figure 3.7. By using input variables and output variables, rules will be created. In fuzzy inference process, these rules will be used, and output will be generated.

After creating the fuzzy logic controller, it can be used as a position controller for the proposed AMB model as it is a modern controller so there is no tuning of control variables is required and a little disturbance in the system can be easily controlled by the fuzzy logic controller [8]. A simulation of fuzzy logic controller as a position controller for the proposed model is shown in Figure 3.8.

Figure 3.7 Rule Editor of Fuzzy tool of MATLAB.

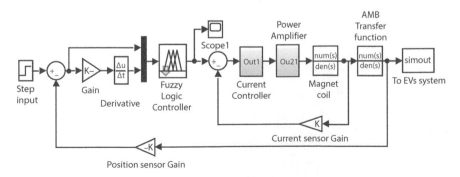

Figure 3.8 Simulation of proposed AMB with FLC as a position controller for EVs.

3.4.2 Artificial Neural Network (ANN)

Neural systems (NN), which are rearranged models of the organic neuron framework, is an enormously parallel disseminated handling framework made up of exceptionally interconnected neural computing components that have the capacity to learn and along these lines gain information and make it accessible for use. Different learning component exists to empower the NN procure information. NN models have been ordered into different kinds, depending on their learning components and different highlights. A few classes of NN allude to this learning procedure as preparing and the capacity to take care of an issue utilizing the information procured as derivation [24, 26].

NNs are disentangled impersonations of the focal sensory system, and clearly in this manner, have been roused by the sort of registering performed by the human cerebrum. The auxiliary constituents of a human mind named neurons are the substances, which perform calculations, for example, comprehension, consistent derivation, design acknowledgment, etc. Thus, the innovation, which has been based on a disentangled impersonation of figuring by neurons of a mind, has been named Artificial neural systems (ANS) innovation or, Artificial neural system (ANN) or, essentially Neural Network (NN) [36]. A diagram to understand the various layers of ANN is shown in Figure 3.9 and a flowchart of ANN is shown in Figure 3.10.

3.4.2.1 Artificial Neural Network Using MATLAB

Artificial neural network (ANN) is a tool using which parameters of controlling variables of any classical controller can be calculated. The advantage of ANN is, they are easy to understand and implement even

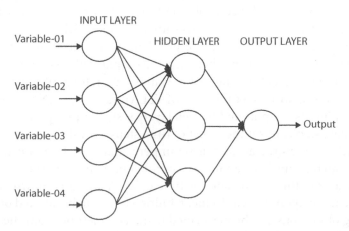

Figure 3.9 Various layers of ANN.

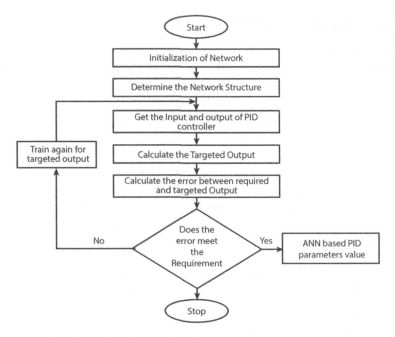

Figure 3.10 Flow chart of working and implementation of ANN.

by non-experts [15, 17]. The tedious mathematical observations for calculating values of controlling variables in the classical controller like K_p (Proportional gain), K_D (Derivative gain) and K_I (Integral gain) can quickly be calculated by this tool [16].

In MATLAB, the ANN tool is available, which can be used to create an ANN-based classical controller; in this case, ANN-based Proportional-Integral-Derivative (PID) controller [14, 35]. The first step is to select the dynamic time-series application. As shown in Figure 3.11.

Later, after selecting the type of problem from a given list, inputs are entered in a matrix form and then targeted output is also entered in matrix form. Through, MATLAB stands for Matrix Laboratory, all the data given and observed is in matrix form. A MATLAB layout of ANN tool which consist of inputs, outputs and hidden layers is shown in Figure 3.12.

The next step is to set the target of time steps for validation and testing for which the required amount is set in percentage. Further, it is to design network architecture by defining the number of neurons in the system, the hidden layer of the system, and the time delay. A layout is shown below.

Depending upon the requirement, hidden layer can be allotted on which training of neurons can be performed using any method from the following training algorithm [37].

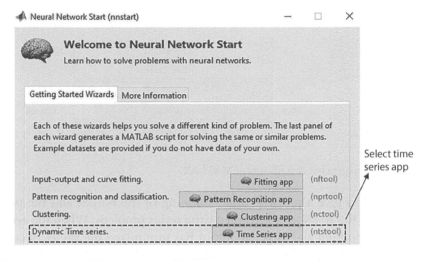

Figure 3.11 Neural Network Tool of MATLAB.

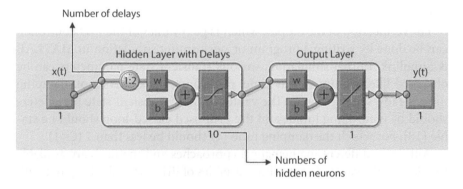

Figure 3.12 A layout of ANN tool of MATLAB.

1. Levenberg–Marquardt
2. Bayesian Regularization
3. Scaled Conjugate Gradient

Training can be performed up to several time until the error between the output and targeted output is minimized. The number of iterations can set accordingly to it. During training, a progress toll will open in which various parameters can be observed in real-time scenario as shown in Figure 3.13.

After the progress will be finished for the set values of the number of iterations. Different plots can be observed in plot window like the plot of error, performance plot, regression, time-series responses, etc. A list of available various plots is shown in Figure 3.14.

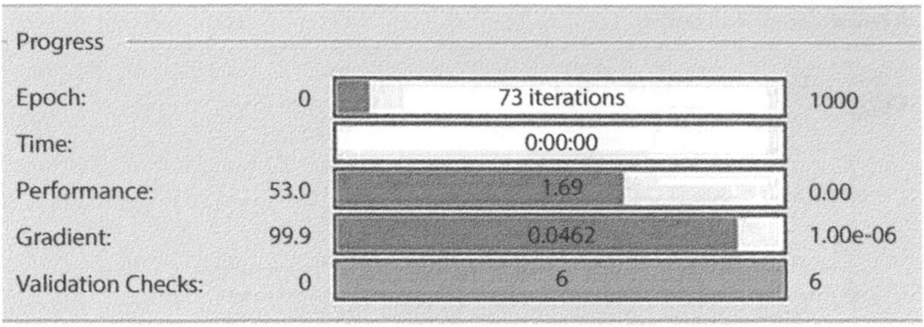

Progress			
Epoch:	0	73 iterations	1000
Time:		0:00:00	
Performance:	53.0	1.69	0.00
Gradient:	99.9	0.0462	1.00e-06
Validation Checks:	0	6	6

Figure 3.13 Progress bar of ANN tool of MATLAB.

Those plots give a pictorial understanding of the output and the performance of the ANN for the trained time series problem. When the error between the output and targeted output has minimized the values of controlling variables of PID controller will be found. Using those values of controlling parameters PID controller for the Proposed AMB model can be designed in which the values of the controlling variable have been calibrated by ANN [19, 40, 41].

For verification of the output, which is gain values of the PID controller, can be done by writing a program or performing simulation in MATLAB & Simulink. In that simulation, various transient state parameters can be observed like rise time, delay time, peak time, peak overshoot, damping ratio, steady-state error, etc. The values of these transient state parameters should be controlling limits, and the proposed closed-loop should be stable [18]. For which the damping ratio (ζ) should be less than 1 ($\zeta < 1$).

Although, different mathematical approaches and methods are available to calculate the value of controlling variables of PID controller [27]. But with

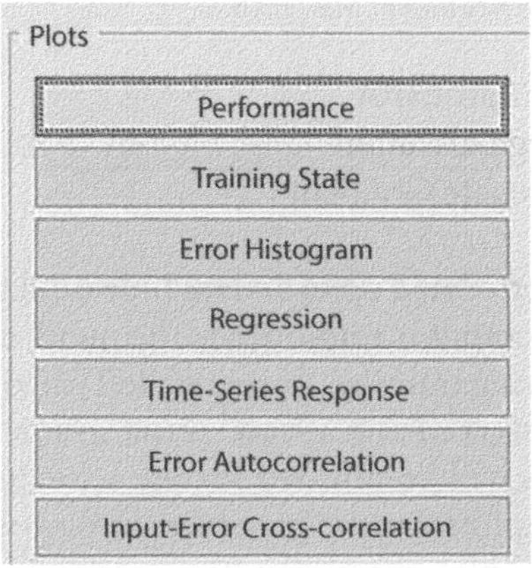

Plots
Performance
Training State
Error Histogram
Regression
Time-Series Response
Error Autocorrelation
Input-Error Cross-correlation

Figure 3.14 Various Plots of ANN tool of MATLAB.

the use of ANN that tedious and resilient mathematical calculation can be easily eliminated and the results are more accurate as compared to the results of a classical mathematical approach.

3.4.3   Particle Swarm Optimization (PSO)

Particle Swarm Optimization (PSO) described in the area of Artificial Intelligence. The term 'Artificial Intelligence' or 'Artificial Life' alludes to the hypothesis of re-enacting human conduct through calculation. It includes planning such PC frameworks that can execute errands that require human knowledge. For e.g., prior just people had the ability to perceive the discourse of an individual. Be that as it may, presently, discourse acknowledgment is a typical component of any computerized gadget. This has gotten conceivable through computerized reasoning. Different instances of human insight may incorporate basic leadership, language interpretation, and visual discernment and so forth. There are different procedures that make it conceivable. These techniques to implement artificial intelligence into computers are popularly known as approaches to artificial intelligence [34].

PSO is initially ascribed to Kennedy, Eberhart, and Shi and was first expected for intimidating social conduct, as appeared in Figure 3.15, as an adapted portrayal of the development of living beings in a flying creature rush or fish school. The calculation was improved and it was seen to perform streamlining. The book by Kennedy and Eberhart depicts numerous philosophical parts of PSO and swarm insight. A broad overview of PSO applications is made by Poli [7].

PSO is a metaheuristic as it makes not many or no suspicions about the issue being upgraded and can look through enormous spaces of applicant arrangements. In any case, metaheuristics, for example, PSO do not

(a)   (b)

Figure 3.15 (a) Fish school and (b) Flying creatures rush. Basic algorithm as proposed by Kennedy and Eberhart (1995).

Table 3.2 List of variables used in PSO.

y_k^i	Position of particle
v_k^i	Velocity of particle
p_k^i	Best "remembered" individual particle position
p_k^g	Best "remembered" swarm position
c_1, c_2	Cognitive parameters and social parameters
r_1, r_2	Random numbers between 0 and 1

ensure an ideal arrangement is ever found. All the more explicitly, PSO does not utilize the inclination of the issue being upgraded, which implies PSO does not necessitate that the advancement issue is differentiable as is required by exemplary streamlining techniques, for example, angle plummets and quasi newton strategies. PSO is, in this way, additionally utilized on enhancement issues that are somewhat irregular, boisterous, change after some time, and so on [29, 39].

3.4.4   Particle Swarm Optimization (PSO) Algorithm

A fundamental variation of the PSO calculation works by having a populace (called a swarm) of competitor arrangements (called particles). These particles are moved around in the hunt space as per a couple of basic formulae. The developments of the particles are guided by their own best-referred to position in the pursuit space just as the whole swarm's best-known position. At the point when improved positions are being found these will at that point come to control the developments of the swarm, the model appears in Figure 3.15. This figure shows a swarm or a school of winged creatures flying together, from the start they fly arbitrarily yet after, in some cases, when they find their ideal situation with the flawless speed they improved their position. The procedure is rehashed, and by doing so, it is trusted, yet not ensured, that an acceptable arrangement will, in the end, be found [30–32].

Considering the list of variables used in PSO as shown in Table 3.2 and after setting up the values of the particles and velocity using the following equation, the position of individual updates as:

$$y_{k+1}^i = y_k^i + v_{k+1}^i \tag{3.1}$$

And the velocity calculated as:

$$v_{k+1}^i = v_k^i + c_1 r_1 \left(p_k^i - y_k^i \right) c_2 r_2 \left(p_k^g - y_k^i \right) \tag{3.2}$$

A flow diagram for PSO algorithm flow is shown in Figure 3.16:

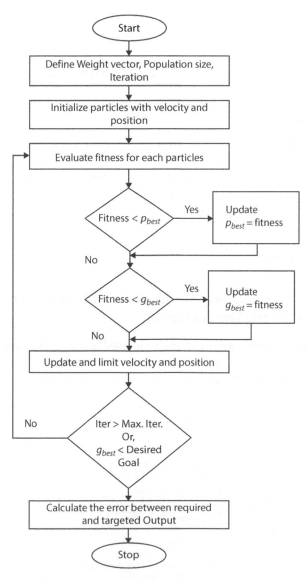

Figure 3.16 Flow chart of working and implementation of PSO.

Which can be explained by the following steps,

1. Initialization
a) Set the values of constants k_{maz}, c_1, c_2
b) Initialization of position of particles randomly, $y_o^i \in D$ in IR^n for $i = 1,...,p$
c) Initialization of velocity of particles randomly, $0 \le v_o^i \le v_o^{max}$ for $i = 1,...,p$
d) Set the value, $k = 1$

2. Optimization
a) Evaluate function value f_k^i using design space coordinates x_k^i
b) If $f_k^i \le f_{best}^i$ then $f_{best}^i = f_k^i$, $p_k^i = y_k^i$
c) If $f_k^i \le f_{best}^g$ then $f_{best}^g = f_k^i$, $p_k^g = y_k^i$
d) If the termination condition is satisfied, then go to step 3, termination
e) Updating all position of particles v_k^i for $i = 1,.....,p$
f) Updating all velocities of particles y_k^i for $1,.....,p$
g) Increment in value of k
h) Go to (a)

3. Termination

3.4.4.1   Implementation of Particle Swarm Optimization for Electric Vehicles System

Particle swarm optimization technique is used to calculate gain values of a conventional controller like PID controller. The calculated value of the gains is fed to the PID controller for controlling the AMB as shown in Figure 3.17.

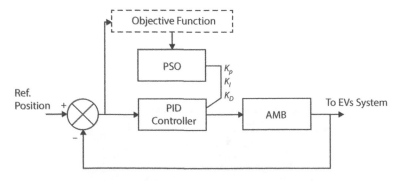

Figure 3.17 Implementation of PSO in AMB for EVs system.

Table 3.3 List of parameters.

S No.	Parameters
1.	Weight Factor
2.	Iterations
3.	Population Size
4.	Lower Translation Frequency
5.	Higher Translation frequency
6.	Order of Approximation
7.	Performance Index (ISE)

Before operating the PSO for calculation of gains value, various performance index parameters and constant values have to be set [33]. A list of those parameters is shown in Table 3.3.

Here, for performance index, Integral of squared error (ISE) is selected and depending upon the observation weight factor is selected, which should be below 1. Number of iterations increases the accuracy of the calculation, so almost 50–100 iterations are performed. Lower translation and higher translation frequency are selected depending upon the lower and upper bound of the system.

3.5   Conclusion

Active magnetic bearings are inherently unstable and extremely nonlinear systems. Using this system in any application like electric vehicles requires controllers to achieve a smooth and successful bearing performance. From the conventional point of view, classical controllers are efficient, but the tuning of the controlling variables is always creating a huge problem. Implementation of an artificial control technique for the different conditions in active magnetic bearing along with EV system is added a significant advantage in its applications. As nowadays, various optimization techniques are developed, among which three most useful optimization techniques, which are Fuzzy logic, Artificial neural network, and Particle swarm Optimization techniques is briefly described in this review. Apart from these optimization techniques, others can also be implemented for this system, and they have their advantages. But due to the word limit, only three control techniques are discussed in this chapter. Most of the Electric vehicles are battery-powered EVs (BEVs), so they require long-lasting battery storage, low losses, and efficient performance, which can be continuously provided by the flywheel energy storage system (FESS). However, with the use of conventional bearing in FESS, losses increase mostly due to friction and in the harsh environment, the performance of bearing degraded. With the use of AMB, these problems can be eliminated as there is no contact between the stationary and rotatory parts and in a very harsh environment the AMB performance does not degrade. In the Fuzzy logic controller, tuning is done automatically because the rules of fuzzy inference system are designed for the very same purpose. But the remaining two optimization techniques are used to calculate the controlling parameters or, the gains value of Proportional-Integral-Derivative (PID) controller, unlike fuzzy logic controller. Although there is a various combination of gain values for which the proposed AMB model is stable among them which one is best can be easily obtained by those two optimization techniques.

Every controller or, optimization techniques which are explained, have their advantages and disadvantages. If a controller or an optimization technique is useful in some aspects, it may be or may not be performing properly in other aspects. To get rid of these difficulties, hybrid optimization techniques can be used means two different optimization technique is used to optimize the system. This will eliminate the short coming of one optimization technique and improve the final output response.

References

1. Maslen, E.H. and Schweitzer, G., *Magnetic bearings: theory, design, and application to rotating machinery*, pp. 1–17, Springer-Verlag Berlin Heidelberg, Berlin, Heidelberg, 2009.
2. Pichot, M.A. *et al.*, Active magnetic bearings for energy storage systems for combat vehicles. *IEEE Trans. Magn.*, 37, 1, 318–323, 2001.
3. Abrahamson, J. and Bernhoff, H., Magnetic bearings in kinetic energy storage systems for vehicular applications. *J. Electr. Syst.*, 7, 2, 225–236, 2011.
4. Wang, Z. and Zhu, C., Active Control of Active Magnetic Bearings for Maglev Flywheel Rotor System Based on Sliding Mode Control. *2016 IEEE Vehicle Power and Propulsion Conference (VPPC)*, pp. 1–6, 2016.
5. Ren, M., Shen, Y., Li, Z., Nonami., K., Modeling and Control of a Flywheel Energy Storage System Using Active Magnetic Bearing for Vehicle. In *2009 International Conference on Information Engineering and Computer Science*, pp. 1–5, 2009.

6. Chau, K.-T., Jiang, C., Han, W., Lee, C.H.T., State-of-the-Art Electromagnetics Research in Electric and Hybrid Vehicles (Invited Paper). *Prog. Electromagn. Res.*, 159, 139–157, 2017.

7. Zhang, Y., Wang, S., Ji, G., A Comprehensive Survey on Particle Swarm Optimization Algorithm and Its Applications. *Math. Probl. Eng.*, vol. 2015, 38 pages, 2015. https://doi.org/10.1155/2015/931256

8. Koskinen, H., Fuzzy control schemes for active magnetic bearings, Fuzzy Logic in Artificial Intelligence. FLAI 1993, in: *Lecture Notes in Computer Science (Lecture Notes in Artificial Intelligence)*, vol. 695, E.P. Klement and W. Slany (Eds.), Springer, Berlin, Heidelberg, 1993.

9. Applications of Fuzzy Logic, in: *Introduction to Fuzzy Logic using MATLAB*, Springer, Berlin, Heidelberg, 2007.

10. Yixin, S., Xuan, L., Zude, Z. *et al.*, Fuzzy-immune PID control for AMB systems. *Wuhan Univ. J. Nat. Sci.*, Volume 11, 3, 637–641, 2006.

11. Liu, D., Zhang, K., Dong, J., Optimization of a Fuzzy PID Controller, in: *Electrical Engineering and Control. Lecture Notes in Electrical Engineering*, vol. 98, M. Zhu (Ed.), Springer, Berlin, Heidelberg, 2011.

12. Hong, S.-K. and Langari, R., Robust fuzzy control of a magnetic bearing system subject to harmonic disturbances. In: *IEEE Trans. Control Syst. Technol.*, 8, 2, 366–371, 2000.

13. Moulton, K.M., Cornell, A., Petriu, E., A fuzzy error correction control system. In: *IEEE Trans. Instrum. Meas.*, 50, 5, 1456–1463, 2001.

14. Cozma, A. and Pitica, D., Artificial neural network and PID based control system for DC motor drives. *2008 11th International Conference on Optimization of Electrical and Electronic Equipment*, Brasov, pp. 161–166, 2008.

15. Thangaraju, I., Muruganandam, M., Nagarajan, C., Implementation of PID Trained Artificial Neural Network Controller for Different DC Motor Drive. *Middle East J. Sci. Res.*, 23, 4, 606–618, 2015.

16. Ayomoh, M.K.O. and Ajala, M.T., Neural Network Modelling of a Tuned PID Controller. *Eur. J. Sci. Res.*, 71, 2, 283–297, 2012.

17. Jacob, R. and Murugan, S., Implementation of neural network based PID controller. *International Conference on Electrical, Electronics, and Optimization Techniques (ICEEOT)*, Chennai, pp. 2769–2771, 2016.

18. Sui, D. and Jiao, Z., Application of Neural Network in Optimization of PID Controller, *Metallurgical & Mining Industry*, 7, Ukraine, 2015.

19. Rivera-MejÃa, J., LÃ-Rubio, A.G., Arzabala-Contreras., E, PID Based on a Single Artificial Neural Network Algorithm for Intelligent Sensors. *J. Appl. Res. Technol.*, 10, 262–282, 2012.

20. Wu, H. and Shen, S., Application of PID Control and Theory. *Control Eng.*, 10, 1, 37–42, 2003.

21. Zhao, R. and Wang, X., Fuzzy PID Controller in Air-conditioning Temperature Control. *Comput. Simul.*, 23, 11, 311–313, 2006.

22. Rashid, H.M., *Power Electronics Handbook*, pp. 169, Academic Press, San Diego, California, 2001.
23. Ogata, K., *Discrete-Time Control Systems*, Prentice Hall Inc, New Jersey, 1996.
24. Rajasekaran, S. and Pai, G.V., *Neural networks, fuzzy logic and genetic algorithm: synthesis and applications (with cd)*, PHI Learning Pvt. Ltd, New Delhi, India, 2003.
25. Ogata, K., *Modern Control Engineering*, 4th Edition, Pearson Education (Singapore), Pvt. Ltd, India, 2004.
26. Yildirim, S., Vibration control of suspension systems using a proposed neural network. *J. Sound Vib.*, 277, 4–5, 1059–1069, 2004.
27. Leva, A. and Maggio, M., A systematic way to extend ideal PID tuning rules to the real structure. *J. Process Control*, 21, 1, 130–136, 2011.
28. Zadeh, L. A., Fuzzy sets, *Information and Control*, 8(3), pp. 338–353, 1965.
29. Eberhart, R.C. and Shi, Y., Comparing inertia weights and constriction factors in particle swarm optimization. *Proc. Congress on Evolutionary Computation 2000*, San Diego, CA, pp. 84–88, 2000.
30. Kennedy, J., The behavior of particles. In V. W. Porto, N. Saravanan, D. Waagen, and A. E. Eiben, Eds. *Evolutionary Programming VII: Proc. 7th Ann. Conf. on Evolutionary Programming Conf.*, San Diego, CA, Berlin: Springer-Verlag, pp. 581–589, 1998.
31. Kennedy, J., Thinking is social: experiments with the adaptive culture model. *J. Conflict Resolut.*, 42, 1, 56–76, 1998.
32. He, Z., Wei, C., Yang, L., Gao, X., Yao, S., Eberhart, R., Shi, Y., Extracting rules from fuzzy neural network by particle swarm optimization. *Proc. IEEE International Conference on Evolutionary Computation*, Anchorage, Alaska, USA. 1998.
33. Shi, Y. and Eberhart, R.C., Parameter selection in particle swarm optimization, in: *Evolutionary Programming VII: Proc. EP98*, pp. 591–600, Springer-Verlag, New York, 1998a.
34. Kennedy, J. and Eberhart, R.C., The particle swarm: social adaptation in information processing systems, in: *New Ideas in Optimization*, D. Corne, M. Dorigo, F. Glover (Eds.), McGraw-Hill, London, 1999.
35. Zhi-gang, Y. and Jun-lei, Q., PID Neural Network Adaptive Predictive Control for Long Time Delay System, in: *Information Computing and Applications. ICICA 2013. Communications in Computer and Information Science*, vol. 391, Y. Yang, M. Ma, B. Liu (Eds.), Springer, Berlin, Heidelberg, 2013.
36. Li, H.-J. and Xiao, B., Multistep recurrent neural network model predictive controller without constraints. *Control Theory Appl.*, 29, 5, 642–648, 2012.
37. Zhang, Y., Wang, F., Song, Y. *et al.*, *Recurrent neural networks-based multivariable system PID predictive control*, Volume 2, Issue 2, pp. 197–201, Frontiers of Electrical and Electronic Engineering, China, 2007.
38. Savran, A., Multivariable predictive fuzzy PID control system. *Appl. Soft Comput.*, 13, 5, 2658–2667, Elsevier, Netherlands, 2013.

39. Chavoshian, M., Taghizadeh, M., Mazare, M., Hybrid Dynamic Neural Network and PID Control of Pneumatic Artificial Muscle Using the PSO Algorithm. *Int. J. Autom. Comput.*, 1–11, 2019. https://doi.org/10.1007/s11633-019-1196-5

40. Yuan, X. and Wang, Y., Neural networks based self-learning PID control of electronic throttle. *Nonlinear Dynamics*, 55, 4, 385–393, Springer, Netherlands, 2009.

41. Zhai, L. and Chai, T., Nonlinear decoupling PID control using neural networks and multiple models. *J. Control Theory Appl.*, 4, 1, 62–69, 2006.

4

Small-Signal Modelling Analysis of Three-Phase Power Converters for EV Applications

Mohamed G. Hussien[1]*, Sanjeevikumar Padmanaban[2],
Abd El-Wahab Hassan[1] and Jens Bo Holm-Nielsen[2]

[1]Department of Electrical Power and Machines Engineering, Faculty of Engineering,
Tanta University, Tanta, Egypt
[2]Center for Bioenergy and Green Engineering, Department of Energy Technology,
Aalborg University, Esbjerg, Denmark

Abstract

This chapter aims at proposing a complete mathematical analysis and derivation of the small signal model for voltage-source inverter (VSI) with surface-mounted PMSM (SPMSM). The basic equations of the SPMSM model were developed and simulated using MATLAB/SIMULINK environment. In addition, the switch state functions were used to express the motor phase voltage and then develop mathematical model for VSI. In order to control the machine speed from standstill to rated speed with rated load, the vector control strategy was applied. To design the speed loop and current loop, anti-windup PI controllers were used. To verify the effectiveness of the presented analysis, some of obtained simulation results were discussed.

Keywords: Surface mounted PM synchronous motor (SPMSM), voltage-source inverter (VSI), average model, small signal model, bode diagram

4.1 Introduction

Power stages of PWM converters are nonlinear owing to the presence of at least one transistor and a diode [1–13]. In order to apply the known knowledge of linear control theory, the power stages need to be averaged and linearized [1]. Nonlinear power stages of PWM converters have been averaged

---

**Corresponding author*: mohamed.hussien3@f-eng.tanta.edu.eg

Chitra A, P. Sanjeevikumar, Jens Bo Holm-Nielsen and S. Himavathi (eds.) *Artificial Intelligent Techniques for Electric and Hybrid Electric Vehicles,* (77–102) © 2020 Scrivener Publishing LLC

by predominantly two methods: the state-space averaging technique and the circuit averaging technique [1, 14]. Both methods have been employed extensively in the past with respect to numerous PWM converters [1, 15–20].

Three-phase voltage-source inverter (VSI) as shown in Figure 4.1 employs a three-leg six-switch network fed by a voltage source [3, 4]. The six switches which are typically MOSFETs or IGBTs are switched in a specified sequence based on the modulation technique employed to synthesize the required ac output voltage.

State-space averaging [15] and circuit-averaging [14] methods have been two of the popular methods for obtaining small-signal models of PWM power converters. The state-space averaging technique involves the averaging of the state equations associated with the different switching states of a converter. In the circuit-averaging technique, the averaging is performed on the switching component waveforms. The circuit-averaging technique tends to give a better physical insight into the circuit behavior. The primary aspect in the circuit-averaging technique is to replace the non-linear switching network of the converter by an equivalent averaged and linearized network [1, 2, 16].

The aim of this chapter is to propose a complete mathematical analysis and derivation of the small signal model for VSI with SPMSM. In addition, the switch state functions were used to express the motor phase voltage and then develop mathematical model for VSI. Moreover, the speed loop and current loop are designed based on the anti-windup PI controllers.

The constant switching frequency is considered as 2.5 kHz.

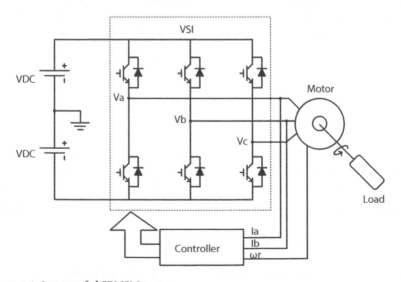

Figure 4.1 Inverter-fed SPMSM system.

Adopt $i_d = 0$ vector control strategy to control the machine from standstill to rated speed with rated load [21]. Use PI controller to design speed loop and current loop [22–25] with bandwidth $f_s = 10$ Hz and $f_c = 300$ Hz, respectively. The speed overshoot is required less than 5% and the settling time is within 0.5 s, and the limited current for the inverter is 50 A. The switching frequency is chosen as 2.5 kHz.

4.2   Overall System Modelling

4.2.1   PMSM Dynamic Model

The dynamic model of surface-mounted PMSM (SPMSM) in the rotor synchronous d-q coordinate can be expressed as:

The voltage equation of the machine in the *abc*-coordinate is written as:

$$v_{abc} = R_s\, i_{abc} + \frac{d}{dt}\psi_{abc} \tag{4.1}$$

In the rotating reference frame:

$$\theta_r = \omega_r t$$

where, ω_r is the electrical angular rotor-speed.

The *abc* reference frame to transformation rotor reference frame can be obtained using the following transformation matrix, T^r and the angle θ_r based on the phase-axis relationship shown in Figure 4.2.

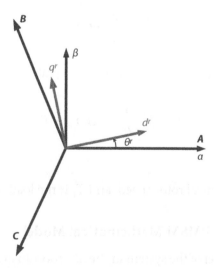

Figure 4.2 Phase–axis relationship of SPMSM.

$$T^r = \frac{2}{3} \begin{bmatrix} \cos \omega_r t & \cos\left(\omega_r t - \frac{2\pi}{3}\right) & \cos\left(\omega_r t + \frac{2\pi}{3}\right) \\ -\sin \omega_r t & -\sin\left(\omega_r t - \frac{2\pi}{3}\right) & -\sin\left(\omega_r t + \frac{2\pi}{3}\right) \end{bmatrix}$$

From which, the dq-axis voltage equations can be expressed as:

$$\left. \begin{aligned} v_d^r &= R\, i_d^r + \frac{d}{dt}\psi_d - \omega_r \psi_q \\ v_q^r &= R\, i_q^r + \frac{d}{dt}\psi_q + \omega_r \psi_d \end{aligned} \right\} \tag{4.2}$$

In addition, the stator dq-axis flux linkages can be written as:

$$\left. \begin{aligned} \psi_d &= L\, i_d^r + \psi_f \\ \psi_q &= L\, i_q^r \end{aligned} \right\} \tag{4.3}$$

where, ψ_f is the flux of the magnets.

Moreover, the electromagnetic-torque expression is represented as:

$$T_e = \frac{3}{2} p \psi_f i_q \tag{4.4}$$

Furthermore, the electromechanical torque equation is given as:

$$T_e = J \frac{d\omega_{rm}}{dt} + B\omega_{rm} + T_L \tag{4.5}$$

where,

ω_{rm} is the mechanical rotor speed, and T_L is the load torque, N·m.

4.2.2   VSI-Fed SPMSM Mathematical Model

The switching model of the system in the *abc* coordinates can be expressed, based on Figure 4.3, as:

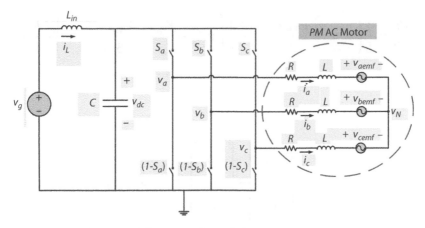

Figure 4.3 Switching model circuit of VSI-fed SPMSM.

By applying Kirchhoff Voltage Law:

$$
\left.
\begin{aligned}
v_a - v_N &= L\frac{di_a}{dt} + R\,i_a + v_{a_{emf}} \\[2mm]
v_b - v_N &= L\frac{di_b}{dt} + R\,i_b + v_{b_{emf}} \\[2mm]
v_c - v_N &= L\frac{di_c}{dt} + R\,i_c + v_{c_{emf}}
\end{aligned}
\right\} \tag{4.6}
$$

By summing the phase voltage equations in Equation (4.6),
  Using, $i_a + i_b + i_c = 0$
Then,

$$
v_N = \frac{v_a + v_b + v_c}{3} - \frac{v_{a_{emf}} + v_{b_{emf}} + v_{c_{emf}}}{3}
$$

From which,

$$
\frac{di_a}{dt} = \frac{1}{L}\left(v_a - \frac{v_a + v_b + v_c}{3}\right) - \frac{1}{L}\left(v_{a_{emf}} - \frac{v_{a_{emf}} + v_{b_{emf}} + v_{c_{emf}}}{3}\right) - \frac{R}{L}\,i_a
$$

$$
\frac{di_b}{dt} = \frac{1}{L}\left(v_b - \frac{v_a + v_b + v_c}{3}\right) - \frac{1}{L}\left(v_{b_{emf}} - \frac{v_{a_{emf}} + v_{b_{emf}} + v_{c_{emf}}}{3}\right) - \frac{R}{L}\,i_b
$$

$$\frac{di_c}{dt} = \frac{1}{L}\left(v_c - \frac{v_a + v_b + v_c}{3}\right) - \frac{1}{L}\left(v_{c_{emf}} - \frac{v_{a_{emf}} + v_{b_{emf}} + v_{c_{emf}}}{3}\right) - \frac{R}{L}i_c$$

By using,

$$\vec{v}_{ph} = \begin{bmatrix} v_a \\ v_b \\ v_c \end{bmatrix} = \begin{bmatrix} s_a \\ s_b \\ s_c \end{bmatrix} \cdot v_{dc} = \vec{s}_{ph} \cdot v_{dc}$$

$$\vec{v}_{emf} = \begin{bmatrix} v_{a_{emf}} \\ v_{b_{emf}} \\ v_{c_{emf}} \end{bmatrix},$$

$$\vec{i}_{ph} = \begin{bmatrix} i_a \\ i_b \\ i_c \end{bmatrix}$$

Then,

$$\frac{d\vec{i}_{ph}}{dt} = \frac{1}{L}\left(E - \frac{1}{3}X\right)\vec{s}_{ph} \cdot v_{dc} - \frac{1}{L}\left(E - \frac{1}{3}X\right)\vec{v}_{emf} - \frac{R}{L}\vec{i}_{ph} \qquad (4.7)$$

which,

$$E = \begin{bmatrix} 1 & 0 & 0 \\ 0 & 1 & 0 \\ 0 & 0 & 1 \end{bmatrix}, X = \begin{bmatrix} 1 & 1 & 1 \\ 1 & 1 & 1 \\ 1 & 1 & 1 \end{bmatrix}$$

On the other hand, the DC-side relations can be given as

$$v_g - L_{in}\frac{di_L}{dt} - v_{dc} = 0$$

$$i_L = C\frac{dv_{dc}}{dt} + i_{dc}$$

$$i_{dc} = \begin{bmatrix} s_a & s_b & s_c \end{bmatrix} \cdot \begin{bmatrix} i_a \\ i_b \\ i_c \end{bmatrix} = \vec{s}_{ph}^{T} \cdot \vec{i}_{ph}$$

From which,

$$\left.\begin{array}{l} \dfrac{di_L}{dt} = \dfrac{1}{L_{in}}\left(v_g - v_{dc}\right) \\[3mm] \dfrac{dv_{dc}}{dt} = \dfrac{1}{C}\left(i_L - \vec{s}_{ph}^{T} \cdot \vec{i}_{ph}\right) \end{array}\right\} \qquad (4.8)$$

By applying the average operator:

$$\frac{d\bar{\vec{i}}_{ph}}{dt} = \frac{1}{L}\left(E - \frac{1}{3}X\right)\bar{\vec{d}}_{ph} \cdot \bar{v}_{dc} - \frac{1}{L}\left(E - \frac{1}{3}X\right)\bar{\vec{v}}_{emf} - \frac{R}{L}\bar{\vec{i}}_{ph} \quad (4.9)$$

$$\left.\begin{array}{l} \dfrac{d\bar{i}_L}{dt} = \dfrac{1}{L_{in}}\left(\bar{v}_g - \bar{v}_{dc}\right) \\[3mm] \dfrac{d\bar{v}_{dc}}{dt} = \dfrac{1}{C}\left(\bar{i}_L - \bar{\vec{d}}_{ph}^{T} \cdot \bar{\vec{i}}_{ph}\right) \end{array}\right\} \qquad (4.10)$$

$$\vec{d}_{ph} = \begin{bmatrix} d_a \\ d_b \\ d_c \end{bmatrix} = \begin{bmatrix} \bar{s}_a \\ \bar{s}_b \\ \bar{s}_c \end{bmatrix}$$

where,

Based on Equation (4.9), the dqo model can be obtained, aided with the matrix, T, and the angle θ_r, as follows:

Coordinate transformation:

$$x_{dqo} = T x_{abc}; \; x_{abc} = T^{-1} x_{dqo}$$

From the average-model in Equation (4.9),

$$\frac{d(T^{-1} \, \overline{\vec{i}}_{dqo})}{dt} = \frac{1}{L_s}\left(E - \frac{1}{3}X\right)T^{-1}\,\vec{d}_{dqo} \cdot \overline{v}_{dc}$$
$$- \frac{1}{L}\left(E - \frac{1}{3}X\right)T^{-1}\,\overline{v}_{dqo_{emf}} - \frac{R}{L}T^{-1}\,\overline{\vec{i}}_{dqo}$$

From which,

$$\frac{d(T^{-1})}{dt}\overline{\vec{i}}_{dqo} + T^{-1}\frac{d\left(\overline{\vec{i}}_{dqo}\right)}{dt} = \frac{1}{L}\left(E - \frac{1}{3}X\right)T^{-1}\,\vec{d}_{dqo} \cdot \overline{v}_{dc}$$
$$- \frac{1}{L}\left(E - \frac{1}{3}X\right)T^{-1}\,\overline{v}_{dqo_{emf}} - \frac{R}{L}T^{-1}\,\overline{\vec{i}}_{dqo}$$

$$T\frac{d(T^{-1})}{dt}\overline{\vec{i}}_{dqo} + T\,T^{-1}\frac{d\left(\overline{\vec{i}}_{dqo}\right)}{dt} = \frac{1}{L}T\left(E - \frac{1}{3}X\right)T^{-1}\,\vec{d}_{dqo} \cdot \overline{v}_{dc}$$
$$- \frac{1}{L}T\left(E - \frac{1}{3}X\right)T^{-1}\,\overline{v}_{dqo_{emf}} - \frac{R}{L}TT^{-1}\,\overline{\vec{i}}_{dqo}$$

Then,

$$T\frac{d(T^{-1})}{dt}\vec{\bar{i}}_{dqo} + \frac{d\left(\vec{\bar{i}}_{dqo}\right)}{dt} = \frac{1}{L}\vec{d}_{dqo}\cdot\vec{\bar{v}}_{dc} - \frac{1}{3L}Q\,\vec{d}_{dqo}\cdot\vec{\bar{v}}_{dc}$$

$$-\left(\frac{1}{L}\vec{\bar{v}}_{dqo_{emf}} - \frac{1}{3L}Q\,\vec{\bar{v}}_{dqo_{emf}}\right) - \frac{R}{L}\vec{\bar{i}}_{dqo}$$

where, $Q = \begin{bmatrix} 0 & 0 & 0 \\ 0 & 0 & 0 \\ 0 & 0 & 3 \end{bmatrix}$

Using, $T\dfrac{d(T^{-1})}{dt} = \begin{bmatrix} 0 & -\omega_r & 0 \\ \omega_r & 0 & 0 \\ 0 & 0 & 0 \end{bmatrix}$

Then,

$$\frac{d\left(\vec{\bar{i}}_{dqo}\right)}{dt} = \frac{1}{L}\vec{d}_{dqo}\cdot\vec{\bar{v}}_{dc} - \frac{1}{3L}Q\,\vec{d}_{dqo}\cdot\vec{\bar{v}}_{dc} - \left(\frac{1}{L}\vec{\bar{v}}_{dqo_{emf}} - \frac{1}{3L}Q\,\vec{\bar{v}}_{dqo_{emf}}\right)$$

$$-\begin{bmatrix} 0 & -\omega_r & 0 \\ \omega_r & 0 & 0 \\ 0 & 0 & 0 \end{bmatrix}\vec{\bar{i}}_{dqo} - \frac{R}{L}\vec{\bar{i}}_{dqo}$$

For the DC-side,

$$\frac{d\bar{v}_{dc}}{dt} = \frac{1}{C}\left(\bar{i}_L - \vec{d}_{dqo_{ph}}^{T}\;.T\;T^{-1}.\vec{\bar{i}}_{dqo_{ph}}\right)$$

Then,

$$\frac{d\bar{v}_{dc}}{dt} = \frac{1}{C}\left(\bar{i}_L - \vec{d}_{dqo_{ph}}^{T}\;.\vec{\bar{i}}_{dqo_{ph}}\right)$$

$$\frac{d\overline{i_L}}{dt} = \frac{1}{L_{in}}\left(\overline{v}_g - \overline{v}_{dc}\right)$$

By omitting the zero-sequence component for balanced system, the dq-axis model of the VSI-fed SPMSM can be summarized as:

$$\left.\begin{array}{l} d_d \cdot \overline{v}_{dc} = R\overline{i_d} + L\dfrac{d\overline{i_d}}{dt} - \omega_r\, L\,\overline{i_q} + \overline{v}_{d_{emf}} \\[4mm] d_q \cdot \overline{v}_{dc} = R\overline{i_q} + L\dfrac{d\overline{i_q}}{dt} + \omega_r\, L\,\overline{i_d} + \overline{v}_{q_{emf}} \end{array}\right\} \tag{4.11}$$

Using, $\overline{v}_{d_{emf}} = 0;\ \overline{v}_{q_{emf}} = \omega_r\,\psi_f$

Then, the final dq-axis model of VSI-fed SPMSM can be expressed as:

$$\left.\begin{array}{l} d_d \cdot \overline{v}_{dc} = R\,\overline{i_d} + L\dfrac{d\overline{i_d}}{dt} - \omega_r\, L\,\overline{i_q} \\[4mm] d_q \cdot \overline{v}_{dc} = R\,\overline{i_q} + L\dfrac{d\overline{i_q}}{dt} + \omega_r\, L\,\overline{i_d} + \omega_r\,\psi_f \end{array}\right\} \tag{4.12}$$

4.3   Mathematical Analysis and Derivation of the Small-Signal Model

4.3.1   The Small-Signal Model of the System

From the dq-model,

$$\frac{d}{dt}\begin{bmatrix} \overline{i}_{d\,ph} \\ \overline{i}_{q\,ph} \end{bmatrix} = \frac{1}{L}\begin{bmatrix} d_{d\,ph} \\ d_{q\,ph} \end{bmatrix} \cdot \overline{v}_{dc} - \frac{1}{L}\begin{bmatrix} \overline{v}_{d_{emf}} \\ \overline{v}_{q_{emf}} \end{bmatrix} - \begin{bmatrix} 0 & -\omega \\ \omega & 0 \end{bmatrix} \cdot \begin{bmatrix} \overline{i}_{d\,ph} \\ \overline{i}_{q\,ph} \end{bmatrix}$$

$$-\frac{R}{L}\begin{bmatrix} \overline{i}_{d\,ph} \\ \overline{i}_{q\,ph} \end{bmatrix} \qquad \frac{d\overline{v}_{dc}}{dt} = \frac{1}{C}\left(\overline{i}_L - \begin{bmatrix} d_{d\,ph} & d_{q\,ph} \end{bmatrix} \cdot \begin{bmatrix} \overline{i}_{d\,ph} \\ \overline{i}_{q\,ph} \end{bmatrix}\right)$$

$$\frac{d\overline{i}_L}{dt} = \frac{1}{L_{in}}\left(\overline{v}_g - \overline{v}_{dc}\right)$$

Applying small-signal model,

$$\frac{d}{dt}\begin{bmatrix} \tilde{i}_{d_{ph}} \\ \tilde{i}_{q_{ph}} \end{bmatrix} = \frac{1}{L}\begin{bmatrix} D_{d_{ph}} \\ D_{q_{ph}} \end{bmatrix} \cdot \tilde{v}_{dc} + \frac{1}{L}\begin{bmatrix} \tilde{d}_{d_{ph}} \\ \tilde{d}_{q_{ph}} \end{bmatrix} \cdot V_{dc} - \frac{1}{L}\begin{bmatrix} \tilde{v}_{d_{emf}} \\ \tilde{v}_{q_{emf}} \end{bmatrix}$$

$$- \begin{bmatrix} 0 & -\omega \\ \omega & 0 \end{bmatrix} \cdot \begin{bmatrix} \tilde{i}_{d_{ph}} \\ \tilde{i}_{q_{ph}} \end{bmatrix} - \frac{R}{L}\begin{bmatrix} \tilde{i}_{d_{ph}} \\ \tilde{i}_{q_{ph}} \end{bmatrix}$$

$$\tag{4.13}$$

$$\frac{d\tilde{v}_{dc}}{dt} = \frac{1}{C}\left(\tilde{i}_L - \begin{bmatrix} D_{d_{ph}} & D_{q_{ph}} \end{bmatrix} \cdot \begin{bmatrix} \tilde{i}_{d_{ph}} \\ \tilde{i}_{q_{ph}} \end{bmatrix} - \right.$$

$$\left. \begin{bmatrix} \tilde{d}_{d_{ph}} & \tilde{d}_{q_{ph}} \end{bmatrix} \cdot \begin{bmatrix} I_{d_{ph}} \\ I_{q_{ph}} \end{bmatrix} \right)$$

$$\frac{d\tilde{i}_L}{dt} = \frac{1}{L_{in}}\left(\tilde{v}_g - \tilde{v}_{dc} \right)$$

$$\tag{4.14}$$

4.3.2   Small-Signal Model Transfer Functions

From the small-signal model in dq-coordinates in Equations (4.13) and (4.14),

$$\frac{d}{dt}\begin{bmatrix} \tilde{i}_{d_{ph}} \\ \tilde{i}_{q_{ph}} \end{bmatrix} = \frac{1}{L}\begin{bmatrix} D_{d_{ph}} \\ D_{q_{ph}} \end{bmatrix} \cdot \tilde{v}_{dc} + \frac{1}{L}\begin{bmatrix} \tilde{d}_{d_{ph}} \\ \tilde{d}_{q_{ph}} \end{bmatrix} \cdot V_{dc}$$

$$- \frac{1}{L}\begin{bmatrix} \tilde{v}_{d_{emf}} \\ \tilde{v}_{q_{emf}} \end{bmatrix} - \begin{bmatrix} 0 & -\omega \\ \omega & 0 \end{bmatrix} \cdot \begin{bmatrix} \tilde{i}_{d_{ph}} \\ \tilde{i}_{q_{ph}} \end{bmatrix} - \frac{R}{L}\begin{bmatrix} \tilde{i}_{d_{ph}} \\ \tilde{i}_{q_{ph}} \end{bmatrix}$$

$$\frac{d\tilde{v}_{dc}}{dt} = \frac{1}{C}\left(\tilde{i}_L - \begin{bmatrix} D_{d_{ph}} & D_{q_{ph}} \end{bmatrix} \cdot \begin{bmatrix} \tilde{i}_{d_{ph}} \\ \tilde{i}_{q_{ph}} \end{bmatrix} - \begin{bmatrix} \tilde{d}_{d_{ph}} & \tilde{d}_{q_{ph}} \end{bmatrix} \cdot \begin{bmatrix} I_{d_{ph}} \\ I_{q_{ph}} \end{bmatrix} \right)$$

$$\frac{d\tilde{i}_L}{dt} = \frac{1}{L_{in}}\left(\tilde{v}_g - \tilde{v}_{dc} \right)$$

From which, put $\tilde{v}_g = 0$

$$
\frac{d}{dt}\begin{bmatrix} \tilde{i}_{d_{ph}} \\ \tilde{i}_{q_{ph}} \\ \tilde{v}_{dc} \\ \tilde{i}_L \end{bmatrix} = \begin{bmatrix} \dfrac{-R}{L} & \omega & \dfrac{D_d}{L} & 0 \\[2mm] -\omega & \dfrac{-R}{L} & \dfrac{D_q}{L} & 0 \\[2mm] \dfrac{-D_d}{C} & \dfrac{-D_q}{C} & 0 & \dfrac{1}{C} \\[2mm] 0 & 0 & \dfrac{-1}{L_{in}} & 0 \end{bmatrix} \begin{bmatrix} \tilde{i}_{d_{ph}} \\ \tilde{i}_{q_{ph}} \\ \tilde{v}_{dc} \\ \tilde{i}_L \end{bmatrix}
$$

$$
+ \begin{bmatrix} \dfrac{V_{dc}}{L} & 0 \\[2mm] 0 & \dfrac{V_{dc}}{L} \\[2mm] \dfrac{-I_d}{C} & \dfrac{-I_q}{C} \\[2mm] 0 & 0 \end{bmatrix} \begin{bmatrix} \tilde{d}_{d_{ph}} \\ \tilde{d}_{q_{ph}} \end{bmatrix}
$$

$$
+ \begin{bmatrix} \dfrac{-1}{L} & 0 \\[2mm] 0 & \dfrac{-1}{L} \\[2mm] 0 & 0 \\[2mm] 0 & 0 \end{bmatrix} \begin{bmatrix} \tilde{v}_{d_{emf}} \\ \tilde{v}_{q_{emf}} \end{bmatrix}
$$

Applying Laplace Transformation:

$$
\begin{bmatrix}
s & 0 & 0 & 0 \\
0 & s & 0 & 0 \\
0 & 0 & s & 0 \\
0 & 0 & 0 & s
\end{bmatrix}
\cdot
\begin{bmatrix}
\tilde{i}_{d_{ph}} \\
\tilde{i}_{q_{ph}} \\
\tilde{v}_{dc} \\
\tilde{i}_{L}
\end{bmatrix}
$$

$$
=
\begin{bmatrix}
\dfrac{-R}{L} & \omega & \dfrac{D_d}{L} & 0 \\
-\omega & \dfrac{-R}{L} & \dfrac{D_q}{L} & 0 \\
\dfrac{-D_d}{C} & \dfrac{-D_q}{C} & 0 & \dfrac{1}{C} \\
0 & 0 & \dfrac{-1}{L_{in}} & 0
\end{bmatrix}
\begin{bmatrix}
\tilde{i}_{d_{ph}} \\
\tilde{i}_{q_{ph}} \\
\tilde{v}_{dc} \\
\tilde{i}_{L}
\end{bmatrix}
$$

$$
+
\begin{bmatrix}
\dfrac{V_{dc}}{L} & 0 \\
0 & \dfrac{V_{dc}}{L} \\
\dfrac{-I_d}{C} & \dfrac{-I_q}{C} \\
0 & 0
\end{bmatrix}
\begin{bmatrix}
\tilde{d}_{d_{ph}} \\
\tilde{d}_{q_{ph}}
\end{bmatrix}
$$

$$
+
\begin{bmatrix}
\dfrac{-1}{L} & 0 \\
0 & \dfrac{-1}{L} \\
0 & 0 \\
0 & 0
\end{bmatrix}
\begin{bmatrix}
\tilde{v}_{d_{emf}} \\
\tilde{v}_{q_{emf}}
\end{bmatrix}
$$

From which,

$$
\begin{bmatrix}
s+\dfrac{R}{L} & -\omega & \dfrac{-D_d}{L} & 0 \\[2ex]
\omega & s+\dfrac{R}{L} & \dfrac{-D_q}{L} & 0 \\[2ex]
\dfrac{D_d}{C} & \dfrac{D_q}{C} & s & \dfrac{-1}{C} \\[2ex]
0 & 0 & \dfrac{1}{L_{in}} & s
\end{bmatrix}
\begin{bmatrix}
\tilde{i}_{d_{ph}} \\[1ex]
\tilde{i}_{q_{ph}} \\[1ex]
\tilde{v}_{dc} \\[1ex]
\tilde{i}_L
\end{bmatrix}
$$

$$
=
\begin{bmatrix}
\dfrac{V_{dc}}{L} & 0 \\[2ex]
0 & \dfrac{V_{dc}}{L} \\[2ex]
\dfrac{-I_d}{C} & \dfrac{-I_q}{C} \\[2ex]
0 & 0
\end{bmatrix}
\begin{bmatrix}
\tilde{d}_{d_{ph}} \\[1ex]
\tilde{d}_{q_{ph}}
\end{bmatrix}
$$

$$
+
\begin{bmatrix}
\dfrac{-1}{L} & 0 \\[2ex]
0 & \dfrac{-1}{L} \\[2ex]
0 & 0 \\[1ex]
0 & 0
\end{bmatrix}
\begin{bmatrix}
\tilde{v}_{d_{emf}} \\[1ex]
\tilde{v}_{q_{emf}}
\end{bmatrix}
$$

Then,

$$
\begin{bmatrix}
\tilde{i}_{d_{ph}} \\
\tilde{i}_{q_{ph}} \\
\tilde{v}_{dc} \\
\tilde{i}_L
\end{bmatrix}
=
\begin{bmatrix}
s+\dfrac{R}{L} & -\omega & \dfrac{-D_d}{L} & 0 \\[2mm]
\omega & s+\dfrac{R}{L} & \dfrac{-D_q}{L} & 0 \\[2mm]
\dfrac{D_d}{C} & \dfrac{D_q}{C} & s & \dfrac{-1}{C} \\[2mm]
0 & 0 & \dfrac{1}{L_{in}} & s
\end{bmatrix}^{-1}
$$

$$
\begin{bmatrix}
\dfrac{V_{dc}}{L} & 0 \\[2mm]
0 & \dfrac{V_{dc}}{L} \\[2mm]
\dfrac{-I_d}{C} & \dfrac{-I_q}{C} \\[2mm]
0 & 0
\end{bmatrix}
\begin{bmatrix}
\tilde{d}_{d_{ph}} \\
\tilde{d}_{q_{ph}}
\end{bmatrix}
+
\begin{bmatrix}
s+\dfrac{R}{L} & -\omega & \dfrac{-D_d}{L} & 0 \\[2mm]
\omega & s+\dfrac{R}{L} & \dfrac{-D_q}{L} & 0 \\[2mm]
\dfrac{D_d}{C} & \dfrac{D_q}{C} & s & \dfrac{-1}{C} \\[2mm]
0 & 0 & \dfrac{1}{L_{in}} & s
\end{bmatrix}^{-1}
$$

$$
\begin{bmatrix}
\dfrac{-1}{L} & 0 \\[2mm]
0 & \dfrac{-1}{L} \\[2mm]
0 & 0 \\[2mm]
0 & 0
\end{bmatrix}
\begin{bmatrix}
\tilde{v}_{d_{emf}} \\
\tilde{v}_{q_{emf}}
\end{bmatrix}
$$

Using the following matrix inverse,

$$
\begin{bmatrix}
s+\dfrac{R}{L} & -\omega & \dfrac{-D_d}{L} & 0 \\[2mm]
\omega & s+\dfrac{R}{L} & \dfrac{-D_q}{L} & 0 \\[2mm]
\dfrac{D_d}{C} & \dfrac{D_q}{C} & s & \dfrac{-1}{C} \\[2mm]
0 & 0 & \dfrac{1}{L_{in}} & s
\end{bmatrix}^{-1}
$$

$$
= \frac{1}{X}
\begin{bmatrix}
A_1 & B_1 & C_1 & D_1 \\
A_2 & B_2 & C_2 & D_2 \\
A_3 & B_3 & C_3 & D_3 \\
A_4 & B_4 & C_4 & D_4
\end{bmatrix}
$$

where,

$$
X = s^4 + \frac{2R}{L}s^3 + \left(\frac{R^2}{L^2} + \frac{1}{L_{in}C} + \frac{D_q^2}{LC} + \frac{D_d^2}{LC} + \omega^2 \right)s^2
$$

$$
+ \left(\frac{2R}{LL_{in}C} + \frac{RD_q^2}{L^2 C} + \frac{RD_d^2}{L^2 C} \right)s + \left(\frac{R^2}{L^2 L_{in}C} + \frac{\omega^2}{L_{in}C} \right)
$$

$$A_1 = s^3 + \frac{R}{L}s^2 + \left(\frac{1}{L_{in}C} + \frac{D_q^2}{LC}\right)s + \frac{R}{LL_{in}C}$$

$$A_2 = -\left(\omega s^2 + \frac{D_d D_q}{LC}s + \frac{\omega}{L_{in}C}\right)$$

$$A_3 = -\frac{D_d}{C}s^2 + \left(\frac{\omega D_q}{C} - \frac{D_d R}{LC}\right)s$$

$$A_4 = \frac{D_d}{L_{in}C}s + \left(\frac{RD_d}{LL_{in}C} - \frac{\omega D_q}{L_{in}C}\right)$$

$$B_1 = \omega s^2 - \frac{D_d D_q}{LC}s + \frac{\omega}{L_{in}C}$$

$$B_2 = s^3 + \frac{R}{L}s^2 + \left(\frac{1}{L_{in}C} + \frac{D_d^2}{LC}\right)s + \frac{R}{LL_{in}C}$$

$$B_3 = -\left(\frac{D_q}{C}s^2 + \left(\frac{RD_q}{LC} + \frac{D_d\omega}{C}\right)s\right)$$

$$B_4 = \frac{D_q}{L_{in}C}s + \left(\frac{R D_q}{LL_{in}C} + \frac{D_d\omega}{L_{in}C}\right)$$

$$C_1 = \frac{D_d}{L}s^2 + \left(\frac{\omega D_q}{L} + \frac{R\,D_d}{L^2}\right)s$$

$$C_2 = \frac{D_q}{L}s^2 + \left(\frac{R\,D_q}{L^2} - \frac{\omega\,D_d}{L}\right)s$$

$$C_3 = s^3 + \frac{2R}{L}s^2 + \left(\left(\frac{R}{L}\right)^2 + \omega^2\right)s$$

$$C_4 = -\left(\frac{1}{L_{in}}s^2 + \frac{2R}{LL_{in}}s + \left[\frac{R^2}{L^2 L_{in}} + \frac{\omega^2}{L_{in}}\right]\right)$$

$$D_1 = \frac{D_d}{LC}s + \left(\frac{RD_d}{L^2C} + \frac{\omega D_q}{LC}\right)$$

$$D_2 = \frac{D_q}{LC}s + \left(\frac{RD_q}{L^2C} - \frac{\omega D_d}{LC}\right)$$

$$D_3 = \frac{1}{C}s^2 + \frac{2R}{LC}s + \left(\frac{R^2}{L^2C} + \frac{\omega^2}{C}\right)$$

$$D_4 = s^3 + \frac{2R}{L}s^2 + \left(\frac{R^2}{L^2} + \frac{D_q^2 + D_d^2}{LC} + \omega^2\right)s + \frac{R\left(D_q^2 + D_d^2\right)}{L^2C}$$

From which,

$$
\begin{bmatrix} \tilde{i}_{d_{ph}} \\ \tilde{i}_{q_{ph}} \\ \tilde{v}_{dc} \\ \tilde{i}_{L} \end{bmatrix} = \begin{bmatrix} \left(\dfrac{V_{dc}}{L} \dfrac{A_1}{X} - \dfrac{I_d}{C} \dfrac{C_1}{X} \right) \\ \left(\dfrac{V_{dc}}{L} \dfrac{A_2}{X} - \dfrac{I_d}{C} \dfrac{C_2}{X} \right) \\ \left(\dfrac{V_{dc}}{L} \dfrac{A_3}{X} - \dfrac{I_d}{C} \dfrac{C_3}{X} \right) \\ \left(\dfrac{V_{dc}}{L} \dfrac{A_4}{X} - \dfrac{I_d}{C} \dfrac{C_4}{X} \right) \end{bmatrix} \begin{bmatrix} \tilde{d}_{d_{ph}} \\ \tilde{d}_{q_{ph}} \end{bmatrix}
$$

$$
+ \begin{bmatrix} \dfrac{-A_1}{L\,X} & \dfrac{-B_1}{L\,X} \\ \dfrac{-A_2}{L\,X} & \dfrac{-B_2}{L\,X} \\ \dfrac{-A_3}{L\,X} & \dfrac{-B_3}{L\,X} \\ \dfrac{-A_4}{L\,X} & \dfrac{-B_4}{L\,X} \end{bmatrix} \begin{bmatrix} \tilde{v}_{d_{emf}} \\ \tilde{v}_{q_{emf}} \end{bmatrix}
$$

Therefore,

$$
\frac{\tilde{i}_{d_{ph}}}{\tilde{d}_{d_{ph}}} = \frac{\dfrac{V_{dc}}{L}s^3 + \left(\dfrac{RV_{dc}}{L^2} - \dfrac{I_d D_d}{LC} \right)s^2 + \left(\dfrac{V_{dc}}{LL_{in}C} + \dfrac{V_{dc}\,D_q^2}{L^2C} - \dfrac{\omega D_q I_d}{LC} - \dfrac{R\,D_d I_d}{L^2C} \right)s + \dfrac{RV_{dc}}{L^2 L_{in}C}}{s^4 + \dfrac{2R}{L}s^3 + \left(\dfrac{R^2}{L^2} + \dfrac{1}{L_{in}C} + \dfrac{D_q^2}{LC} + \dfrac{D_d^2}{LC} + \omega^2 \right)s^2 + \left(\dfrac{2R}{LL_{in}C} + \dfrac{RD_q^2}{L^2C} + \dfrac{RD_d^2}{L^2C} \right)s + \left(\dfrac{R^2}{L^2 L_{in}C} + \dfrac{\omega^2}{L_{in}C} \right)}
$$

$$
\frac{\tilde{i}_{d_{ph}}}{\tilde{d}_{q_{ph}}} = \frac{\left(\dfrac{V_{dc}}{L}\omega - \dfrac{I_q D_d}{LC} \right)s^2 - \left(\dfrac{V_{dc}D_d D_q}{L^2C} + \dfrac{\omega D_q I_q}{LC} + \dfrac{R\,D_d I_q}{L^2C} \right)s + \dfrac{\omega V_{dc}}{LL_{in}C}}{s^4 + \dfrac{2R}{L}s^3 + \left(\dfrac{R^2}{L^2} + \dfrac{1}{L_{in}C} + \dfrac{D_q^2}{LC} + \dfrac{D_d^2}{LC} + \omega^2 \right)s^2 + \left(\dfrac{2R}{LL_{in}C} + \dfrac{RD_q^2}{L^2C} + \dfrac{RD_d^2}{L^2C} \right)s + \left(\dfrac{R^2}{L^2 L_{in}C} + \dfrac{\omega^2}{L_{in}C} \right)}
$$

$$
\frac{\tilde{i}_{q_{ph}}}{\tilde{d}_{q_{ph}}} = \frac{\dfrac{V_{dc}}{L}s^3 + \left(\dfrac{RV_{dc}}{L^2} - \dfrac{I_q D_q}{LC} \right)s^2 + \left(\dfrac{V_{dc}}{LL_{in}C} + \dfrac{V_{dc}D_d^2}{L^2C} - \dfrac{R\,I_q D_q}{L^2C} + \dfrac{\omega I_q\,D_d}{LC} \right)s + \dfrac{RV_{dc}}{L^2 L_{in}C}}{s^4 + \dfrac{2R}{L}s^3 + \left(\dfrac{R^2}{L^2} + \dfrac{1}{L_{in}C} + \dfrac{D_q^2}{LC} + \dfrac{D_d^2}{LC} + \omega^2 \right)s^2 + \left(\dfrac{2R}{LL_{in}C} + \dfrac{RD_q^2}{L^2C} + \dfrac{RD_d^2}{L^2C} \right)s + \left(\dfrac{R^2}{L^2 L_{in}C} + \dfrac{\omega^2}{L_{in}C} \right)}
$$

$$
\frac{\tilde{i}_{q_{ph}}}{\tilde{d}_{d_{ph}}} = \frac{-\left[\left(\dfrac{\omega V_{dc}}{L} + \dfrac{I_d D_q}{LC} \right)s^2 + \left(\dfrac{V_{dc}D_d D_q}{L^2C} + \dfrac{R\,I_d D_q}{L^2C} - \dfrac{\omega I_d\,D_d}{LC} \right)s + \dfrac{\omega V_{dc}}{LL_{in}C} \right]}{s^4 + \dfrac{2R}{L}s^3 + \left(\dfrac{R^2}{L^2} + \dfrac{1}{L_{in}C} + \dfrac{D_q^2}{LC} + \dfrac{D_d^2}{LC} + \omega^2 \right)s^2 + \left(\dfrac{2R}{LL_{in}C} + \dfrac{RD_q^2}{L^2C} + \dfrac{RD_d^2}{L^2C} \right)s + \left(\dfrac{R^2}{L^2 L_{in}C} + \dfrac{\omega^2}{L_{in}C} \right)}
$$

4.3.3   Bode Diagram Verification

In order to validate the proposed derivation of the transfer functions, some comparative results with that obtained by Matlab/Simulink toolbox are presented in this subsection, as illustrated for the bode diagrams in Figure 4.4 to Figure 4.7.

- Case 1: $\dfrac{\tilde{i}_{d_{ph}}}{\tilde{d}_{d_{ph}}}$

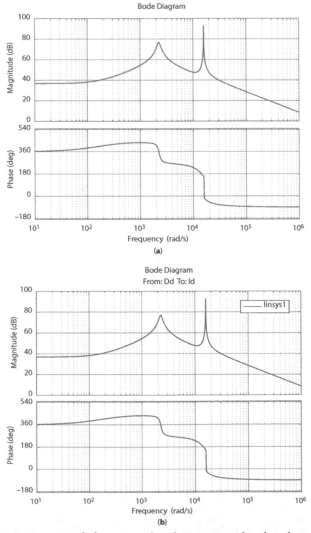

Figure 4.4 Bode diagram with the proposed analysis compared to that obtained by the Matlab toolbox. (a) Using the proposed derivation and analysis. (b) Using Matlab toolbox.

- *Case 2:* $\dfrac{\tilde{i}_{d_{ph}}}{\tilde{d}_{q_{ph}}}$

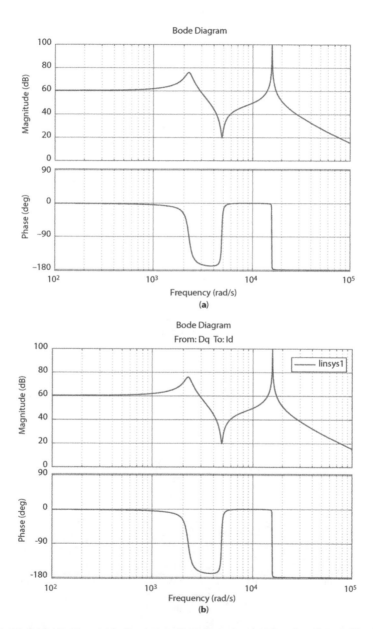

Figure 4.5 Bode diagram with the proposed analysis compared to that obtained by the Matlab toolbox. (a) Using the proposed derivation and analysis.(b) Using Matlab toolbox.

- *Case 3:* $\dfrac{\tilde{i}_{q_{ph}}}{\tilde{d}_{q_{ph}}}$

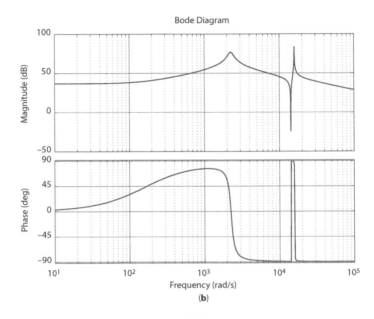

(b)

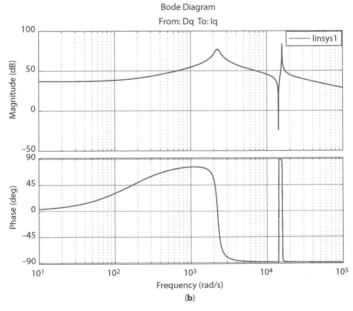

(b)

Figure 4.6 Bode diagram with the proposed analysis compared to that obtained by the Matlab toolbox. (a) Using the proposed derivation and analysis. (b) Using Matlab toolbox.

- *Case 4:* $\dfrac{\tilde{i}_{q_{ph}}}{\tilde{d}_{d_{ph}}}$

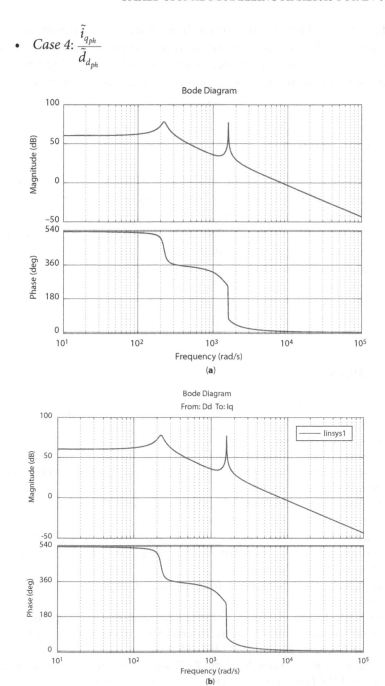

Figure 4.7 Bode diagram with the proposed analysis compared to that obtained by the Matlab toolbox. (a) Using the proposed derivation and analysis. (b) Using Matlab toolbox.

All the results obtained and verified through the bode diagram confirms that there is a close correlation between the proposed analysis and derivation of the small-signal transfer functions and that obtained from the Matlab/Simulink toolbox. This ensures the efficacy of the proposed mathematics for the adopted system modelling.

4.4   Conclusion

In this chapter, the small signal model of a SPMSM fed with a voltage-source inverter (VSI) has been completely analyzed. In order to control the machine speed from standstill to the rated speed with rated load, the vector control strategy has been applied. In order to validate the efficacy of the presented mathematical analysis of the adopted model for VSI, some of the obtained simulation results have been discussed. The obtained results have confirmed, through the bode diagram, the efficacy of the proposed mathematical derivations for the small signal model transfer functions compared with that obtained aided with Matlab/Simulink toolbox.

References

1. Kazimierczuk, M.K., *Pulse-width modulated dc-dc power converters*, John Wiley & Sons, USA, 2008.
2. Erickson, R.W. and Maksimovi, D., *Fundamentals of Power Electronics*, Kluwer Academic Pub, USA, 2001.
3. Bose, B., *Power electronics and ac drives*, vol. 1, Englewood Cliffs, NJ, Prentice-Hall, USA, 1986.
4. Mohan, N. and Undeland, T.M., *Power electronics: Converters, applications, and design*, Wiley-India, India, 2007.
5. Blaabjerg, F., Chen, Z., Kjaer, S.B., Power electronics as efficient interface in dispersed power generation systems. *IEEE Trans. Power Electron.*, 19, 5, 1184–1194, Sept. 2004.
6. Peng, F.Z., Z-source inverter. *IEEE Trans. Ind. Appl.*, 39, 2, 504–510, Mar. 2003.
7. Shen, M., Joseph, A., Wang, J., Peng, F.Z., Adams, D.J., Comparison of traditional inverters and Z-Source inverter for fuel cell vehicles. *IEEE Trans. Power Electron.*, 22, 4, 1453–1463, Jul. 2007.
8. Peng, F., Yuan, X., Fang, X., Qian, Z., Z-source inverter for adjustable speed drives. *IEEE Power Electron. Lett.*, 1, 2, 33–35, Jun. 2003.
9. Loh, P.C., Vilathgamuwa, D.M., Lai, Y.S., Chua, G.T., Li, Y., Pulse-width modulation of z-source inverters. *IEEE Trans. Power Electron.*, 20, 6, 1346–1355, Nov. 2005.

10. Peng, F.Z., Shen, M., Qian, Z., Maximum boost control of the z-source inverter. *IEEE Trans. Power Electron.*, 20, 4, 833–838, Jul. 2005.
11. Huang, Y., Shen, M., Peng, F., Wang, J., Z-source inverter for residential photovoltaic systems. *IEEE Trans. Power Electron.*, 21, 6, 1776–1782, 2006.
12. Peng, F.Z., Shen, M., Holland, K., Application of z-source inverter for traction drive of fuel cell-battery hybrid electric vehicles. *IEEE Trans. Power Electron.*, 22, 3, 1054–1061, May 2007.
13. Zhou, Z.J., Zhang, X., Xu, P., Shen, W.X., Single-phase uninterruptible power supply based on Z-source inverter. *IEEE Trans. Ind. Electron.*, 55, 8, 2997–3004, Aug. 2008.
14. Wester, G.W. and Middlebrook, R.D., Low-frequency characterization of switched dc-dc converters. *IEEE Trans. Aerosp. Electron. Syst.*, 9, 376–385, 1973.
15. Middlebrook, R.D. and Cuk, S., A general unified approach to modelling switching-converter power stages. *IEEE Power Electronics Specialists Conf. (PESC)*, 18–34, 1976.
16. Galigekere, V. and Kazimierczuk, M., Analysis of PWM Z-source dc-dc converter in CCM for steady state. *IEEE Trans. Circuits Syst. I, Reg. Papers*, 59, 4, 854–863, April 2012.
17. Vorperian, V., Tymerski, R., Lee, F.C.Y., Equivalent circuit models for resonant and PWM switches. *IEEE Trans. Power Electron.*, 4, 2, 205–214, Apr. 1989.
18. Vorp´erian, V., Simplified analysis of PWM converters using the model of the PWM switch: Parts I and II. *IEEE Trans. Aerosp. Electron. Syst.*, 26, 3, 490–505, May 1990.
19. Czarkowski, D. and Kazimierczuk, M., Energy-conservation approach to modeling PWM DC-DC converters. *IEEE Trans. Aerosp. Electron. Syst.*, 29, 3, 1059–1063, July 1993.
20. Van Dijk, E., Spruijt, J.N., O'sullivan, D.M., Klaassens, J.B., PWM-switch modeling of DC-DC converters. *IEEE Trans. Power Electron.*, 10, 6, 659–665, Nov. 1995.
21. Jiang, D. and Wang, F., Current Ripple Prediction for Three-phase PWM Converters. *IEEE Trans. Ind. Appl.*, 50, 1, 531–538, Jan.-Feb. 2014.
22. Mousa, M.G., Allam, S.M., Rashad, E.M., Sensored and sensorless scalar-control strategy of a wind-driven BDFRG for maximum wind-power extraction. *J. Control Decis.*, 5, 209–227, 2018.
23. Hussien, M.G., Xu, W., Liu, Y., Allam, S.M., Rotor speed observer with extended current estimator for sensorless control of induction motor drive systems. *Energies*, 12, 3613, 2019.
24. Jiang, D. and Wang, F., Variable Switching Frequency PWM for Three-phase Converters Based on Current Ripple Prediction. *IEEE Trans. Power Electron.*, 28, 11, 4951–4961, Nov. 2013.
25. Jiang, D., Li, Q., Han, X., Qu, R., Variable switching frequency PWM for torque ripple control of AC motors. *2016 19th Int. Conf. Electrical Machines and Systems (ICEMS)*, 1–5, Chiba, Japan, 2016.

5

Energy Management of Hybrid Energy Storage System in PHEV With Various Driving Mode

S. Arun Mozhi[1]*, S. Charles Raja[1], M. Saravanan[1]
and J. Jeslin Drusila Nesamalar[2]

[1]*Department of Electrical and Electronics Engineering, Thiagarajar
College of Engineering, Madurai, India*
[2]*Department of Electrical and Electronics Engineering, Kamaraj
College of Engineering, Virudhunagar, India*

Abstract

The diminution of fossil fuel due to substantial consumption has hastened the improvement of the electric vehicle. So, Plug-in Hybrid Electric Vehicle (PHEV) is widely used for transportation system to lessen the fossil fuel utilization. This is recognized to be the finest short-term solution to lessen greenhouse gas emission. In PHEV, the Energy Storage System (ESS) plays a key role. Even though some batteries supply both high power and high energy, they may overheat and their lifetime is short. Therefore, various power sources have to be implicated. Ultra-capacitors, due to extended life cycle and instantaneous high power properties, are a prominent appendage for the energy storage system. An ultra-capacitor is incorporated in hybrid energy storage system to provide instant high power to the vehicle. In this chapter, battery and ultra-capacitors are modeled as a hybrid energy storage system of plug-in hybrid electric vehicle and they have been simulated using MATLAB Simulink. Various cases such as acceleration and deceleration of the vehicle have been discussed and results are analyzed. Simulation result corroborates that peak power demand requisite for the vehicle is delivered by the ultra-capacitor, thereby the main grid stress is reduced.

Keywords: Battery, ultra-capacitor, energy management, hybrid energy storage system, plug-in hybrid electric vehicle, acceleration, deceleration, driving mode

*Corresponding author: arunmozhi49@gmail.com

Chitra A, P. Sanjeevikumar, Jens Bo Holm-Nielsen and S. Himavathi (eds.) Artificial Intelligent Techniques for Electric and Hybrid Electric Vehicles, (103–114) © 2020 Scrivener Publishing LLC

5.1   Introduction

In the past, various types of vehicles were available which used gasoline, diesel, biodiesel, compressed natural gases, etc., as fuel sources. Due to the usage of fossil fuel for vehicle transportation, the environment got affected. Environmental pollution and degradation became a major problem in the world. The main reason was the emission of greenhouse gases and industrial waste. The problem cannot be eliminated but it can be reduced with the use of alternate source of energy for the vehicle i.e. from non-renewable source to renewable source. So, an electric vehicle was recognized to be the finest short-term solution.

The electric cars were invented in different countries by different inventors. It is very hard to pinpoint the year of invention of electric vehicle. In 18th century, the first electric vehicle was designed. But the positive result was gained by William Morrison of Des Moines, Iowa in 1890–1891 in the United States. Its top speed is 23 kmph. Battery is the main source for driving the electric car and it gets exhausted easily. As charging stations are not available everywhere, it's very difficult to charge the electric vehicle. To boost the capacity of the battery in an electric vehicle, the size of the battery must be increased which increases the total vehicular mass.

Another type called Hybrid Electric Vehicle (HEV) came into existence which uses both fuel and battery as a source for running the vehicle. The chemical energy of the fuel is transformed to mechanical energy to run the vehicle. Fuel source not only drives the vehicle but also charges the battery. The fuel to wheel efficiency of the hybrid electric vehicle is too low. To overcome this drawback, the alternate type of vehicle called Plug-In Hybrid Electric Vehicle (PHEV) is designed [1].

The experimental study about the battery—super-capacitor incorporated energy storage system [2, 3] for the electric vehicle application helps to find the solution for the installation of charging station [4–6]. Energy management [7–16] in and out of electric vehicle i.e. energy management in the energy storage system, energy management between the electric vehicle and charging station, etc., is essential to ensure the reliability of supply. The penetration of electric vehicles into the distribution system within the permissible limit i.e. optimal integration [17–20] reduces the main grid stress.

5.1.1   Architecture of PHEV

The fuel economy is improved in PHEV due to the Charge-Depletion (CD) mode of the vehicle. In CD form, the vehicle is driven only with the energy

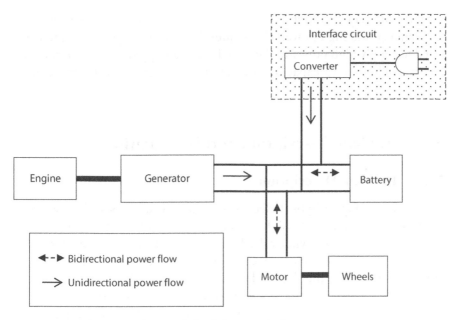

Figure 5.1 Architecture of plug-in hybrid electric vehicle.

obtained from electric motor. Another mode called Charge-Sustaining mode, where the vehicle is operated like a traditional HEV. This is the main advantage of PHEV. If charging station is available everywhere, the progress of PHEV will be increased.

Owing to the direct charging of battery at the charging station, use of fuel source was trimmed down. While the State of Charge (SOC) of the battery is reduced to its threshold value, the energy requisite is supplied by the engine.

Figure 5.1 shows the architecture of Plug-in hybrid electric vehicle with the power flow directions. The sources of PHEV are fuel and energy storage system. The fuel source is generally an Engine–Generator set, where the chemical energy of the fossil fuel or natural gases is converted to mechanical energy by the engine and the generator converts this mechanical energy into electrical energy. The energy storage system consists of battery. The battery is charged from the charging station via interface circuit. The electrical energy from these sources is converted to mechanical energy via motor.

5.1.2   Energy Storage System

The performance of PHEV varies depends on the Energy Storage System present in it. ESS consists of only battery in the normal EV. This ESS supplies the required high energy to the vehicle. But vehicles need both high energy and high power. Consequently, an ultra-capacitor is incorporated to supply high power to the vehicle. The energy storage system which consists of both ultra-capacitor and battery is recognized as Hybrid energy storage system (HESS).

5.2   Problem Description and Formulation

5.2.1   Problem Description

Now-a-days, plug-in hybrid electric vehicle is widely used for transportation system to reduce fossil fuel consumption. But in PHEV, the energy storage system plays a vital role. For the ESS of plug-in hybrid electric vehicle, energy is not the only requirement for an electric vehicle to drive. While driving along the slopes, the vehicle requires high power. So, HESS is brought in which is incorporated with the ultra-capacitor.

In the Plug-In Hybrid Electric Vehicle, the fuel to wheel efficiency is enhanced with the presence of Hybrid Energy Storage System i.e. Battery–Ultra-capacitor model (BA–UC model). To increase the efficiency of the vehicle, the structure of HESS of PHEV is designed carefully as it mainly depends on the battery and the ultra-capacitor connection. And the power allocation between them reduces the energy loss in the vehicle. Thereby it enriches the fuel economy of the vehicle.

5.2.2   Objective

The main contribution is to allocate the power between battery and the ultra-capacitor, and to evaluate a best power delivery between ultra-capacitor and battery pack in order to increase the reliability of energy storage system of the plug-in hybrid electric vehicle.

5.2.3   Problem Formulation

The inappropriate power allotment between the battery pack and the ultra-capacitor leads to high energy loss as it depends on the structure of HESS. If the energy loss is high, the energy output of the HESS to the vehicle is low. Therefore the efficiency of the system is affected. Accordingly, the performance of the vehicle is diminished.

5.3   Modeling of HESS

The presence of electric motor in the plug-in hybrid electric vehicle miti-
gates the use of internal combustion engine. By this means emission of pol-
lutants and the fuel efficiency of the vehicle are increased. In the proposed
system, the hybrid energy storage system of the PHEV consisting of both
ultra-capacitor pack and battery pack are modeled.

The super-capacitor and the battery are connected in series with the
boost converter and buck/boost converter respectively. The characteristics
of both the energy sources are analyzed with the help of scope. The power
required for the vehicle is calculated from the driving cycle pattern of the
vehicle.

The battery parameters such as voltage, current and state of charge are
monitored with the scope and the battery power is calculated from the battery voltage and battery current. Likewise, the super-capacitor parameters
are also monitored and power of super-capacitor is calculated from the
super-capacitor voltage and current. The power of HESS is calculated by
adding the source powers i.e. an adder block is used. The voltage amplitude
of the DC voltage source is set to 42 V.

The battery and the ultra-capacitor which are connected in series as
shown in Figure 5.2 with the converters supplies the power required for
the electric vehicle. Both the energy sources are charged and discharged
according to the requirement. At the time of starting the SOC of the battery

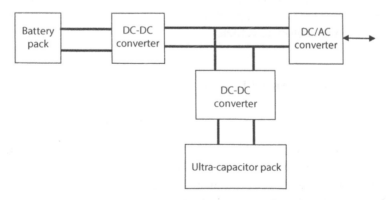

◄───► CAN Bus (Connects the energy storage system and electric vehicle)

Figure 5.2 Structure of proposed system.

Table 5.1 Battery parameters.

Rated capacity	6.6 Ah
Nominal voltage	26.4.V
Initial state of charge	100%
Internal resistance	0.04

Table 5.2 Ultra-capacitor parameters.

Rated capacitance	500 F
Equivalent DC series resistance	2.1.mΩ
Number of series capacitor	6
Operating temperature	25 °C

is 100%. When the vehicle gets started, the SOC of the battery decreases i.e. the battery starts discharging. While applying brake, ultra-capacitor gets charged due to regenerative braking. The incorporation of ultra-capacitor with the battery ensures the reliability of power supply to the vehicle.

The parameters of both the battery pack and the ultra-capacitor are given in Tables 5.1 and 5.2. The state of charge (SOC) of battery is initially 100%. The parameters given in the table are used to identify the type of battery pack and the ultra-capacitor to be used in the energy storage system of plug-in hybrid electric vehicle.

5.4   Results and Discussion

5.4.1   Case 1: Gradual Acceleration of Vehicle

The characteristics of battery pack such as SOC, current and voltage for the gradual acceleration of the vehicle is plotted in Figure 5.3(a). The battery voltage was very high at initial stage and it was nominal due to constant load. In Figure 5.3(b), the characteristics of super-capacitor such as current, voltage and SOC is plotted. The super-capacitor voltage was very high at initial stage and decreases due to load.

Figure 5.3(c) shows the power delivered by the super-capacitor and the battery pack to the load. At the peak time the power required for the load is

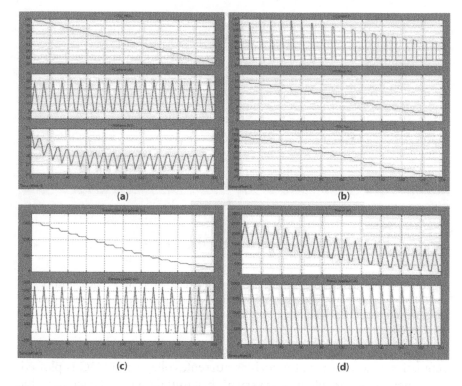

(a)   (b)

(c)   (d)

Figure 5.3 Characteristics of gradually accelerated vehicle: (a) Battery characteristics and (b) ultra-capacitor characteristics (c) power of ultra-capacitor pack and battery pack (d) power output of HESS and power required.

delivered by the ultra-capacitor. The power supplied by the super-capacitor is 1,500 W and the battery supplies 1,100 W. This power is calculated from the voltage and current values of the battery and super-capacitor. Figure 5.3(d) shows the power supplied by the energy storage system and the power required for the electric vehicle. This power is the sum of the powers of both battery and super-capacitor and it is 2,600 W. The power required for the electric vehicle tracks the driving cycle pattern of the vehicle. In this the power required is set as 2,000 W.

5.4.2   Case 2: Gradual Deceleration of Vehicle

In Figure 5.4(a), the characteristics of battery pack such as SOC, current and voltage for the gradual deceleration of the vehicle is plotted. Initially the battery voltage was very high. Suddenly the voltage is decreased to a low value and then it increases gradually. The current is initially high

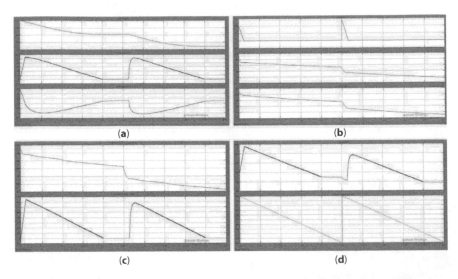

(a)   (b)

(c)   (d)

Figure 5.4 Characteristics of gradually decelerated vehicle: (a) Battery characteristics and (b) ultra-capacitor characteristics (c) power of ultra-capacitor pack and battery pack (d) power output of HESS and power required.

and decreases gradually due to deceleration. In Figure 5.4(b), the characteristics of super-capacitor such as current, voltage and SOC is plotted. The super-capacitor voltage was very high at initial stage and decreases due to load.

Figure 5.4(c) shows the power delivered by the super-capacitor and the battery pack to the load. Due to deceleration of vehicle, the battery power is zero as no power required for the vehicle at braking. Figure 5.4(d) shows the power supplied by the energy storage system and the power required for the electric vehicle. During deceleration, the power required for the vehicle is negative.

5.4.3   Case 3: Unsystematic Acceleration and Deceleration of Vehicle

The unsystematic acceleration and deceleration of the electric vehicle is shown in Figure 5.5. In Figure 5.5(a), the characteristics of battery pack such as SOC, current and voltage for sudden acceleration and deceleration of the vehicle is plotted. The battery current was zero at initial stage and it varies according to the unsystematic changes in the speed of the vehicle. In Figure 5.5(b), the characteristics of super-capacitor such as current, voltage and SOC is plotted. The super-capacitor voltage was high and then maintained constant.

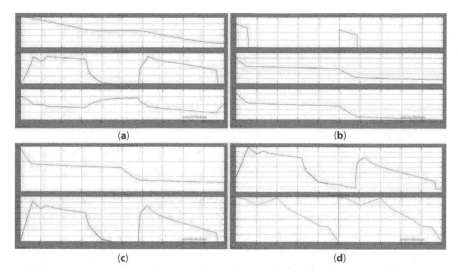

Figure 5.5 Characteristics of unsystematically accelerated and decelerated vehicle: (a) Battery characteristics and (b) ultra-capacitor characteristics (c) power of ultra-capacitor pack and battery pack (d) power output of HESS and power required.

Figure 5.5(c) shows the power delivered by the super-capacitor and the battery pack to the load. Due to the unsystematic acceleration and deceleration of vehicle, the battery power variation is high and it is zero during deceleration as no power is required for the vehicle at the time of braking. Figure 5.5(d) shows the power supplied by the energy storage system and the power required for the electric vehicle. During sudden application of acceleration and deceleration, the power required for the vehicle changes rapidly. During braking the vehicle power requirement is negative.

5.5   Conclusion

In this chapter, hybrid energy storage system of plug-in hybrid electric vehicle is modeled in MATLAB Simulink. The simulation result infers that the ultra-capacitor supply power during peak power demand. Due to the variation of speed, the electrical vehicle was driven in two modes such as acceleration mode and deceleration mode. These modes are analyzed from the simulation results. During acceleration, the battery SOC starts decreasing i.e. battery is discharged as the vehicle consumes energy and during deceleration the battery power is zero as there is no power required for the vehicle while applying brake.

References

1. Fathabadi, H., Plug-in Hybrid Electric Vehicles (PHEVs): Replacing Internal Combustion Engine with Clean and Renewable Energy Based Auxiliary Power Sources. *IEEE T. Power Electr.*, 33, 11, 9611–9618, 2018.
2. Xiong, R., Duan, Y., Cao, J., Yu, Q., Battery and Ultra-capacitor in-the-loop approach to validate a real time power management method for an all-climate electric vehicle. *Appl. Energy*, Elsevier. 217, 153–165, 2018.
3. Zhang, Q. and Li, G., Experimental Study on A Semi-active Battery-Supercapacitor Hybrid Energy Storage System for Electric Vehicle Application. *IEEE T. Power Electr.*, 35, 1, 1014–1021, 2020.
4. Laha, A., Yin, B., Cheng, Y., Cai, L.X., Wang, Y., Game Theory Based Charging Solution for Networked Electric Vehicles: A Location-Aware Approach. *IEEE T. Veh. Technol.*, 68, 7, 6352–6364, 2019.
5. Mohamed, A., Salehi, V., Ma, T., Mohammed O., Real-Time Energy Management Algorithm for Plug-In Hybrid Electric Vehicle Charging Parks Involving Sustainable Energy. *IEEE Trans. Sustain. Ener.*, 5, 2, 577–586, 2014.
6. Chis, A., Lundén, J., Koivunen, V., Reinforcement Learning-Based Plug-in Electric Vehicle Charging With Forecasted Price. *IEEE T. Veh. Technol.*, 66, 5, 3674–3684, 2017.
7. Li, S.G., Sharkh, S.M., Walsh, F.C., Zhang, C.N., Energy and Battery Management of a Plug-In Series Hybrid Electric Vehicle Using Fuzzy Logic. *IEEE T. Veh. Technol.*, 60, 8, 3571–3585, 2011.
8. Zheng, C., Li, W., Liang, Q., An Energy Management Strategy of Hybrid Energy Storage Systems for Electric Vehicle Applications. *IEEE Trans. Sustain. Ener.*, 9, 4, 1880–1888, 2018.
9. Xiong, R., Cao, J., Yu, Q., Reinforcement learning-based real-time power management for hybrid energy storage system in the plug-in hybrid electric vehicle. *Appl. Energy*, Elsevier. 211, 538–548, 2018.
10. Wang, X. and Liang, Q., Energy Management Strategy for Plug-In Hybrid Electric Vehicles *via* Bidirectional Vehicle-to-Grid. *IEEE Syst. J.*, 11, 3, 1789–1798, 2017.
11. Martinez, C. M., Hu, X., Cao, D., Velenis, E., Gao, B., Wellers, M., Energy Management in Plug-in Hybrid Electric Vehicles: Recent Progress and a Connected Vehicles Perspective. *IEEE T. Veh. Technol.*, 66, 6, 4534–4549, 2017.
12. Liu, J., Chen, Y., Zhan, J., Shang, F., Heuristic Dynamic Programming Based Online Energy Management Strategy for Plug-In Hybrid Electric Vehicles. *IEEE T. Veh. Technol.*, 68, 5, 4479–4493, 2019.
13. Tian, H., Wang, X., Lu, Z., Huang, Y., Tian, G., Adaptive Fuzzy Logic Energy Management Strategy Based on Reasonable SOC Reference Curve for Online Control of Plug-in Hybrid Electric City Bus. *IEEE Trans. Intell. Transp. Syst.*, 19, 5, 1607–1617, 2018.

14. Liu, T., Hu, X., Hu, W., Zou, Y., A Heuristic Planning Reinforcement Learning-Based Energy Management for Power-Split Plug-in Hybrid Electric Vehicles. *IEEE Trans. Industr. Inform.*, 15,12,6436–6445, 2019.
15. Chen, Z., Mi, C.C., Xu, J., Gong, X., You, C., Energy Management for a Power-Split Plug-in Hybrid Electric Vehicle Based on Dynamic Programming and Neural Networks. *IEEE T. Veh. Technol.*, 63, 4, 1567–1580, 2014.
16. Zou, Y., Liu, T., Liu, D., Sun, F., Reinforcement learning-based real-time energy management for a hybrid tracked vehicle. *Appl. Energy*, Elsevier. 171, 372–382, 2016.
17. Sun, G., Zhang, F., Liao, D., Yu, H., Du, X., Guizani, M., Optimal Energy Trading for Plug-in Hybrid Electric Vehicles based on Fog Computing. *IEEE Internet of Things J.*, 6, 2, 2309–2324, 2019.
18. Sun, W., Kadel, N., Alvarez-Fernandez, I., Nejad, R.R., Golshani, A., Optimal distribution system restoration using PHEVs. *IET Smart Grid*, 2, 1, 42–49, 2019.
19. Eldeeb, H.H., Elsayed, A.T., Lashway, C.R., Mohammed, O., Hybrid Energy Storage Sizing and Power Splitting Optimization for Plug-In Electric Vehicles. *IEEE Trans. Ind. Appl.*, 55, 3, 2252–2262, 2019.
20. Zeng, X. and Wang, J., Optimizing the Energy Management Strategy for Plug-In Hybrid Electric Vehicles With Multiple Frequent Routes. *IEEE Trans. Control Syst. Technol.*, 27, 1, 394–400, 2019.

6

Reliability Approach for the Power Semiconductor Devices in EV Applications

Krishnachaitanya, D.[1], Chitra, A.[1]* and Biswas, S.S.[2]

[1]School of Electrical Engineering, Vellore Institute of Technology, Vellore, India
[2]Engineer and R&D In Charge, BHAVINI, Kalpakkam, India

Abstract

Due to the increasing importance of the power electronic devices in industrial applications, it becomes necessary to consider the reliability and predict the life of the components. This paper initially discusses the general reliability prediction methods for power converters. In a converter, the life of the power electronic devices depends on the failure rate of the individual device. For the evaluation of failure rate of power semiconductor device temperature, current rating, voltage stress, application, quality and environment factors are considered. Life period of the device is decided by the bathtub curve. All the quantitative analysis projected in this work are based on the standard of MIL-217F N2.

Keywords: Reliability, power electronic devices, failure rate, MIL-217F N2, reliability prediction

6.1   Introduction

Nowadays, the usage of power electronic equipment has been widely increasing in industries. The operation time of the electronic equipment is directly proportional to the failure rate of the power electronic component. The failure of the power electronic component affects the overall reliability of the power electronic equipment [1–4]. To assess the reliability of the equipment, failure rate analysis is used. Most of the electronic equipment has more number of electronic components and power semiconductor

---

*Corresponding author: chitra.a@vit.ac.in

Chitra A, P. Sanjeevikumar, Jens Bo Holm-Nielsen and S. Himavathi (eds.) *Artificial Intelligent Techniques for Electric and Hybrid Electric Vehicles,* (115–124) © 2020 Scrivener Publishing LLC

devices. Redundancy of electronic components is not included in electronic equipment. Hence the failure rate analysis can assume that if one of the component performance fails, the whole system has failed. Therefore, the reliability of the each component must be determined [5]. The reliability of the component is dependent on the specified function in a given environment. All design phases of electronic equipment should be considered in reliability. In conceptual design stress cannot be determined exactly, the part count or part-stress methods can be applied. These methods consider the environment conditions and quality of the product and it permits to the detailed investigation of the system reliability [6–8]. The part-stress method needs the knowledge on the stresses and temperature profile of the component, but this method is applicable to the later phase of design process. In semiconductor material temperature and its variations influence the reliability of the component because it changes the thermal conditions in power semiconductor devices [9].

The paper aims at presenting a reliability prediction of the power semiconductor devices and quantitative evaluation of the reliability prediction. Here temperature, environment factors, voltage stress and current rating factor have been considered for reliability prediction.

6.2   Conventional Methods for Prediction of Reliability for Power Converters

The product failure rate and lifecycle describes the reliability. Failure rate depends on the probability of the particular product at operational time interval. Failure chances in the device $[t, t + \Delta t]$ where $\Delta t = 0$. It gives the failure chances in a certain time interval for defined boundary conditions of particular product. Failure rate is denoted by 'λ' [1, 10–14].

$$\text{Failure rate w.r.t time } \lambda(t) = \frac{\text{failure chances}}{10^9 \text{ hours}} \qquad (6.1)$$

In most cases reliability $R(t)$ of the electronic component can be assumed to decrease exponentially.

Let us consider

The failure rate $\lambda(t)$ constant value $= \lambda$

Total failure rate λ_{total}, number of components in a circuit 'k' k is sum of the all the individual failure rates λ_i in Equation (6.3)

$$\lambda_{total} = \sum_{i=1}^{k} \lambda_i \tag{6.2}$$

Mean time to failure (MTTF) also considered for the reliability,

$$\text{MTTF} = \frac{1}{\lambda_{total}} \tag{6.3}$$

There are dissimilar methods for quantitative estimation of reliability. Few methods will be explained and compared. Widely used and accepted method is dependent on failure rate catalogs [15]. There are different failure rate catalogs which are based on the electronics and large empirical investigations [1, 16, 17]. Reliability prediction methods are mainly classified into three types:

1. Bottom-up statistical methods
2. Top-Down similarity analysis methods
3. Bottom-up physics of failure methods.

Bottom-up statistical method is applicable and provides the electronic component field failure rate and defect densities. It is a good indicator for the field reliability. The main disadvantage in this method is difficult to keep up to date and difficult to collect the good quality field data to use in method [18]. Difficult to compare the correlated variables (e. g. Quality vs Environment). Failure rate of the component is decided by the historical operational data of the component.

Top-Down similarity analysis method (e. g. TRACS) is dependent on the external failure rate data base of the particular product. This method reflect the actual reliability by employing the test data of the product but it should be performed before the system or product is commercialized [1, 16]. The main disadvantages are the conversion of actual reliability data into field value is required and acceleration models are needed.

Bottom-up physics of failure method (e.g. FIDES) is useful for evaluation of the specific failure mechanisms and life time prediction of the product. The main disadvantages are it is not applicable to the prediction of field reliability, expensive and complex to apply on the system. Also it is not extendable to dynamic assessment of the reliability parameters for a real-time system [19].

This paper explains about the failure rate of the electronic component by considering the historical data. Several methods are available to calculate the reliability of the electronic components. Each method project a wide range of variation in reliability prediction. These methods are not comparable in terns because the each method have different sensitive parameters and each method has different assumptions [4]. Here reliability of the electronic component has been calculated by using the bottom-up statistical method. Electronic components reliability depends on the chances of failure.

6.3   Calculation Process of the Electronic Component

Failing of number of units in a particular unit time is called failure rate. Every product has a failure rate defined over a specific periods of time and this failure rate chance is dependent in turn on the operational period of the component. It effects the operational life span of the product and producing the failure period curve called as bath curve as shown in Figure 6.1.

Bathtub curve has divided the failure rate into three portions. The first portion is known as early failure rate period and it has greater failure rate because of the manufacture errors.

The manufacturers are mainly concentrated on the reduction of failure chances to reach the customer level. The second portion is known as useful life period [5]. In commercial applications focus on enhancing the duration of the life time to a satisfactory level. The existence of the product beyond the useful life time corresponds to the wear out period. The product failure in this wear out portion is mainly due to the deterioration of time material, temperature, oxidization, deionization of material and chemical damage. The first and second sections provide the manufacturer warranty. The failure of the product depends on many heads namely such

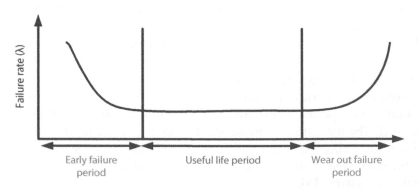

Figure 6.1 Bathtub curve.

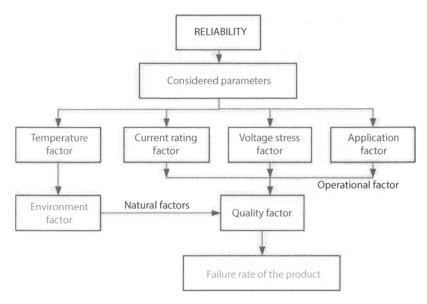

Figure 6.2 Failure rate based reliability process flow chart.

as thermal, environment, quality and electrical stress on the component [6]. Component failure rate is denoted by λ_p, base failure rate of the component λ_b, quality factor N_i. All components failure rate as shown in Equation (6.5).

$$\lambda = \sum_{i=1}^{n} N_i \lambda_p \tag{6.4}$$

Where λ = failure rate of the whole system.

The reliability process for the failure method is dependent on which parameters have been considered. The involved factors in the failure rate of the product as shown in Figure 6.2.

The main influencing factors of reliability are shown in Figure 6.2. Some of the factors are dependent on the manufacturer end while other factors are dependent on the operational and natural factor (environment). The paper aims at presenting an evaluation of reliability to the power semiconductor device. Reliability evaluation has been presented for the MOSFET.

6.4   Reliability Prediction for MOSFETs

Several factors influence the reliability of the electronic components. The product of the effecting factor is called the failure rate of the product.

Failure rate of the component

$$\lambda_p = \lambda_b \, \pi_T \, \pi_R \, \pi_S \, \pi_A \, \pi_Q \, \pi_E \, \text{Failure/10}_6 \, h \tag{6.5}$$

Where:

π_T: Temperature factor
π_R: Current rating factor
π_S: Voltage stress factor
π_A: Application factor
π_Q: Quality factor
π_E: Environment factor

Temperature is a main affecting factor on the life time of electronic components. It is a dependent factor, which means it depends on the current and voltage applied to the component. Here the temperature factor is junction temperature [18, 19].

$$\pi_T = \exp\left(-3082\left(\frac{1}{T_j + 273} - \frac{1}{298}\right)\right) \tag{6.6}$$

Where: T_j = Junction temperature

0 °C is equal to the 273 K.
23 °C considered as the room temperature.

Application factor and environment factors are important for the selection of the power electronic components. The constant value of the environment factor depends on the application of the product. Let us consider the marine application (N_s) [18].

$$\text{Environment factor } (\pi_E) = N_S = \text{constant value.} \tag{6.8}$$

Manufactured material of the product decides the quality and life of the product (material e.g. JANTXV, JANTX, JAN). Quality has a direct effect on the component failure rate and it appear as a product quality factor. It is denoted by π_Q [18, 19].

$$\text{Quality factor } (\pi_Q) = \text{material} = \text{constant} \tag{6.9}$$

The operating failure rate of the product is dependent on the applied voltage across the power semiconductor device. Possibilities of the failure rates maximum caused due to the blocking voltage and peak currents. It appears as current rating factor π_R and voltage stress factor π_S [18, 19].

$$\text{Current rating factor } (\pi_R) = (I_{rms})^{0.40} \tag{6.10}$$

Where I_{rms} = RMS rated forward current

$$\text{Voltage stress factor } \pi_S = (V_s)^{1.9} \tag{6.11}$$

Where V_s = voltage stress

6.5   Example: Reliability Prediction for Power Semiconductor Device

Let us consider one model of the IGBT and the assumed data of the power semiconductor device is maximum temperature across the junction 150 °C, RMS current of the IGBT is 30 A and the IGBT is manufactured by the material of JANTX. The maximum applicable input voltage is 500 V, case temperature is 75 °C. This model is used in the marine application. Reliability estimation has been done below

Formula for failure rate Equation (6.5),

$$\lambda_p = \lambda_b \cdot \pi_T \cdot \pi_Q \cdot \pi_E \cdot \pi_R \cdot \pi_S$$

λ_b is base failure rate = 0.002 (for all type devices same value)
π_T is temperature factor = 150 °C

$$= e^{\left(-3082\left(\frac{1}{Tj+273} - \frac{1}{298}\right)\right)} = e^{\left(-3082\left(\frac{1}{150+273} - \frac{1}{298}\right)\right)} = 21$$

Where T_j = junction temperature.

  0 °C temperature converted into Kelvin = 273
  At room temperature 25 °C converted into Kelvin = 273 + 25 = 298
  π_Q is quality factor   = 1.0
  π_E is environmental factor = N_s = marine application = 9.0
  π_R is current rating factor = 30 A

$$= (i_{rms})^{0.40} = (30)^{0.40} = 3.9$$

π_S is voltage stress factor
$$= 500 \text{ V} = 0.5$$
$$= (V_s)^{1.9} = (0.5)^{1.9} = 0.27$$

$$\lambda_p = \lambda_b . \pi_T . \pi_Q . \pi_E . \pi_R . \pi_S = 0.002 * 21 * 1.0 * 9.0 * 3.9 * 0.27 = 0.437$$
failure/10^6 h

Failure rate for assumed model switch = 0.437 failure/10^6 h.

6.6   Example: Reliability Prediction for Resistor

Let us consider the resistor for the reliability prediction. Model number of the resistor is RC0603 1/10 W, operating temperature range is −55 °C to 155 °C, maximum working voltage is 75 V, maximum overload voltage is 150 V, dielectric withstand voltage is 100 V and ambient temperature is 70 °C.

Formula for failure rate Equation (6, 5),

$$\lambda_p = \lambda_b . \pi_R . \pi_Q . \pi_E$$

λ_b is base failure rate

$$= 4.5 \times 10^{-3} \exp\left(12\left(\frac{T+273}{343}\right)\exp\left(\frac{s}{0.6}\left(\frac{T+273}{273}\right)\right)\right)$$

$$= 4.5 \times 10^{-3} \exp\left(12\left(\frac{70+273}{343}\right)\exp\left(\frac{\frac{1}{10}}{0.6}\left(\frac{70+273}{273}\right)\right)\right)$$

$$= 0.00090$$

π_Q is quality factor = R quality = 0.1
π_E is environmental factor = N_s = marine application = 5.0
Resistor factor 1MΩ π_R = 1.1

$$\lambda_p = \lambda_b . \pi_R . \pi_Q . \pi_E$$

Failure rate of the resistor λ_p = 0.00090×1.1×5.0×0.1
= 0.000495 or 4.95× 10^{-4} W−s

The failure rate based reliability prediction has been done for the considered model of the power semiconductor and resistor. The procedure of the failure rate calculation and reliability dependent parameters are explained. The power semiconductor failure rate depends on the ambient temperature of the device.

6.7 Conclusions

Several methods are used for reliability prediction. Some methods have their own data and other methods are depend on the additional data from other sources. The reliability prediction methods are not comparable because each method has own sensitive consideration parameters and focused on different assumptions. Failure rate or mean time failure rate are considered for the electronic component reliability. The reliability has been explained and evaluated with the considerations namely JANTX material, maximum temperature, environment factor and application factors. By following MLI-217F N2 standards failure rate of the IGBT has been calculated.

References

1. Hirschmann, D., Tissen, D., Schroder, S., De Doncker, R.W., Reliability prediction for inverters in hybrid electrical vehicles. *IEEE T. Power Electr.*, 22, 6, pp. 2511–2517, 2007.
2. Kumar, G.R., Zhu, G.R., Lu, J., Chen, W., Li, B., Thermal analysis and reliability evaluation of cascaded H-bridge MLPVI for grid-connected applications. *IET The 6th International Conference on Renewable Power Generation*, pp. 1595–1599, Oct. 2017.
3. Babaie, A., Karami, B., Abrishamifar, A., Improved equations of switching loss and conduction loss in SPWM multilevel inverters. *proc. IEEE 7th Power Electronics and Drive Systems Technologies Conf.*, pp. 559–564, Feb. 2016.
4. Chaturvedi, P.K., Jain, S., Agrawal, P., Nema, R.K., Sao, K.K., Switching losses and harmonic investigations in multilevel inverters. *IETE J. Res.*, vol. 54, no. 4, pp. 297–307, Jul-Aug. 2008.
5. Obeidat, F. and Shuttleworth, R., PV inverters reliability prediction. *World Appl. Sci. J.*, vol. 35, no. 2, pp. 275–287, 2017.

6. Denson, W., The history of reliability prediction. *IEEE T. Reliab.*, vol. 47, no. 3, pp. SP321–SP328, Sep. 1998.
7. Jones, J. and Hayes, J., A comparison of electronic-reliability prediction models. *IEEE T. Reliab.*, vol. 48, no. 2, pp. 127–134, Jun. 1999.
8. Jahan, H.K., Naseri, M., Haji-Esmaeili, M.M., Abapour, M., Zare, K., Low component merged cells cascaded-transformer multilevel inverter featuring an enhanced reliability. *IET Power Electron.*, vol. 10, no. 8, pp. 855–862, Feb. 2017.
9. Farokhina, N., Fathi, S.H., Yousefpoor, N., Bakshizadeh, M.K., Minimisation of total harmonic distortion in a cascaded multilevel inverter by regulating of voltages dc sources. *IET Power Electron.*, vol. 5, no. 1, pp. 106–114, Jan 2012.
10. Ramani, K. and Krishan, A., New hybrid multilevel inverter fed induction motor drive-A diagnostic study. *Int. Rev. Electr. Eng. (IREE)*, vol. 5, no. 6, pp. 2562–2569, Dec. 2010.
11. Du, Z., Tolbert, L.M., Chiasson, J.N., Active Harmonic elimination for multilevel converters. *IEEE T. Power Electr.*, vol. 21, no. 2, pp. 459–469, Mar. 2006.
12. Malinowski, M., Gopakumar, K., Rodriguez, J., Perez, M.A., A survey on cascaded multilevel inverters. *IEEE T. Ind. Electron.*, vol. 57, no. 7, pp. 2197–2206, Jul. 2010.
13. Ma, K., Wang, H., Blaabjerg, F., New approaches to reliability assessment: Using physics-of-failure for prediction and design in power electronics systems. *IEEE Power Electron. Mag.*, vol. 3, no. 4, pp. 28–41, Dec. 2016.
14. Chan, F. and Calleja, H., Reliability estimation of three single-phase topologies in grid-connected PV systems. *IEEE T. Ind. Electron.*, vol. 58, no. 7, pp. 2683–2689, Jul. 2011.
15. Niazi, A., Dai, J.S., Balabani, S., Seneviratne, L., Product cost estimation: Technique classification and methodology review. *J. Manuf. Sci. Eng.*, vol. 128, no. 2, pp. 563–575, May 2006.
16. Yu, X. and Khambadkone, A.M., Reliability analysis and cost optimization of parallel-inverter system. *IEEE T. Ind. Electron.*, vol. 59, no. 10, pp. 3881–3889, Oct. 2012.
17. Jayabalan, M., Jeevarathinam, B., Sandirasegarane, T., Reduced switch count pulse width modulated multilevel inverter. *IET Power Electron.*, vol. 10, no. 1, pp. 10–17, Jan. 2017.
18. M. Handbook, *Reliability Prediction of Electronic Equipment (MIL-HDBK-217F)*, US Government Printing Office, Washington DC, 1986, Sec. 4.
19. F. I. D. E. S. Guide, *A Reliability Methodology for Electronic Systems*, UTE-C 80811, France, 2009.

7

Modeling, Simulation and Analysis of Drive Cycles for PMSM-Based HEV With Optimal Battery Type

Chitra, A.[1]*, Srivastava, Shivam[1], Gupta, Anish[1], Sinha, Rishu[1], Biswas, S.S.[2] and Vanishree, J.[1]

[1]*School of Electrical Engineering, Vellore Institute of Technology, Vellore, India*
[2]*Engineer and R&D In charge, BHAVINI, Kalpakkam, India*

Abstract

The current automotive industry is facing a huge transition from ICE to electric propulsion. However, the current infrastructure is not that EV-friendly so that majority of the population can trust this segment. This is where the Hybrid Electric Vehicle (HEV) comes into the picture offering a high fuel economy without compromising the vehicle driving dynamics. It becomes increasingly important to have a comprehensive understanding of the working of HEV under different drive cycles and also the knowledge of an optimal battery type to prevent range anxiety. This paper presents a modeling of PMSM-based HEV with comparative evaluation of three different drive cycles viz. acceleration cruising and deceleration for three distinct state of charge values for each drive cycle considering six major vehicle performance defining parameters namely—vehicle speed, battery power, torque sharing, final SOC value, ICE power and switching ON of hybrid mode. Additionally, a comparison on three different battery types—Lead acid, Li-ion and Ni-MH is presented based on their sizing and cost considerations for the proposed HEV model.

Keywords: Battery, comparative study, degree of hybridness (H), hybrid electric vehicle (HEV), permanent magnet synchronous motor (PMSM), state of charge (SOC)

*Corresponding author: chitra.a@vit.ac.in

Chitra A, P. Sanjeevikumar, Jens Bo Holm-Nielsen and S. Himavathi (eds.) *Artificial Intelligent Techniques for Electric and Hybrid Electric Vehicles*, (125–142) © 2020 Scrivener Publishing LLC

7.1   Introduction

The electric vehicle technology is capable of reducing the pollution level as well as not requiring fossil fuels and hence, they appear to be the best for green transportation. However, the current infrastructure is not perfectly suitable for such a segment to attract more market primarily because of the range anxiety issue of the EVs. Hybrid electric vehicles are currently one of the most favorable technologies and are attracting more and more attention [1]. HEVs have multiple power sources, and their fuel economy and emissions can be optimized through an optimal power distribution called an energy management strategy [2, 3]. Possible combination of such power sources can be: fuel cell—battery, gasoline—flywheel and diesel—electric. As a result, HEVs should make transitions between different modes to achieve an optimal power distribution [4].

For low power applications and economically low-end cars Permanent Magnet Synchronous Motor (PMSM) serves as a perfect option. They can be designed to operate over wide torque—speed range with superior torque density and power density [5]. Fast electrical torque response is required to ensure quick dynamic performance of the whole system in these applications. And dynamic current response directly affects the dynamic performance of torque [6]. Conventional energy system of HEV can only be a single battery module with low power density and short cycle life [7]. The single battery can lead to driving range as well as poor acceleration performance. The common solution is to design a large battery by increasing the size of battery to meet the requirements of high-power density [8]. But the cost of this kind of battery is bound to rise, and it would result in a waste of battery's capacity and huge volume [9]. Hence, a comparative study on different battery types depending on their sizing and cost parameters becomes imperative.

The series-parallel architecture incorporates power-split devices allowing for power paths from Internal Combustion Engine (ICE) and batteries to the wheels that can be either mechanical, electromechanical or both of them [10].

In this study, authors have presented a PMSM based HEV simulation model which is capable to simulate different driving cycles depending upon the acceleration curve given as input in the signal builder block of Simulink. Additionally, a comparison on three different battery types—Lead acid, Li-ion and Ni-MH is presented based on their sizing and cost considerations for the proposed HEV model.

7.2   Modeling of Hybrid Electric Vehicle

The HEV system being proposed consists of two main blocks viz. the Energy management system and the Electrical Subsystem. Figure 7.1 shows the block diagram of the proposed system. The energy management system block further contains the Battery Management System (BMS) and the Hybrid Management System (HMS). The BMS is modeled such that it is responsible to maintain the SOC level of the battery between 40 and 80%. The HMS is responsible for switching ON/OFF the hybrid mode of the vehicle. This switching takes place depending upon the need for dynamic response of the vehicle like—requirement of excess torque while cruising, better power requirement while accelerating, etc.

The major parameters that were considered for modeling the HEV system were torque and state of charge (SOC). The general electromagnetic torque equation for the PMSM motor is expressed as

$$T_e = \frac{3p}{4}\left[\frac{1}{2}\left(L_d - L_q\right)I_m^2 \sin 2\alpha + \varphi I_m \sin \alpha\right] \qquad (7.1)$$

In order to get maximum torque, the α has to be made equal to 90° and hence the above equation can be rewritten as

$$T_e = \frac{3p}{4}\varphi I_q \qquad (7.2)$$

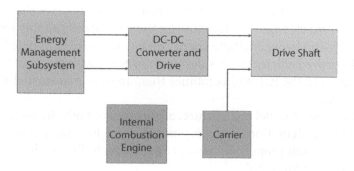

Figure 7.1 General block diagram of the proposed system.

"Cost-killing" policies from automotive part-makers contribute to rethink the EV electric propulsion so that new optimizations and new topologies would be proposed [11]. This is where the hybrid machine has to be designed very carefully. The degree of hybridness (H) of a vehicle plays a very important role in this. H can be expressed by the equation

$$H = \frac{Sum\ of\ all\ traction\ power\ \left(Electric\ motor\right)}{Sum\ of\ trction\ power\ of\ motor + ICE\ power} \qquad (7.3)$$

The hybrid vehicle is characterized by two types on energy, fuel and electricity and the other model is totally based on electrical power source [12]. If the H value is around 50% then the HEV is considered as fully hybrid and it has almost equal propulsion power from both the sources. In the modeled system, the H value is 46.72% as the two traction powering components are IC Engine (57 kW @ 5,000rpm) and an electric motor (50 kw, 500 V). The different architectures of HEVs are discussed in the section below.

7.2.1   Architectures Available for HEV

Hybrid Electrical Vehicles are generally implemented by different hybrid architectures such as: Series hybrid architecture, Parallel hybrid architecture, Series-parallel hybrid architecture and Complex hybrid architecture. In series hybrid architecture the ICE is coupled with the generator to yield electricity for fully electric vehicle propulsion. The mechanical decoupling between the IC engine and the driven wheels allows the IC engine operating at its very narrow optimal region [13].

In parallel hybrid architecture both the ICE and electric motor are coupled with the transmission system using the same drive shaft to propel the hybrid electric vehicle, allowing them to directly supply torque to the wheels and hence multiple energy conversions are eliminated resulting in improved efficiency. This design utilizes the advantages of the electric motor and the ICE and combines them to form a more fuel-efficient vehicle [14].

In the series-parallel architecture, advantages of both the series as well as parallel configuration are incorporated. Here just like parallel hybrid architecture, both propulsion devices are mechanically coupled to wheels and provide traction [15].

7.3 Series—Parallel Hybrid Architecture

The proposed system uses two electrical machines—an electric motor and a generator. Figure 7.2 shows the architecture of the proposed HEV model for the purpose of analysis. In the series-parallel architecture, the power from the combustion engine is split up into a part (nearly) directly sent to the wheels and a part sent through power electronic converters [16]. The Toyota Prius is a well-known example of such a system. In this case, a planetary gear is used for the power split [17, 18]. Although this architecture is more expensive than any of its parent architectures, it is one of the most preferred topologies for HEVs, especially when automakers target excellent dynamic performance for their models. Similar to the parallel HEVs, the degree of hybridness is adjusted as a trade-off of performance, cruising speed, fuel economy, drivability, and driver's comfort. Therefore, using the two electrical machines provides quiet and smooth running at lower speeds as in case of series hybrid architecture, as well as provides effortless high-speed cruising as in case of parallel hybrid architecture.

7.4 Analysis With Different Drive Cycles

In this study, authors have followed a specific protocol for analyzing different drive cycles. Each drive cycle is divided into 3 distinct cases depending upon the SOC values viz. 30%, 60% and 90%. Each of these cases is analyzed for 6 different parameters viz. Battery power, SOC, ICE power, Status of hybrid mode, car speed and torque sharing. The drive cycle input

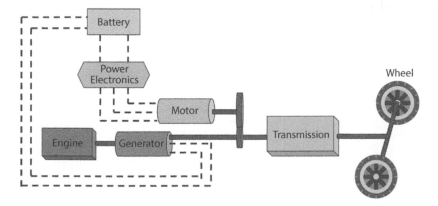

Figure 7.2 Proposed architecture of the HEV system.

is given through the signal builder block of the Simulink and the results are simulated. The analysis sections are presented below shows the simulation results for 4 major vehicle parameters.

7.4.1   Acceleration Drive Cycle

In this cycle it is assumed that the vehicle is going to start from rest and the driver is accelerating the vehicle from 0 to 80% throttle (ramp signal) in 16 s of simulation time. Figure 7.3 shows the input signal given to the signal builder for this drive cycle. Each of the cases has been discussed in the sections below.

7.4.1.1   For 30% State of Charge

For SOC value below the BMS level (30%) the performance of the model vehicle is not at par the normal conditions. The battery power shows a negative value (−21 kW) as the SOC is below the BMS limit so it cannot power the wheels instead it acts as a load. The maximum vehicle speed attained in this case is 55.59 kmph which is considerably low since only ICE is powering the wheels and also its fraction of power is responsible for charging the battery due to the low SOC level. The percentage sharing of torque between the electric motor and IC Engine is dominated by electric motor which is attributed to the fact that the proposed model has a H value of 46.72% which comes under the fully hybrid category where electric motor dominates the ICE. The electric motor torque is 100.7 N·m and the ICE torque is 80.98 N.m. This share of torque for the electric motor will increase as the SOC value increases. The final SOC is recorded as 31.93% which is greater than the initial SOC value as the battery is being charged. Figure 7.4 shows the simulation results for this case.

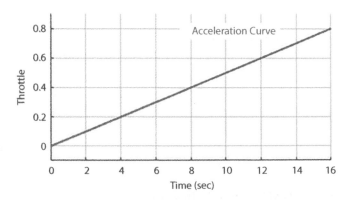

Figure 7.3 Acceleration curve in the signal builder.

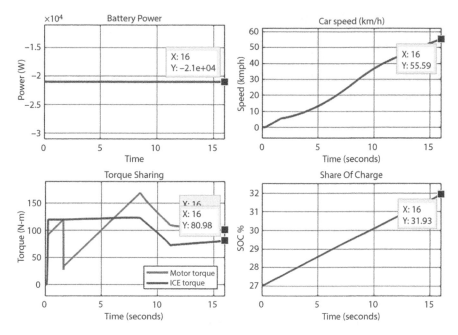

Figure 7.4 Acceleration drive cycle with SOC = 30%.

7.4.1.2   For 60% State of Charge

This case meets the SOC limit of the BMS and shows desired results for the vehicle parameters. The battery power is positive (17.44 kW) as the SOC level is adequate, the battery acts as a source and supplies power to the electric motor. This case meets the SOC limit of the BMS and shows desired results for the vehicle parameters. The battery power is positive (17.44 kW) as the SOC level is adequate, the battery acts as a source and supplies power to the electric motor. The vehicle attains a higher speed (80.74 kmph) compared to the 30% SOC case as both the electric motor and ICE will contribute in powering the wheels. The percentage share of motor torque is increased, having electric motor torque as 224.9 N.m and ICE torque as 99.89 N.m. The final SOC value is recorded as 55.77% which is less than the initial SOC value as the battery is supplying power to the electric motor. Figure 7.5 shows the simulation results for this case.

7.4.1.3   For 90% State of Charge

This case also has the enough initial SOC value as per the BMS limits. All the vehicle parameters showed the same results as in the case of 60% SOC which perfectly matched the expectations as there should not be any

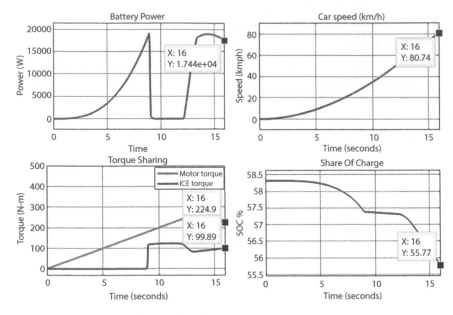

Figure 7.5 Acceleration drive cycle with SOC = 60%.

variation if the SOC value is adequate as per the BMS. The only parameter which was changed is the final SOC value at the end of simulation time which is recorded as 87.18%. Table 7.1 shows the summarized simulation results for the acceleration drive cycle.

7.5   Cruising Drive Cycle

In this cycle the vehicle is in a constant cruising mode at 80% of throttle. The initial vehicle speed is made to be 0 kmph. The simulation time is kept as 16 s and the constant 0.8 is given as input in the signal builder block of Simulink. Figure 7.6 shows the input signal given to the signal builder for this drive cycle. This drive cycle showed similar results as that acceleration drive cycle but with improved magnitude of the parameters under study as in this drive cycle vehicle will be accelerating constantly at a higher acceleration value. Simulation results for this drive cycle have been summarized in the Table 7.2.

7.6   Deceleration Drive Cycle

In this cycle, the vehicle is given with a short duration (5 s) cruising at 80% throttle so that a certain positive speed is attained and for the next 25 s the

Table 7.1 Comparitive evaluation for acceleration drive cycle.

SOC (in %)	Hybrid mode (ON state in s)	Battery power (kW)	Vehicle speed (kmph)	Battery-motor torque (N•m)	ICE torque (N•m)	Final SOC %	Vehicle power (kW)
30	0.072–16	−21	55.59	100.7	80.98	31.93	42.4
60	7.632–16	17.44	80.74	224.9	99.89	55.77	52.3
90	7.632–16	17.44	80.74	224.9	99.89	87.18	52.3

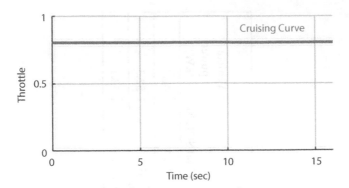

Figure 7.6 Cruising curve in the signal builder.

vehicle is provided with a deceleration from 80% to −80% (ramp profile) so that deceleration can be studied. The initial vehicle speed is made to be 0 kmph. The simulation time is kept as 30 s. Figure 7.7 shows the input signal given to the signal builder for this drive cycle. Each of the cases has been discussed in the sections below.

7.6.1   For 30% State of Charge

For SOC value below the BMS level (30%) the performance of the model vehicle is again not par the normal conditions. The battery power shows a negative value (−21 kW) same as that of earlier drive cycles, as the SOC is below the BMS limit so it cannot power the wheels instead it acts as a load. The vehicle attains the maximum speed of 64.46 kmph at 16.32 s, as at this instant the vehicle acceleration changes its sign from positive to negative. The final speed is recorded as −28.43 kmph at the end of simulation time. The speed is negative because the vehicle

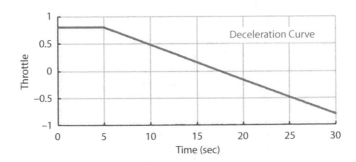

Figure 7.7 Deceleration curve in the signal builder.

Table 7.2 Comparitive evaluation for cruising drive cycle.

SOC (in %)	Hybrid mode (ON state in s)	Battery power (kW)	Vehicle speed (kmph)	Battery-motor torque (N·m)	ICE torque (N·m)	Final SOC %	Vehicle power (kW)
30	0.05–16	–21	65.81	99	86.33	31.99	45.89
60	0.927–16	18.8	117.5	168.3	108.8	50.86	56.98
90	0.927–16	18.8	117.5	168.3	108.8	83.92	56.98

decelerates. There is equal percentage sharing of torque magnitude between the electric motor and IC Engine but the electric motor offers a negative torque (−186.3 N·m) due to the regenerative action of the electric motor, its magnitude is almost the same as that of ICE torque (186.8 N·m). The final SOC is recorded as 37.58% which is greater than the final SOC value achieved in other drive cycles this is due to the regenerative action of the electric motor. Figure 7.8 shows the simulation results for this case.

7.6.2   For 60% State of Charge

This case meets the SOC limit of the BMS, but the battery shows a negative value (−21 kW) which is due to the regenerative action of electric motor similar to the earlier cases and the battery gets charged (acts as load). The vehicle attains a maximum speed of 101.9 kmph at 16.32 s, as at this instant the vehicle acceleration changes its sign from positive to negative, similar to the earlier case. The final speed is recorded as 46.47 kmph at the end of simulation time. This speed is positive because the vehicle has the sufficient SOC so that it can power the electric motor helping the vehicle attain a

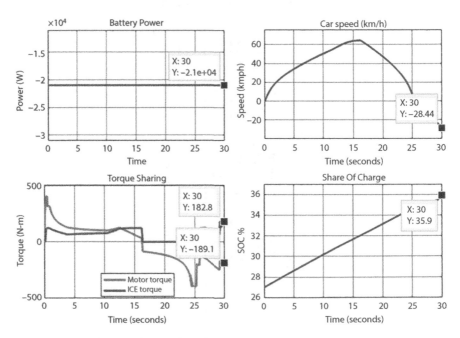

Figure 7.8 Deceleration drive cycle with SOC = 30%.

very high speed until 16.32 s and then it needs more time to come to rest. The net torque is −118.7 N.m which is purely due to the electric motor. The final SOC is recorded as 57.71% which is greater than the final SOC value achieved in other drive cycles of this SOC value (60%), due to the regenerative action of the electric motor. Figure 7.9 shows the simulation results for this case.

7.6.3   For 90% State of Charge

This case also has enough initial SOC value as per the BMS limits. All the vehicle parameters showed the same results as in the case of 60% SOC as there should not be any variation if the SOC value is adequate as per the BMS. The only parameter which was changed is the final SOC value at the end of simulation time which is recorded as 88.86%. Table 7.3 shows the summarized simulation results for the cruising drive cycle.

The percentage share of torque between the ICE and the electric motor can be summarized in the Table 7.4, for each drive cycle which clearly shows that electric motor dominates ICE torque.

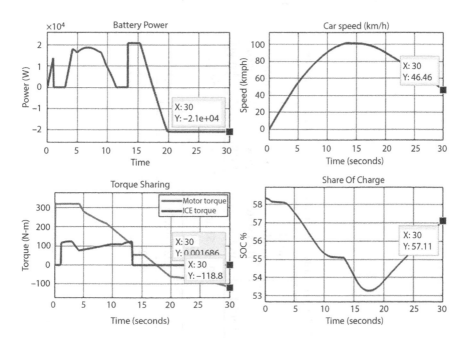

Figure 7.9 Deceleration drive cycle with SOC = 60%.

Table 7.3 Comparitive evaluation for deceleration drive cycle.

SOC (in %)	Hybrid mode (ON state in sec)	Battery power (kW)	Vehicle speed (kmph)	Battery-motor torque (N•m)	ICE torque (N•m)	Final SOC %	Vehicle power (kW)
30	0–17.51 and 25.66–30	–21	–28.43	–186.3	186.8	37.58	72.41
60	0.927–16.39	–21	46.47	–118.7	0	57.71	0
90	0.927–16.39	–21	46.47	–118.7	0	88.86	0

Table 7.4 Torque sharing.

Drive cycle	SOC (in %)	Battery-motor torque (in %)	ICE torque (in %)
Acceleration	30	55.247	44.57
	60	69.24	30.75
	90	69.24	30.75
Cruising	30	53.41	46.58
	60	60.73	39.26
	90	60.73	39.26
Deceleration	30	50	50
	60	100	0
	90	100	0

7.7 Analysis of Battery Types

Batteries are very complex electrochemical systems and their detailed review is beyond the scope of this work. In the present study, authors have presented a summarized comparison of battery types depending on their sizing and cost parameters.

Two parameters viz. gravimetric energy density (GED) and volumetric energy density (VED) are used to analyze the battery sizing. These can be given by the equations below:

$$Gravimetric\ energy\ density\left(\frac{Wh}{kg}\right) = \frac{Energy(Wh)}{Weight(kg)} \qquad (7.4)$$

$$Volumetric\ energy\ density\left(\frac{Wh}{lit}\right) = \frac{Energy(Wh)}{Volume(lit)} \qquad (7.5)$$

For the price-based comparison, price energy density has been taken into account for each battery type. This is given by the equation given below:

$$Price\ energy\ density\left(\frac{Wh}{n}\right) = \frac{Energy(Wh)}{Price(n)} \qquad (7.6)$$

Table 7.5 Optimal battery type.

Parameter	Energy density	Lead acid	Ni-MH	Li-ion
Size	Wh/Kg	32.69	98	209.3
	Wh/lit	91.6	391.48	541.14
Cost	Wh/₹	0.05083	0.00979	0.01950

The necessary data for calculating these parameters have been referred from the website amazon.com. Table 7.5 shows a numerical tabulation of these parameters.

On the basis of these parameters it is evident that the Li Ion battery is the most compact and has highest energy density among the 3 batteries. The Lead Acid battery has the maximum size for the same rated energy density. Nickel Metal Hydride has intermediate compactness but has almost thrice the energy density of the Lead Acid battery. From the cost parameter row in Table 7.5 it can be deduced that One rupee produces 0.05083 Wh of energy by Lead Acid Battery which is the cheapest among all. Ni–MH appears to be the most expensive battery type with one rupee producing 0.00979 Wh of energy.

7.8   Conclusion

In this chapter authors have presented a side-by-side comparison of different drive cycles viz. Acceleration, Cruising and Deceleration for multiple SOC values. Different driving topologies are considered for PMSM-based HEV model. Also, three different battery types are considered for the HEV model and are compared based on their sizing and cost parameters to present the most optimal battery type for the proposed model. Comparative evaluation indicates that the system performs better when adequate amount of SOC is available to the system; all the parameters have shown better responses.

Based on the gravimetric and volumetric analysis of the battery types for the sizing comparison, the Li-ion battery offers maximum energy density for the same battery rating and hence is the most compact battery type considered for the comparison. The cost analysis of the battery portrays that the lead acid battery offers highest energy making it the most economical battery type considered. Considering both the sizing and cost parameters simultaneously and also the current trends in decreasing price of Li-ion battery, the most optimal battery is undoubtedly the Li-ion battery for the HEV model considered. However, there are certain safety issues like battery leakage, overcharge, etc. which have to be taken care of seriously while using the Li-ion battery.

References

1. Wang, G., Yang, P., Zhang, J., Fuzzy optimal control and simulation of battery-ultracapacitor dual-energy source storage system for pure electric vehicle. *2010 Int. Conf. Intell. Control Inf. Process.*, pp. 555–560, 2010.
2. Plug-in, O.B., Charge-depleting control strategies and fuel hybrid electric vehicles. *IEEE Trans. Veh. Technol.*, 60, 4, 1516–1525, 2011.
3. Wang, Y., Optimal control of the transient emissions and the fuel efficiency of a diesel hybrid electric vehicle. *P. I. Mech. Eng. D.*, 227, 11, 1546–1561, 2013.
4. Zhang, H., Zhang, Y., Yin, C., Hardware-in-the-Loop Simulation of Robust Mode Transition Control for a Series – Parallel Hybrid Electric Vehicle. 65, 3, 1059–1069, 2016.
5. Yang, Z., Shang, F., Member, S., Brown, I.P., Comparative study of interior permanent magnet, induction, and switched reluctance motor drives for EV and HEV applications. *IEEE Trans. Transp. Electrif.*, 1, 3, 245–254, 2015.
6. Wang, H. and Leng, J., Summary on development of permanent magnet synchronous motor. *2018 Chinese Control Decis. Conf.*, pp. 689–693, 2018.
7. Camara, M.B., Gualous, H., Gustin, F., Berthon, A., Design and New Control of DC/DC Converters to Share Energy Between Supercapacitors and Batteries in Hybrid Vehicles. 57, 5, 2721–2735, 2008.
8. Qi, W., Yu-kun, S., Yong-hong, H., Study on the experiment of ultracapacitor in HES for HEV. *26th Chinese Control Decis. Conf. (2014 CCDC)*, pp. 4707–4710, 2014.
9. Lukic, Srdjan M., Sanjaka G. Wirasingha, Fernando Rodriguez, Jian Cao, and Ali Emadi, Power management of an ultracapacitor/battery hybrid energy storage system in an HEV. in: *2006 IEEE Vehicle Power and Propulsion Conference*, pp. 1–6, IEEE, 2006.
10. Chen, Keyu, Walter Lhomme, Alain Bouscayrol, and Alain Berthon, Comparison of two series-parallel hybrid electric vehicles focusing on control structures and operation modes. in: *2009 IEEE Vehicle Power and Propulsion Conference*, pp. 1308–1315, IEEE, 2009.
11. De Sousa, L., Silvestre, B., Bouchez, B., A combined multiphase electric drive and fast battery charger for Electric Vehicles. in: *2010 IEEE Vehicle Power and Propulsion Conference*, Lille, pp. 1–6, 2010.
12. Chau, K.T. and Chan, C.C., Emerging energy-efficient technologies for hybrid electric vehicles. in: *Proc. IEEE*, vol. 95, no. 4, pp. 821–835, April 2007.
13. Ehsani, Mehrdad, Yimin Gao, and John M. Miller., Hybrid electric vehicles: Architecture and motor drives. *Proceedings of the IEEE*, 95.4, 719–728, 2007.

14. Lukic, S.M. and Member, S., Topological Overview of Hybrid Electric and Fuel Cell Vehicular Power System Architectures and Configurations. vol. 54, no. 3, pp. 763–770, 2005.
15. Zia, A. and Member, I., A comprehensive overview on the architecture of Hybrid Electric Vehicles (HEV). *2016 19th Int. Multi-Topic Conf.*, pp. 1–7.
16. Hoeijmakers, M.J. and Ferreira, J.A., The Electric Variable Transmission, IEEE, 42, 4, 1092–1100, 2006.
17. Hermance, D. and Shoichi, S., Hybrid electric vehicles take to the streets, IEEE spectrum 35, no. 11, 48–52, 1998.
18. Sasaki, S., Toyota's newly developed hybrid powertrain. in: *Proceedings of the 10th International Symposium on Power Semiconductor Devices and ICs. ISPSD'98 (IEEE Cat. No. 98CH36212)*, pp. 17–22, IEEE, 1998.

8

Modified Firefly-Based Maximum Power Point Tracking Algorithm for PV Systems Under Partial Shading Conditions

Chitra, A.[1*], Yogitha, G.[1], Karthik Sivaramakrishnan[1], Razia Sultana, W.[1] and Sanjeevikumar, P.[2]

[1]School of Electrical Engineering, Vellore Institute of Technology, Vellore, India
[2]Department of Energy Technology, Aalborg University, Denmark

Abstract

On handling partial shading conditions the power obtained at the output from the PV modules decreases drastically and the P–V characteristics of the photovoltaic modules is non-linear with multiple peaks including several local peaks and giving a single global peak. In such condition, it is challenging to track exact global maximum power point (GMPP). Conventional MPPT methods like Perturbation and Observe, Incremental conductance, Hill-climbing, etc. often lose to track GMPP as they often get confused with local peak and global peak resulting in extracting less power from PV modules. This paper presents modified firefly algorithm which is nature inspired implemented to track the GMPP. Its tracking efficiency is compared with the original firefly and also incremental conductance algorithm. The simulated results shows that the proposed algorithm can track high power, has better tracking quickness, and has effectively faster convergence time. The proposed modified firefly algorithm is fed to a DC–DC converter and the results are simulated.

Keywords: Evolutionary algorithm, partial shading, MPPT, firefly algorithm, GMPP

8.1 Introduction

Energy plays a noticeable part in the economic development and is important for the economy of a nation and even to the society. Future improvement

---

*Corresponding author: chitra.a@vit.ac.in

Chitra A, P. Sanjeevikumar, Jens Bo Holm-Nielsen and S. Himavathi (eds.) *Artificial Intelligent Techniques for Electric and Hybrid Electric Vehicles*, (143–164) © 2020 Scrivener Publishing LLC

and economic development relies upon the long-term accessibility of energy from the sources that are accessible, non-polluting, affordable, secure and non-destructive [1]. At present, non-renewable energy sources are the significant energy provider worldwide. Fossil fuels discharge nitrogen dioxide (NO_2), carbon dioxide (CO_2), carbon monoxide (NO), sulphur dioxide (SO_2), and other different gases which when burnt create adverse impacts on the widely varied flora and fauna exists in the planet. The harmful impacts incorporate, however not restricted to, green-house effect and air pollution. These days, the utilization of sustainable energy sources could diminish the greenhouse emissions and gives positive effect to the world. Among all renewable energy sources, solar photovoltaic standout among the most vital sustainable energy sources in view of the long-term benefits, free maintenance and ecological friendliness. Nonetheless, the low energy conversion efficiency and high initial cost of photovoltaic module have been perceived as the significant prevention in its far spread acknowledgment. Tremendous measure of works have been done to increase the solar energy performance. With enhancing the most extreme power point tracking (MPPT) capacity, the solar system efficiencies can be created. It is one among the most conservative ways that can be possible. The primary challenge in the MPPT is the profoundly nonlinear characteristics curves of PV source which changes in like manner to the environmental impacts like temperature and solar irradiation. Since the V–I characteristics changes continuously, the maximum power point on P–V characteristics curve is not consistent, cause issues in the tracking execution. During partial shading conditions, where PV array receives a non-uniform solar irradiation, the maximum power-point tracking procedure turn out to be more complicated. The impact of partial shading is the PV curve complexity which gives various peaks and it is hard to track the real and exact true MPP. The MPPT procedures can be classified into two kinds which are conventional techniques and soft computing techniques. For the first type, the conventional or traditional techniques which incorporates hill-climbing (HC), P&O, fractional short-circuit and open-circuit voltage, incremental conductance (InCon). While for the second sort depends on soft computing technique which comprises of artificial neural network (ANN). Fuzzy logic controller (FLC) and evolutionary algorithm (EA). The conventional method is most generally utilized because of their advantages and simplicity in implementation. Conventional strategies can give great dynamic and steady-state performance under general conditions. However, they ordinarily show high oscillation around the operating point and unfit to track MPP under fast changing solar irradiance. Moreover, none of the conventional systems have ability to manage partial shading conditions (PSC). This is a result of the ineptitude of the conventional strategies to differentiate local and global peaks. In [2] and [3], the authors recommend that the P&O calculation is a standout among the most generally utilized algorithms in solar energy systems. Reference [3] calls attention to that the customary P&O algorithm neglects to track changing MPP amid changing irradiance and temperature conditions. Authors of [4] depict in detail the confinements of P&O algorithm in consistent ecological conditions and recommend a two-advance P&O strategy to expand the productivity of the regular algorithm. Reference [5] states that the primary utilization of P&O technique for MPP tracking was in the 1970s for aviation applications and states that the irritation period ought to be lower than the system settling time. The algorithm suffers from two major disadvantages. Determination of the ideal perturbation value is difficult. One should carefully perform the trade-off between speed of algorithm and accuracy to determine the perturbation value. A very small perturbation value slows down the algorithm, while a large perturbation value leads to higher oscillations around the MPP. In addition, when the irradiation and/ or cell temperature vary, the error in P&O algorithm is more. The incremental conductance algorithm is more qualified than P&O for varying environment conditions. Nonetheless, the execution is comparatively complex. Moreover, the ΔV can be utilized to increasing the MPP tracking, however a high value of ΔV will make the system away around the MPP, which is not worthy. Executing the incremental conductance requires the current and the voltage output values from the panel. Along this, it requires one current sensor and current sensor. This algorithm is normally actualized utilizing a microcontroller or a DSP. The authors exhibit the issues identified with ordinary P&O and InCon calculations and propose a variable-advance InCon technique for exact MPP tracking. They call the strategy as powerful self-optimization. Researches communicated their inventive by proposing soft computing techniques based on global search algorithm to discover global maxima amid shaded conditions. Among soft computing techniques ANN and FLC ended up proving their better dynamic and steady state execution than conventional techniques. These two strategies are hard to accomplish optimized design. FLC requires a specialist learning while ANN needs a lot of training information. To conquer these constraints, Evolutionary algorithm is the best method to manage the MPPT issue since it work in view of set of points rather than single point utilized as a part of conventional search and optimization strategies. Recently, a few EA techniques have been recommended, for example, the most prevalent ones among are particle swarm optimization (PSO), differential development (DE), Genetic Algorithm (GA). Among the EA methods,

PSO is exceedingly potential because of its simpler structure, fast computation capability and easy implementation. In [6], the writers actualize the PSO algorithm for PV system under the partial shading conditions. The working of the MPPT has been obviously clarified. The standard PSO has additionally been changed to meet the practical contemplations. The writers pass on that the MPPT effectiveness is higher than 99.9%, simple usage and better convergence. In [7], the authors audit the PSO technique with reference to solar PV. The writers say that the PSO algorithm is incredible and non-resistive since they don't require any subordinate estimations. In [8], the author utilizes PSO to decide the exhibit volt-age and afterward track the MPP in an independent PV framework. The effectiveness of following is seen in [9] to be over 98% with a union time of 14 ms. The writers have utilized PSO with the capacity of direct duty ratio to track the MPP of system so as to wipe out the PI controller which is utilized to control the duty cycle. The outcomes demonstrate that the proposed strategy has better execution when compared and the customary hill climbing algorithms. The authors of [10] suggest ant colony based search in the underlying phases of tracking took after by P&O technique. The proposed strategy, the local search capacity of P&O and global search capacity of ACO are both coordinated. This yields better performance, faster convergence and efficiency. The [11] presents the ACO based control technique to tune the PI controller for tracking MPP. The ACO is optimized utilizing fractional open-circuit voltage (FOC) technique to quickly and precisely track the MPP. In this paper, the performance of the system with conventional and evolutionary algorithm under PSC is com-pared. A meta-heuristic algorithm known as firefly algorithm is implemented and the modification is done for the firefly algorithm for tracking quickness, performance, tracking efficiency is improved in comparison with existing firefly algorithm and conventional incremental algorithm.

8.2   System Block Diagram Specifications

The proposed system consists of a solar PV panel as a source. It is connected to DC–DC boost converter with resistive load. The pulses to the boost converter are sent through a MPPT controller. System performance under partial shading conditions is tested with three different MPPT algorithms namely incremental conductance, firefly algorithm and modified firefly algorithm. The system block diagram in shown in the Figure 8.1.

Solar panel is the main source of the system. A solar PV array of two panels is connected in series. The solar panel used is developed through

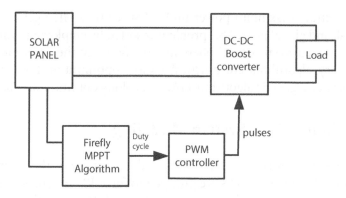

Figure 8.1 System block diagram.

Simulink blocks present in MATLAB library and the panel specifications are taken from KC200GT solar panel data sheet. So two solar panels of a rating of 200 W are connected in series and the performance of the system only under PSC is considered and whether solar PV is operating at global peak and not at local peaks under PSC is observed. The solar specifications are mentioned in Table 8.1.

Boost converter is used to step-up the voltage at the load end. Here boost converter is used to connect with the load. The boost converter parameters L and C are designed using design specifications which are described in detail in *Boost Converter Design* section. Main objective of the work is to observe the modified firefly algorithm to get maximum power from the solar panel.

The MPPT block is used to extract the maximum power from the solar panel. Usually MPPT strategies are divided into 2 types conventional and evolutionary. The most commonly employed MPPT strategies are P&O, incremental conductance, hill-climbing, etc. all these conventional algorithms

Table 8.1 Solar specifications.

Specification	Value
I_{mp}	7.61 A
V_{mp}	26.3 V
I_{sc}	8.21 A
V_{oc}	32.9 V
N_s	54
P_{max}	200.143 W

failed to extract maximum power under PSC as they often get confuse at local peak and global peak. This problem is sorted by employing evolutional algorithm taken from natural phenomenon. Some of the commonly used evolutionary algorithms are practical swarm optimization-PSO, artificial neural network, genetic algorithm-GA, Ant colony optimization-ACO, etc.

8.3   Photovoltaic System Modeling

A Photovoltaic cell is considered as foundation stone of the solar panel. Many such Photovoltaic cells are grouped to form PV modules and thereafter PV arrays are formed by arranging PV modules in parallel and series connection. These PV arrays are usually used in PV generation system to generate electricity. A single diode structure of a Photovoltaic cell is modelled by using a current source, two resistors and a diode [12, 13]. The equivalent circuit of a single-diode photovoltaic cell is shown in Figure 8.2.

It consists of shunting resistance (Rs), series resistance (Rsh), the cell photo-current is represented by the current source Iph and a diode. Mostly, the value of Rs is so small whereas Rsh is very large, thus they are ignored to abridge the analysis. Generally based on the knowledge of semiconductors the main equation is mathematically derived and the V–I characteristic equation of the ideal Photovoltaic cell is given as

$$I = I_{PV,\,cell} - I_{o,cell}\left[\exp\left(\frac{qv}{akT} \right) - 1 \right] \tag{8.1}$$

Equation (8.1) stated above about the fundamental photovoltaic cell does not show the I–V characteristics of Photovoltaic array. The cells connected

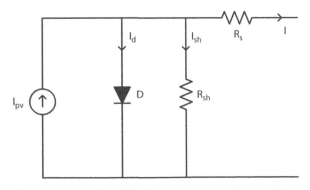

Figure 8.2 Equivalent circuit of single-diode model.

in series will provide high voltage at the output whereas the parallel connected cells increases the current at the output. In practical applications
the arrays consists of numerous PV cells connected and its features at the
endpoints of the Photovoltaic array involves the accumulation of the other
parameters added to main equation as is given as

$$I = I_{sc} - I_o \left[\exp\left(\frac{v + R_s I}{v_t a} \right) - 1 \right] - \frac{v + R_s I}{R_p} \tag{8.2}$$

The cell used in practical areas has a stronger influence of series resistance Rs when the cell is operated in voltage source region and has a stronger influence of shunted resistance Rp when it is operated in current source
region. The prediction Isc ≈ Ipv is usually made during the modeling of
solar PV cell because the parallel resistance Rp is high and serial resistance
Rs is low in practical devices. The equation of diode saturation current is
stated as

$$I_o = \frac{I_{sc,n} + K_i \Delta_T}{\exp\left(\dfrac{V_{oc,n} + K_v \Delta_T}{a v_t} \right) - 1} \tag{8.3}$$

$$I_{PV} = \left(I_{PV,n} + K_i \Delta_T \right) \frac{G}{G_n} \tag{8.4}$$

The saturation current Io depends on temperature so that according
to practical temperature/voltage coefficient the temperature net effect is
directly proportional of open-circuit voltage. Equation (8.3) shortens
the complexity involved in the algorithm by eliminating the model error
which is present near the open-circuit voltages, and thereby also at the
many places on the I–V curve. The PV cell characteristics are the combination of the diode and current source. The diode I–V characteristics are
derived separately and current source I–V characteristics are determined
in separate fashion. In this case the diode and current source are circuited
in parallel, hence by summing both the currents the characteristics of PV
array are achieved. Figures 8.3 and 8.4 represent the P–V and I–V curves
of a Photovoltaic cell.

It is inferred that the Photovoltaic cell functions as constant voltage
source for the corresponding operating current at low values and as constant current source for the corresponding operating voltages at low values.

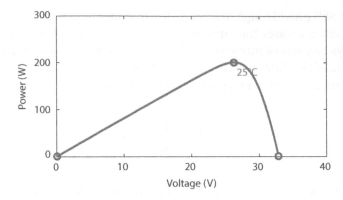

Figure 8.3 P–V characteristics of KC200GT solar panel.

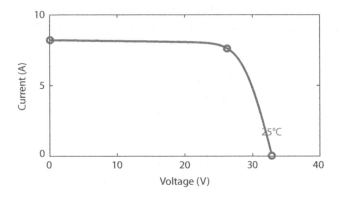

Figure 8.4 I–V characteristics of KC200GT solar panel.

8.4   Boost Converter Design

A DC–DC converter is one of the most important components of an independent Photovoltaic system. The voltage level of PV panels will be continuously varied because of the place of the operating point through which the direct supply of the DC PV power to electric load may be inappropriate. Usually, in a MPPT system the DC–DC converter is utilized to convert varying input power to a regulated power along with the desired level of voltage. Switch-mode DC–DC converters are presently most popular as they possess the advantages of high compatibility and small volume-size in comparison with other existing DC–DC converters. The main process of the DC–DC boost converter is to increase the voltage of the given DC

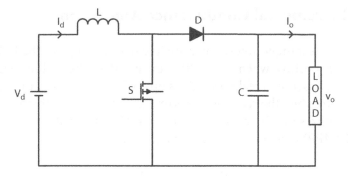

Figure 8.5 Boost converter.

power in the input. The circuitry of the boost converter is shown in the following Figure 8.5.

Diode will be in reverse bias condition when during on state of the switch. The input voltage will be the cause for the inductor current to increase linearly. In this considered case the output will be isolated and capacitor will discharge to supply the load. And when the switch is in off condition, diode will be in forward bias i.e. diode is conducting. At this time the load will get supply from the inductor and the input voltage source. The inductor current waveform during the conduction is given below as we can see that the inductor current is continuous. During the steady state conduction of the converter. Duty ratio is given by Equation (8.5). The following equations calculate the operation of the inductor and capacitor in continuous conduction mode.

$$D = 1 - \frac{V_d}{V_0} \tag{8.5}$$

$$L = \frac{V_d D}{2 \Delta I_L f_S} \tag{8.6}$$

$$C = \frac{I_0 D}{\Delta V_0 f_S} \tag{8.7}$$

From Equation (8.5), we can see that the output voltage is increasing, as the switch's duty cycle is increasing. Also if any change occurs in the duty cycle of the switch there will be changes in the current at the input and output of the above stated converter.

8.5   Incremental Conductance Algorithm

This MPPT technique abides the principle that the slope of the P–V characteristic is positive when the MPP is greater than the real power. When the MPP is lesser than real power the slope of PV curve is negative, and the slope is zero when the real power is same as the MPP. In other words, this strategy utilizes the V–I curve slope to track MPP. Consider the maximum power (PMPP) and power output (P) equations.

$$P_{MPP} = V_{MPP} {}^*I_{MPP} \tag{8.8}$$

$$P = V {}^*I \tag{8.9}$$

Differentiate with respect to voltage,

$$\frac{dP}{dV} = I + \left(V * \frac{dI}{dV} \right) \tag{8.10}$$

The differential of the power have to be equated to zero for the power to be maximum. In other words, this implies,

$$I + \left(V * \frac{dI}{dV} \right) = 0 \tag{8.11}$$

Which is approximated as,

$$\frac{\Delta I}{\Delta V} = \frac{-I_{MPP}}{V_{MPP}} \tag{8.12}$$

By evaluating Equation (8.12), the MPP is tracked. The conditions to track MPP are as explained by Equations (8.13) to (8.15),

$$\frac{dP}{dV} = 0 \rightarrow \frac{\Delta I}{\Delta V} = -\frac{I}{V} \text{ at MPP} \tag{8.13}$$

$$\frac{dP}{dV} > 0 \rightarrow \frac{\Delta I}{\Delta V} > -\frac{I}{V} \text{ left of MPP} \tag{8.14}$$

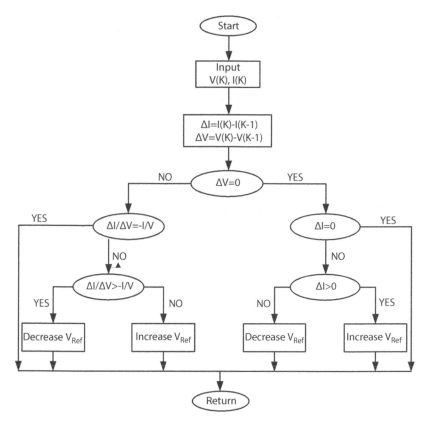

Figure 8.6 Incremental conductance algorithm flowchart.

$$\frac{dP}{dV} < 0 \rightarrow \frac{\Delta I}{\Delta V} < -\frac{I}{V} \text{ right of MPP} \tag{8.15}$$

The incremental conductance algorithm flowchart is stated below in the Figure 8.6.

8.6   Under Partial Shading Conditions

In this condition, the shaded cell in the series connection will block the current from passing through it. To get away with this circumstance a bypass diode is circuited across the cells to make flow the current from the un-shaded cells. Because of this link of bypass diodes there will be multiple peaks formation in I–V and P–V graphs. The above modeled system is now

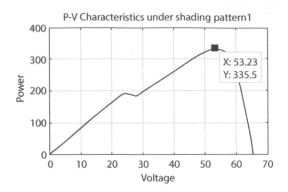

Figure 8.7 P–V characteristics under shading pattern 1.

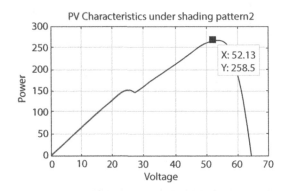

Figure 8.8 P–V characteristics under shading pattern 2.

simulated with the three different solar irradiation levels and the characteristic curves of current, voltage and power are observed. In this report, two different shading patterns are considered for the clear understanding and also for analyzing the behavior of the PV system under different shading conditions. The two different shading patterns are: 1. For 1,000 and 800 w/m² irradiation level; 2. For 800 and 600 w/m² irradiation level. The characteristic curves of I–V and P–V for the two considered shading patterns with multiple peaks are represented in the Figures 8.7 and 8.8.

8.7   Firefly Algorithm

The firefly algorithm, is relatively unique and evolutionary algorithm proposed by Yang in 2008 [14–16]. FA is a bio-inspired stochastic optimization technique based on swarm behavior and the population of fireflies

[17]. It is a meta-heuristic algorithm developed for the optimization of problems from the flashing nature and the movement of fireflies. The fireflies uses their fundamental flashes in order to draw attention of the prey towards them and also to find their coupling partners. The FA mainly consists of two elements which are brightness and attraction degree. The firefly movement, direction and step size are determined by the brightness which is reflected from the location. Once the updating of attraction degree and brightness of fireflies is completed all the fireflies will move towards the brightest firefly in order to achieve optimization goal. In the case of expansion problem, the firefly illumination will be always linear to the objective function value. The following three assumptions are made to simplify the implementation of firefly logic. Firstly, all the fireflies are of same gender so that each one can be get fascinated to the other firefly irrespective of their gender. Secondly, the relative brightness between the two fireflies is directly proportional to the degree of attractiveness which can be defined by calculating the relative distance between them. The firefly with the less brightness will move towards the firefly with more brightness until all the fireflies in the colony are compared except for itself. The firefly move randomly when there is no brighter one in that colony. Lastly the light intensity or brightness of a firefly is completely dependent on the value of objective function. Mathematically, the FA algorithm can be expressed by the following equations. Let i, j be the two fireflies which are located at the positions X_i and X_j, respectively and are separated by the distance rij. The distance between the two fireflies is formulated as

$$r_{ij} = \sqrt{\sum_{K=1}^{d} (X_{ik} - X_{jk})^2} \tag{8.16}$$

Where X_{ik} and X_{jk} are the ith and jth firefly's spatial coordinates of kth component and d is the number of dimensions. For maximum power point applications the number of dimensions is considered as one. Thus, the distance between two fireflies is simplified as

$$r_{ij} = ||X_i - X_j|| \tag{8.17}$$

is the attraction degree which can be determined using the distance rij and is formulated by

$$\beta(r) = \beta_0 * \exp(-\gamma * r_{ij}^m) \tag{8.18}$$

In the above mentioned equation, γ is the parameter which is related to the variations of light intensity and is named as absorption coefficient which has its range [0–10] and m is a integer and is chosen as 2 [18]. $\beta 0$ is initial attractiveness at which is taken as 1. Thus, the brighter firefly definitely decides the other fireflies' position in its particular neighbourhood [19]. For the case, if the brightness of jth is greater than the ith firefly, the position of firefly i is updated by the new position formula which is mentioned as below

$$X_i = X_i + \beta_0 * \exp(-\gamma r_{ij}^2) * (X_j - X_i) + \alpha * \left(rand - \frac{1}{2} \right) \quad (8.19)$$

Where α is random movement value which has range of [0, 1] and it is a constant value throughout the execution of the program. For every single movement of firefly rand is a diffused random number which lies between 0 and 1. Equation (8.19) clearly depicts that the firefly movement is affected by the randomization and the brightness or attractiveness of a brighter firefly. This randomization concept affords a very good way to move in search of global scale by moving away from local search. In general, the large value of α helps in facilitating the firefly globally while the small value tends to local search [20].

8.8   Implementation Procedure

The boost converter poses as a platform between the load and the Photovotaic system. The firefly algorithm controls the operation of the DC–DC converter and directs it to work at its optimum duty cycle which corresponds to the MPP. The implementation steps of firefly algorithm towards MPPT undergo setting of parameter, firefly initialization, evaluation of brightness, updating firefly position, checking for termination criteria and reinitiating. All the mentioned steps are discussed in detail in the following steps:

Step 1: Setting of Parameters: Initialize the constant parameters of the firefly algorithm, namely γ, α, m, $\beta 0$ number of fireflies N i.e. population size of fireflies in the colony, maximum iterations count which is the termination criteria of the algorithm. Duty cycle for the DC–DC converter is taken as the position of firefly. The obtained power from the Photovoltaic module is considered as the bright-ness of every firefly with respect to location of the firefly.

Step 2: Firefly Initialization: All the fireflies are located in the permitted space having upper boundary and lower boundary limitations. Here, the boundary limitations represent Dmax and Dmin which are the two extreme values of duty cycle of the converter. Dmax is set to 98% whereas Dmin in set to 20% in this work. Thus, it is cleared that the duty ratio is represented by the position of the firefly. The population size of fireflies is considered as 6 based on the general analysis that, if the number of fireflies increases it automatically results in the increased computing time, whereas the less population size of fireflies will be resulting in local maximum.

Step 3: Evaluation of Brightness: In this step, depending upon the firefly position, the boost converter is operated and the Photovoltaic module's power obtained at the ouput is considered as respective firefly's light intensity or brightness corresponding to each duty ratio. For the entire population of fireflies this step is repeated and the brightness of each firefly is generated.

Step 4: Updating Firefly Position: The firefly possessing higher or maximum brightness will remain in its respective position while the other fireflies with less brightness will update their position accordingly. The new position of the firefly is calculated with the help of position formula which is mentioned in Equation (8.19).

Step 5: Checking for Termination Criteria: The optimization algorithm continues to execute upto the last iteration as mentioned in step 1 and the program is terminated once the termination criteria is reached. If this is not the case, it will go to step 3 and again the loop gets executed. The algorithm is terminated if all the fireflies' displacement value in successive steps achieves set lowest value. The boost converter works at optimum duty ratio parallel to the global maximum point once the firefly algorithm gets terminated. The flowchart of the algorithm is stated in Figure 8.9.

8.9   Modified Firefly Logic

With reference to the position formula as mentioned previously in Equation (8.19) in which α represents random value of distribution. The position equation represents three major terms which the movements of fireflies consist, they are, current location of firefly i, the locomotion of firefly i towards the other brighter firefly and the random movement of it which persists the period between [0, 1]. T. Niknam introduced modified firefly algorithm for the elucidating of the economic dispatch problems. It can be seen that there are two major parameters that has to be tuned to outperform the firefly algorithm in tracking efficiency and speed of MPP. The stated modified fire-fly algorithm decreases the randomness of all the

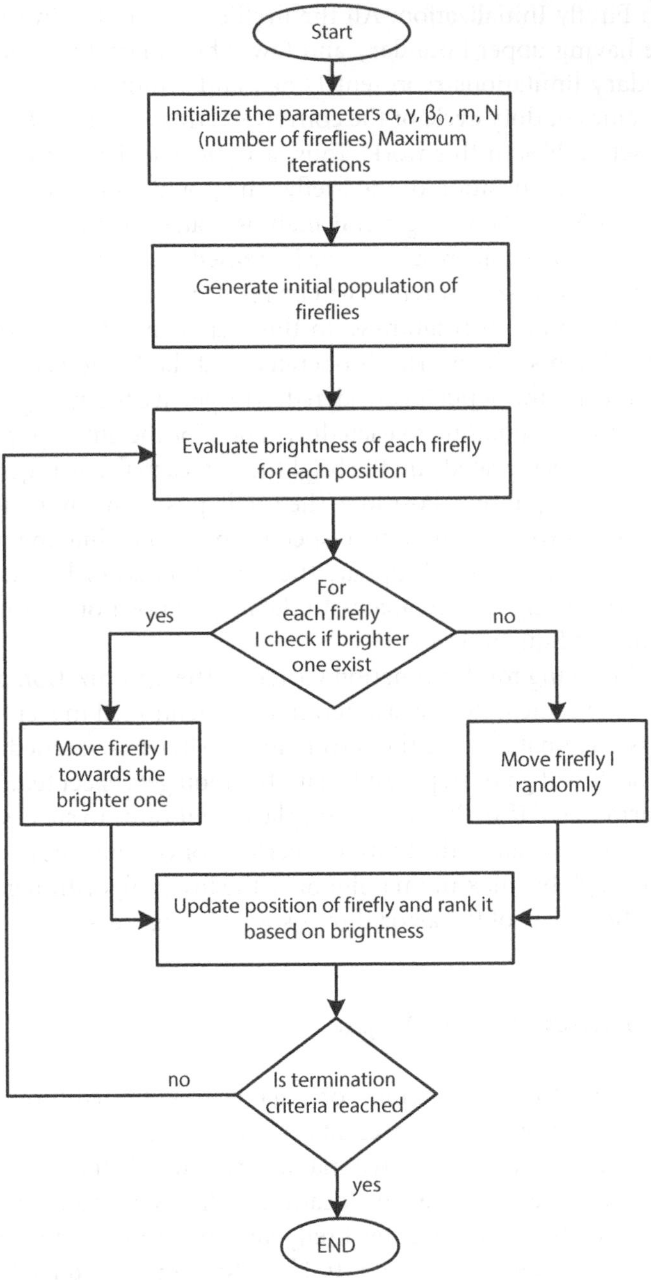

Figure 8.9 Firefly algorithm flowchart.

fireflies by the help of utilizing α which is said to be the randomization parameter. In modified firefly algorithm process, the random parameter α will be updated for every iteration and the change of iterations is achieved by implementing a simple modification to α (randomization parameter). For each iteration, α is decremented by 0.0001. The tracking efficiency of the MPP will be increased by the MFA. By this way when compared to last iteration the firefly will move much faster for every next iteration. This modification improves the convergence rate than that of standard firefly algorithm with the same accuracy and effectiveness of tracking the MPP.

8.10   Results and Discussions

For shading pattern 1: Figure 8.10 represents the power obtained at output, current and voltage from the solar panel with irradiation pattern of 1,000 and 800 w/m² for incremental conductance (a), Firefly (b) and Modified firefly algorithm (c). It can be inferred that with modified firefly algorithm maximum power of 330 W, firefly algorithm is able to trail 326 W from the total power of 335.5 W, whereas conventional algorithm (i.e. Incon) is able to extract 310 W of power only. It can be inferred that with modified firefly algorithm maximum voltage of 51.1 V, firefly algorithm is able to track 50.2 V. Whereas conventional algorithm (i.e. Incon) is able to extract 47.9 V. It can be inferred that with modified firefly algorithm maximum current of

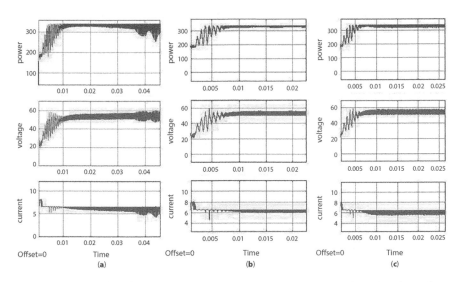

Figure 8.10 Output graphs for (a) Incremental Conductance, (b) Firefly algorithm and (c) Modified firefly algorithm for shading pattern 1.

6.47 A, firefly algorithm is able to track 6.49 A, whereas conventional algorithm (i.e. Incon) is able to extract 6.48 A. For shading pattern 2: Figure 8.11 represents the power obtained at output, current and voltage from the solar panel with irradiation pattern of 800 and 600 w/m² for incremental conductance (a), Firefly (b) and Modified firefly algorithm (c). It can be inferred that with modified firefly algorithm maximum power of 255 W, firefly algorithm is able to track 254 W from the total power of 268.5 W, whereas conventional algorithm (i.e. Incon) is able to extract 247 W of power only. It can be inferred that with modified firefly algorithm maximum voltage of 51.30 V, firefly algorithm is able to track 51.10 V. Whereas conventional algorithm (i.e. Incon) is able to extract 49.59 V. It can be inferred that with modified firefly algorithm maximum current of 4.97 A, firefly algorithm is able to track 4.97 A, whereas conventional algorithm (i.e. Incon) is able to extract 4.98 A. Table 8.2 shows the comparative results between incremental conductions, firefly and modified firefly algorithms. From these outcomes it can be inferred that the tracking efficiency of the modified firefly algorithm is high with 98.36% and 96.847% for the both shading patterns when compared to conventional and firefly algorithm.

With the better tracking speed of 6.4 ms for shading pattern 1 and 1.8 ms for shading pattern 2. From the obtained results we can see that the modified firefly algorithm had higher efficiency and less tracking speed and also maximum power can be utilized from the solar panel.

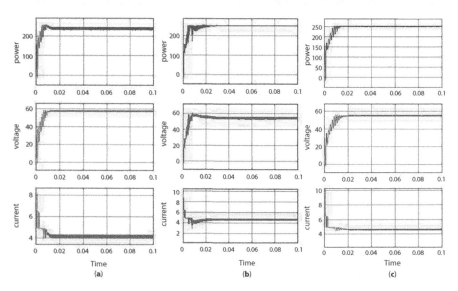

Figure 8.11 Output graphs for (a) Incremental Conductance, (b) Firefly algorithm and (c) Modified firefly algorithm for shading pattern.

Table 8.2 Comparative study of algorithms.

Shading pattern	MPPT Techniques	Power (watts)	Voltage (volts)	Current (amperes)	Maximum Power (watts)	Tracking Efficiency (%)	Tracking speed (ms)
1	Incremental	310.6	47.9	6.48	335.5	92.578	15
	FA	326	50.2	6.49		97.168	8.7
	MFA	330	51.1	6.47		98.360	6.4
2	Incremental	247	49.59	4.98	268.5	93.801	1.2
	FA	254	51.10	4.97		96.467	3.2
	MFA	255	51.30	4.97		96.847	1.8

8.11   Conclusion

The simulation of MPPT strategy with MFA for PV system is implemented with the help of MATLAB/Simulink and the performance analysis of the system is presented. Our concept is to update parameter for each looping step only then to achieve quicker convergence which increases the tracking speed and tracking efficiency. Due to the significance of Photovoltaic systems specifically in the area of renewable energy sources, this paper presents an efficient method for tracking Maximum Power Point for photo-voltaic array using Modified Firefly Algorithm. A better performance is exhibited by the proposed Modified Firefly Algorithm to track MPP even when shading conditions are partial. The performance comparison between incremental conductance, Firefly algorithm and Modified firefly algorithm are tabulated. The proposed algorithm was tested with varying irradiance and temperature conditions in order to simulate the results. Obtained simulated results show that the MFA can accurately track MPP and has superior tracking quickness. The stated algorithm decreases the fluctuations of the Firefly Algorithm in steady state condition.

References

1. Oyedepo, S.O., Energy and sustainable development in Nigeria: The way forward. *Energy Sustain. Soc.* 2, 15, no.1, 2012.
2. Tafticht, T., Agbossou, K., Doumbia, M.L., Cheriti, A., An improved maximum power point tracking method for photovoltaic systems. *Renew. Energy,* 33, 7, 1508–1516, 2008.
3. Hua, C. and Lin, J., An on-line MPPT algorithm for rap-idly changing illuminations of solar arrays. *Renew. Energy,* 28, 7, 1129–1142, 2003.
4. Mamarelis, E., Petrone, G., Spagnuolo, G., A two-steps algorithm improving the P&O steady state MPPT efficiency. *Appl. Energy,* 113, 414–421, 2014.
5. Silva, F.A., Power Electronics and Control Techniques for Maximum Energy Harvesting in Photovoltaic Systems (Femia, N. et al.; 2013) [Book News]. *IEEE Ind. Electron. M.,* 7, 3, 66–67, 2013.
6. Ping, W., Hui, D., Changyu, D., Shengbiao, Q., An improved MPPT algorithm based on traditional incremental conductance method. In *2011 4th International Conference on Power Electronics Systems and Applications,* vol. 1–4, IEEE, 2011.
7. Hare, A. and Rangnekar, S., A review of particle swarm optimization and its applications in solar photovoltaic system. *Appl. Soft Comput.,* 13, 5, 2997–3006, 2013.

8. Azab, M., Optimal power point tracking for stand-alone PV system using particle swarm optimization. In *2010 IEEE International Symposium on Industrial Electronics*, pp. 969–973, 2010.

9. Ishaque, K., Salam, Z., Shamsudin, A., Application of particle swarm optimization for maxi-mum power point tracking of PV system with direct control method. In *IECON 2011-37th Annual Conference of the IEEE Industrial Electronics Society*, pp. 1214–1219, 2011.

10. Besheer, A.H. and Adly, M., Ant colony system based PI maximum power point tracking for standalone photo-voltaic system. *2012 IEEE International Conference on Industrial Technology*, pp. 693–698, 2012.

11. Sundareswaran, K., Vigneshkumar, V., Sankar, P., Simon, S.P., Srinivasa Rao Nayak, P., Palani, S., Development of an improved P&O algorithm assisted through a colony of foraging ants for MPPT in PV system. *IEEE T. Ind. Inform.*, 12, 1, 187–200, 2015.

12. Ramaprabha, R. and Mathur, B.L., Genetic algorithm based maximum power point tracking for partially shaded solar photovoltaic array. *Int. J. Res. Rev. Inf. Sci. (IJRRIS)*, 2, 161–163, 2012.

13. Sridhar, R., Jeevananathan, D., ThamizhSelvan, N., Banerjee, S., Modelling of PV array and performance enhancement by MPPT algorithm. *Int. J. Comput. Appl.*, 7, 5, 0975–8887, 2010.

14. Tsai, H.-L., Tu, C.-S., Su, Y.-J., Development of generalized photovoltaic model using MATLAB/SIMULINK. In *Proceedings of the world congress on Engineering and Computer Science*, pp. 1–6, 2008.

15. Yang, X.-S., Firefly algorithms for multimodal optimization, in: *International symposium on stochastic algorithms*, pp. 169–178, Springer, Berlin, Heidelberg, 2009.

16. Chandrasekaran, K. and Simon, S.P., Optimal deviation based firefly algorithm tuned fuzzy design for multi-objective UCP. *IEEE T. Power Syst.*, 28, 1, 460–471, 2013.

17. Niknam, T., Azizipanah-Abarghooee, R., Roosta, A., Reserve constrained dynamic economic dispatch: a new fast self-adaptive modified firefly algorithm. *IEEE Syst. J.*, 6, 4, 635–646, 2012.

18. Yang, X.-S., Multiobjective firefly algorithm for continuous optimization. *Eng. Comput.*, 29, 2, 175–184, 2013.

19. Milea, L. *et al.*, Theory, Algorithms and Applications for Solar Panel MPP Tracking, in: *Solar Collectors and Panels, Theory and Applications*, pp. 187–210, 2010.

20. Xiao, W., Ozog, N., Dunford, W.G., Topology study of photovoltaic interface for maximum power point tracking. *IEEE Trans. Ind. Electron.*, 54, 3, 1696–1074, 2007.

9

Induction Motor Control Schemes for Hybrid Electric Vehicles/Electric Vehicles

Sarin, M.V.[1], Chitra, A.[1*], Sanjeevikumar, P.[2] and Venkadesan, A.[3]

[1]School of Electrical Engineering, Vellore Institute of Technology, Vellore, India
[2]Department of Energy Technology, Aalborg University, Denmark
[3]AP/EEE, NIT Puducherry, Karaikal, India

Abstract

Due to less consumption of energy and environmental pollution, electric vehicles (EV) have obtaining attention from everywhere the world especially in automobile industry. Nowadays, Induction motor drives are the most appropriate drive for automobile industries to realize the most effective performance. For variable speed applications of Industrial Drives, Induction motors are widely used. The drives used for electric vehicle applications conventionally fed by the voltage source inverter. The two speed control schemes for the induction motor are scalar control and vector control schemes. In ancient time, the motors used for electric vehicle applications is DC motor drives. Implementation of vector control scheme enhanced the performance of electric drives especially it gives a high performance in the drive system. In view of response time and efficiency, scalar control scheme is inferior to modern Vector control schemes, but it requires lesser hardware resources and thus reducing the cost. The decoupling of flux and torque producing component gives high performance in the drive system. The stator current components are decoupled and can control separately. This paper discuss on investigating the closed loop system of voltage source inverter (VSI) fed Induction Motor Drive with scalar method and Vector method has been analyzed and compared. A Sine Pulse Width Modulation (SPWM) technique is used to control the switching action in the drive system. Two decoupled components is controlled by PI controller included in this closed loop system. MATLAB/Simulink has been used to simulate and validate the results. Comparative evaluation of two control schemes have been plotted and analyzed.

*Corresponding author: chitra.a@vit.ac.in

Chitra A, P. Sanjeevikumar, Jens Bo Holm-Nielsen and S. Himavathi (eds.) *Artificial Intelligent Techniques for Electric and Hybrid Electric Vehicles*, (165–178) © 2020 Scrivener Publishing LLC

Keywords: Electric vehicle, induction motor, voltage source inverter, scalar control, field-oriented control, sine PWM, D–Q axes

9.1   Introduction

Conventional automobiles currently in use causes sound pollution, air pollution, global warming and also it causes a rapid decrement of earth's natural resources. Much research work is carrying out in the area of automobiles to reduce the pollution caused by conventional vehicles. The major challenge of this research is to keep high efficiency and safety in automobiles. As per the latest inventions electric vehicles can overcome the majority of the drawback by the conventional vehicles.

The ease of construction and availability of induction motor makes these motors utilize in many of the applications. The domestic appliance is mainly designed to operate at constant speed. So majority of home appliances use induction motors as the workhorse. The selection of motor in an electric vehicle has great importance in its overall performance. It is not advisable for some applications to be in a variable speed environment which affects the total system performance. The best suitable motor for electric vehicle is induction motor because of its easy availability and control. For an electric vehicle the exact speed control is not necessary because of the inertia offered by the mechanical system. So the main aim is that the motor speed has to be maintained in a fixed reference value. The initial transient response has to be improved by the help of controllers and has to achieve a fast response system.

An inverter converts DC input into AC output of required magnitude and frequency. The output from the inverter can be fixed or variable magnitude/ variable frequency. The output obtaining from the inverter purely depends on the switching action performing by the circuit inside the inverter. The switch inside an inverter is controlled by the pulses applied from various pulse generating sources, it is generally accomplished by pulse width modulation (PWM) techniques [17]. There are different types PWMs available, depends on the requirement and most suitable PWMs using for the production of output from the inverter by controlling the switching action. For better results from the inverter it is always advised to reduce the switching losses or harmonics by the switches. The output voltage expected from the inverter is a pure sinusoidal waveform. For large power applications a sinusoidal waveform will give good performance and for medium/low power applications square waveforms also acceptable. Figure 9.1 shows a basic diagram for a single phase inverter with four switches. There are mainly

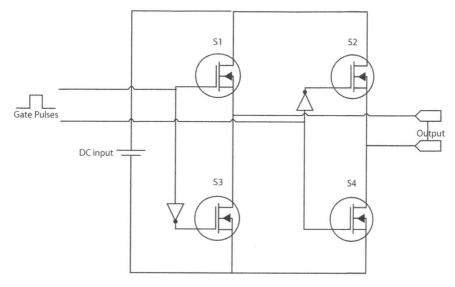

Figure 9.1 Basic diagram of VSI.

two types of inverters: (1) voltage source inverter and (2) current source inverter [4].

In voltage source inverter, the signal produce on the output side functions as a voltage source. Similarly, in current source inverter output signal functions as a current source. Voltage source inverter is the most commonly used type inverter.

9.2   Control Schemes of IM

Speed of induction motor can be controlled in different ways [2, 3]. The speed control methods employed are (1) Scalar control and (2) Vector control [7–9].

9.2.1   Scalar Control

In a scalar control method [1], only magnitudes can be controlled. Induction motor is fed by inverter which is driven by PWM signals. To get a constant torque operation over the working range v/f ratio should be maintained constant. In scalar control method [18], follows an open loop control method so it has less cost compared to any other closed loop system method because of its simplified structure and design. No feedback path makes the practical implementation is easy compared to closed loop

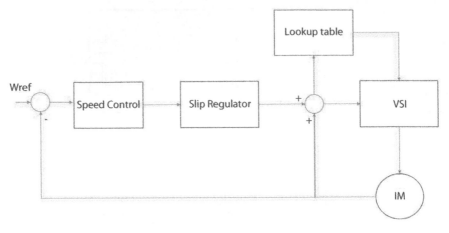

Figure 9.2 Block diagram of Inverter fed IM with scalar control.

system. Figure 9.2 shows scalar control depends only on magnitude of control variable, and does not depend on the coupling effect of machine. The torque and flux are control by the magnitude of frequency/slip and magnitude of voltage respectively.

9.3   Vector Control

Vector control method is also known as flux oriented control [6] or field oriented control. Vector control is mainly designed for control of machines. The main objective of vector control method is decoupling of flux and torque. High performance induction motor drive can be achieved by the vector control method [18]. In induction motor, the stator current is the vector sum of torque producing component and flux producing component. In this method, the stator current is decoupled into torque component (i_{ds}) and flux component (i_{qs}) so each can control individually. A reference frame has to be chosen for different space vector variables. As supply frequency is constant, space variables are moving in the same angular velocity. Both torque and flux components are to be known as orthogonal to each other.

In FOC (Field Oriented Control), the input three axis vectors are converted into two components (d & q). The flux producing stator current component represents by "d" component and the torque producing stator current component represents by "q" component. The input current vectors converts into two dimensional vectors by the theory of Clarke–Park

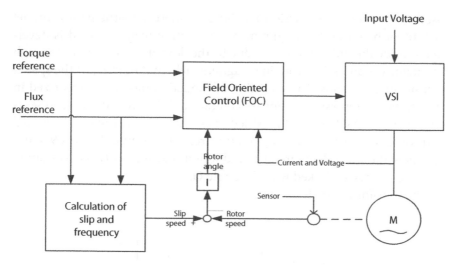

Figure 9.3 Vector control scheme.

transformation. The torque and flux can be independently controlled by PI controllers. By using inverse Clarke–Park transformation, it is transformed back into three dimensional vectors.

Vector control can be implemented by two ways (Figure 9.3) [5, 13]: (1) Direct Field Oriented Control (DFOC) and (2) Indirect Field Oriented Control (IFOC) [10, 15, 16]. In Direct Field Oriented Control, the flux vector position is directly measured by sensor. Use of different sensors makes the system more costly. A special provision has to maintain for proper placement of sensor makes the system more expensive. In Indirect Field Oriented Control (IFOC), the flux vector position is calculated not directly as like DFOC. In IFOC, it is derived from the simple mathematical expressions. From the mathematical modeling of induction motor can calculate the rotor flux position. IFOC technique has more accuracy than other methods. But calculation of rotor flux position from the model of induction motor makes the system more parameter-sensitive and complex. In IFOC, decoupling of torque component and flux component makes both work as individually and can control individually.

9.4   Modeling of Induction Machine

One of the types of induction motor is widely used for the applications in industries. Due to less cost most of the ac machine applications are satisfied by the usage of induction machines. The mathematical modeling has been used to analyze the induction machines. Different mathematical model can adopt based on the requirement. A rotating magnetic field is developed inside the induction motor due to the flow of stator current through the stator windings. The rotating magnetic field in the air gap is the spatial combination of fields. The modeling of induction motor is categorized in two parts one represents stator parameters and the second one represents rotor parameters. Each part modeled uses two separate frames. The model is developed by synchronously rotating reference frame. Figures 9.4 and 9.5 show the equivalent circuit of induction machine in two axis frames. The two frames are linked with the angle Θ.

The transformation leads to:

$$(i_{qd0s})^T = \begin{bmatrix} i_{qs} & i_{ds} & i_{0s} \end{bmatrix}$$
$$(i_{abcs})^T = \begin{bmatrix} i_{as} & i_{bs} & i_{cs} \end{bmatrix}$$

(9.1)

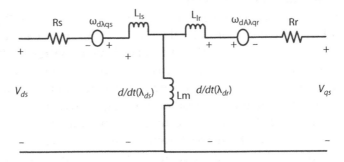

Figure 9.4 D axis equivalent circuit.

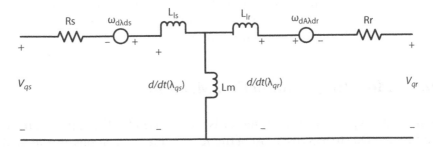

Figure 9.5 Q axis equivalent circuit.

$$V_\alpha = V_m \cos\theta$$
$$V_\beta = V_m \sin\theta \qquad (9.2)$$

$$i_\alpha = i_m \cos(\theta - \varphi)$$
$$i_\beta = i_m \sin(\theta - \varphi) \qquad (9.3)$$

In dq axis frame it can be rewritten as:

$$
\begin{bmatrix} i_d \\ i_q \end{bmatrix} =
\begin{bmatrix} \cos\theta & \sin\theta \\ -\sin\theta & \cos\theta \end{bmatrix}
\begin{bmatrix} i_\alpha \\ i_\beta \end{bmatrix}
\qquad (9.4)
$$

$$i_{qd0s} = K_s i_{abcs} \qquad (9.5)$$

where,

$$\left(i_{qd0s}\right)^T = \begin{bmatrix} i_{qs} & i_{ds} & i_{0s} \end{bmatrix}$$
$$\left(i_{abcs}\right)^T = \begin{bmatrix} i_{as} & i_{bs} & i_{cs} \end{bmatrix} \qquad (9.6)$$

$$
K_s = \frac{2}{3}
\begin{bmatrix}
\cos\theta & \cos\left(\theta - \dfrac{2\pi}{3}\right) & \cos\left(\theta + \dfrac{2\pi}{3}\right) \\[2ex]
\sin\theta & \sin\left(\theta - \dfrac{2\pi}{3}\right) & \sin\left(\theta + \dfrac{2\pi}{3}\right) \\[2ex]
0.5 & 0.5 & 0.5
\end{bmatrix}
\qquad (9.7)
$$

The following equations have been derived from the equivalent circuit shown in the Figures 9.4 and 9.5. So from the equivalent circuit,

$$V_{ds} = R_s i_{ds} + \frac{d}{dt}\lambda_{ds} - \omega_d \lambda_{qs} \qquad (9.8)$$

$$V_{qs} = R_s i_{qs} + \frac{d}{dt} \lambda_{qs} - \omega_d \lambda_{ds} \tag{9.9}$$

$$V_{dr} = R_r i_{dr} + \frac{d}{dt} \lambda_{dr} - \omega_{dA} \lambda_{qr} \tag{9.10}$$

$$V_{qr} = R_r i_{qr} + \frac{d}{dt} \lambda_{qr} - \omega_{dA} \lambda_{dr} \tag{9.11}$$

Where V_{ds} & V_{qs} represents the stator voltage in dq axes and V_{dr} and V_{dr} represents the rotor voltages in dq axes.

The linkage of flux can be shown mathematically below:

$$\begin{bmatrix} \lambda_{ds} \\ \lambda_{qs} \\ \lambda_{dr} \\ \lambda_{qr} \end{bmatrix} = M \begin{bmatrix} i_{ds} \\ i_{qs} \\ i_{dr} \\ i_{qr} \end{bmatrix} \tag{9.12}$$

Where,
$$M = \begin{bmatrix} L_s & 0 & L_m & 0 \\ 0 & L_s & 0 & L_m \\ L_m & 0 & L_r & 0 \\ 0 & L_m & 0 & L_r \end{bmatrix}$$

I_{ds} & I_{qs} represents the stator current in dq axes, I_{dr} & I_{qr} represents the rotor current in dq axes.

L_s, L_r and L_m are stator inductance, rotor inductance and mutual inductance between stator and rotor respectively. The mechanical part of the machine can be represented as by the following equations.

$$
\begin{bmatrix} i_{ds} \\ i_{qs} \\ i_{dr} \\ i_{qr} \end{bmatrix} = \frac{1}{L_m^2 - L_r L_s} \times \left(A \begin{bmatrix} i_{ds} \\ i_{qs} \\ i_{dr} \\ i_{qr} \end{bmatrix} + \begin{bmatrix} L_s & 0 & L_m & 0 \\ 0 & L_s & 0 & L_m \\ L_m & 0 & L_r & 0 \\ 0 & L_m & 0 & L_r \end{bmatrix} \begin{bmatrix} V_{ds} \\ V_{qs} \\ V_{dr} \\ V_{qr} \end{bmatrix} \right) \tag{9.13}
$$

The Electromagnetic torque is given as,

$$
T_{em} = \frac{P}{2}(\lambda_{qr} i_{dr} - \lambda_{dr} i_{qr}) = \frac{P}{2} L_m (i_{qs} i_{dr} - i_{ds} i_{qr}) \tag{9.14}
$$

Differentiating,

$$
\frac{d}{dt} \omega_{Mech} = \frac{T_{em} - T_L}{J_{eq}} = \frac{\frac{P}{2} L_m \left(\lambda_{qs} i_{dr} - i_{ds} i_{qr} \right) - T_L}{J_{eq}} \tag{9.15}
$$

Apply inverse Park transformation:

$$
\begin{bmatrix} \left[P(\theta_s) \right]^{-1} \begin{bmatrix} \lambda_{s_{dq0}} \end{bmatrix} \\ \left[P(\theta_r) \right]^{-1} \begin{bmatrix} \lambda_{s_{dq0}} \end{bmatrix} \end{bmatrix} = \begin{bmatrix} \begin{bmatrix} L_s \end{bmatrix} & \begin{bmatrix} M_{sr}(\theta) \end{bmatrix} \\ \begin{bmatrix} M_{sr}(\theta) \end{bmatrix} & \begin{bmatrix} L_r \end{bmatrix} \end{bmatrix} \begin{bmatrix} \left[P(\theta_s) \right]^{-1} \begin{bmatrix} i_{s_{dq0}} \end{bmatrix} \\ \left[P(\theta_r) \right]^{-1} \begin{bmatrix} i_{r_{dq0}} \end{bmatrix} \end{bmatrix} \tag{9.16}
$$

Rearranging above equation results:

$$
\begin{bmatrix} \begin{bmatrix} \lambda_{s_{dq0}} \end{bmatrix} \\ \begin{bmatrix} \lambda_{r_{dq0}} \end{bmatrix} \end{bmatrix} = \begin{bmatrix} \left[P(\theta_s) \right]\left[L_s \right]\left[P(\theta_s) \right]^T & \left[P(\theta_s) \right]\left[M_{sr}(\theta) \right]\left[P(\theta_r) \right]^T \\ \left[P(\theta_r) \right]\left[M_{sr}(\theta) \right]^T\left[P(\theta_s) \right]^T & \left[P(\theta_r) \right]\left[L_r \right]\left[P(\theta_r) \right]^T \end{bmatrix} \begin{bmatrix} \begin{bmatrix} i_{s_{dq0}} \end{bmatrix} \\ \begin{bmatrix} i_{r_{dq0}} \end{bmatrix} \end{bmatrix} \tag{9.17}
$$

From Equation (9.17) it can be derived the following relation in two axes frame:

$$
\begin{bmatrix} \left[\lambda_{s_{dq0}} \right] \\ \left[\lambda_{r_{dq0}} \right] \end{bmatrix} = \begin{bmatrix} \left[L_{ps} \right] & \left[M_{pSr} \right] \\ \left[M_{sr}(\theta) \right] & \left[L_{pr} \right] \end{bmatrix} \begin{bmatrix} \left[i_{s_{dq0}} \right] \\ \left[i_{r_{dq0}} \right] \end{bmatrix} \tag{9.18}
$$

A mathematical model with constant coefficents has been obtained as shown above in Equation (9.18). The value of mutual inductance does not vary with rotor movement.

9.5   Controller Design

Controller is one of the main parts of a closed loop system. The controller may include some algorithm or processor which generates control signal from the signal it receive from the sensors. The types of controllers include Proportional, Derivative, Integral, Proportional–Derivative, Proportional–Integral and Proportional–Integral–Derivative controllers. Each has its own characteristics. In this system the conventional controller (Proportional–Integral controller) is widely used in electric drive application such as electric vehicles. Proportional–Integral controller improves the steady state response of a system.

The Proportional–Integral controller converts the speed input command into torque component. The current reference components as follows:

$$
\begin{aligned}
i_{qs}^* &= \frac{L_r}{pL_m}\frac{T_{em}^*}{\lambda_r^*} \\
i_{ds}^* &= \frac{1}{L_m}\left(T_r\frac{d\lambda_r^*}{dt} + \lambda_r^* \right)
\end{aligned} \tag{9.20}
$$

The current references were converted to the corresponding voltage references by the following equations,

$$
\begin{aligned}
V_{ds}^* &= R_s i_{ds}^* - \omega_s^* \sigma L_s i_{qs}^* \\
V_{qs}^* &= R_s i_{qs}^* + \omega_s^* \sigma L_s i_{ds}^*
\end{aligned} \tag{9.21}
$$

Where,

$$\omega_s^* = \omega + \omega_{gl}^* ; \omega_{gl}^* = \frac{L_m}{T_r} \frac{i_{qs}^*}{\lambda_r^*} \qquad (9.22)$$

9.6   Simulations and Results

The change of load torque and change of speed were simulated in the platform of MATLAB/Simulink. Both scalar and vector control responses are compared. The vector-controlled induction motor drive was found to get responses very quickly. The initial transients are the result of applying full terminal voltage to the machine. Figures 9.6–9.9 show the torque and speed responses of scalar and vector controlled drives [11, 12].

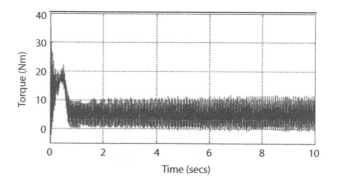

Figure 9.6 Torque Response of a scalar-controlled drive.

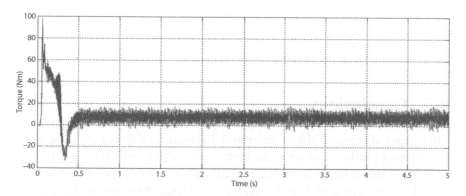

Figure 9.7 Torque Response of a vector-controlled drive.

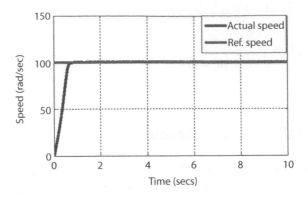

Figure 9.8 Speed Response of a scalar-controlled drive.

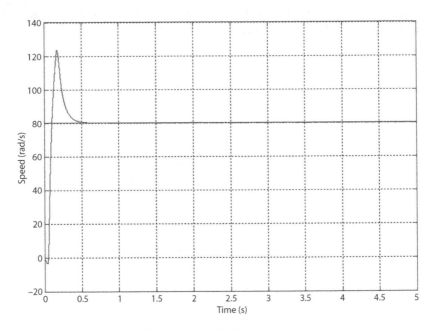

Figure 9.9 Speed Response of vector-controlled drive.

9.7   Conclusions

This paper discussed the comparison between scalar control and vector control methods of an induction motor drive [6]. Both scalar and vector control scheme have been simulated and analyzed in MATLAB/Simulink. Torque and Speed waveforms of induction motor have been simulated by MATLAB/Simulink. Selection of controlling schemes of drive is based on the performance of the speed and torque characteristics. The PI controller in the feedback path improves the dynamic response of the system. From the simulation it is observed that inverter fed induction motor drive [14, 16] with vector control scheme gives high performance compared to scalar control schemeand also the torque ripples were less in vector control scheme compared to scalar control scheme. Even though vector control includes complex calculations, it provides a smooth control over the electric vehicle compared to scalar control scheme.

References

1. De Doncker, R., Pulle, D.W.J., Veltman, A., Control of Induction Machine Drives, in: *Advanced Electrical Drives. Power Systems*, Springer, Dordrecht, 2011.
2. Bose, B.K., Chapter 8—Control and Estimation of Induction Motor Drives, in: *Modern Power Electronics and AC Drives*, Pearson Education, Inc, USA, 2002.
3. Nandi, S., Ahmed, S., Toliyat, H.A., Bharadwaj, R.M., Selection criteria of induction machines for speed-sensorless drive applications. *IEEE Trans. Ind. Appl.*, 39, 3, 704–712, 2003.
4. Richu, S.C. and Rajeevan, P.P., A Load Commutated Multilevel Current Source Inverter Fed Open-End Winding Induction Motor Drive With Regeneration Capability. *IEEE Trans. Power Electron.*, 35, 1, 816–825, 2020.
5. Bimbhra, P.S., Chapter 12–Electric Drives, in: *Power Electronics*, Khanna Publishers, India, 2008.
6. Zerdali, E. and Barut, M., The Comparisons of Optimized Extended Kalman Filters for Speed-Sensorless Control of Induction Motors. *IEEE Trans. Ind. Electron.*, 64, 4340–4351, 2017.
7. Smith, A., Gadoue, S., Armstrong, M., Finch, J., Improved method for the scalar control of induction motor drives. *IET Electr. Power Appl.*, 7, 6, 487–498, 2013.
8. Fan, L. and Zhang, L., An Improved Vector Control of an Induction Motor Based on Flatness. *Procedia Eng.*, 15, 624–628, 2011.
9. Jnayah, S. and Khedher, A., DTC of Induction Motor Drives Fed By Two and Three-Level Inverter: Modeling and Simulation, in: *2019 19th International Conference on Sciences and Techniques of Automatic Control and Computer Engineering (STA)*, pp. 376–381, IEEE, Sousse, Tunisia, 2019.
10. Sayed-Ahmed, A. and Demerdash, N.A.O., Fault-Tolerant Operation of Delta-Connected Scalar- and Vector-Controlled AC Motor Drives. *IEEE T. Power Electron.*, 27, 6, 3041–3049, 2012.

11. Soufi, Y., Bahi, T., Lekhchine, S., Dib, D., Performance analysis of DFIM fed by matrix converter and multilevel inverter. *Energy Convers. Manag.*, 72, 187–193, 2013.
12. Sivakumar, Das, K., Ramchand, A., Patel, R., Gopakumar, C., A Five-Level Inverter Scheme for a Four-Pole Induction Motor Drive by Feeding the Identical Voltage-Profile Windings From Both Sides. *IEEE T. Ind. Electron.*, 57, 8, 2776–2784, 2010.
13. Zhang, Y., Zhao, Z., Zhu, J., A Hybrid PWM Applied to High-Power Three-Level Inverter-Fed Induction-Motor Drives. *IEEE T. Ind. Electron.*, 58, 8, 3409–3420, 2011.
14. Akin, B. and Garg, N., *Scalar(V/f) Control Of 3-Phase Induction Motors, Texas Instruments, Inc*, pp. 1071–1080, C200 Systems and Applications Modelling Practice and Theory 17 Science Direct, Dallas, Texas, 2009.
15. Lekhchine, S., Bahi, T., Soufi, Y., Indirect rotor field oriented control based on fuzzy logic controlled double star induction machine. *Int. J. Electr. Power Energ. Syst.*, 57, 206–211, 2014.
16. Feroura, H., Krim, F., Talbi, B., Laib, A., Belaout, A., Sensorless Field Oriented Control of Current Source Inverter Fed Induction Motor Drive. *Rev. Roum. Sci. Techn.—Électrotechn. Et Énerg.*, 63, 1, 100–105, 2018. Bucarest.
17. de Rossiter Correa, M.B., Jacobina, C.B., da Silva, E.R.C., Lima, A.M.N.A., General PWM Strategy for Four-Switch Three-Phase Inverters. *IEEE T. Power Electron.*, 21, 6, 1618–1627, 2006.
18. Bose, B.K., Scalar Decoupled Control of Induction Motor. *IEEE T. Ind. Appl.*, IA-20, 1, 216–225, 1984.

10

Intelligent Hybrid Battery Management System for Electric Vehicle

Rajalakshmi, M. and Razia Sultana, W.*

School of Electrical Engineering, Vellore Institute of Technology, Vellore, Tamil Nadu, India

Abstract

As the green movement increases in popularity, more and more Electric Vehicles (EVs) of all kinds from electric bicycles, bikes, cars, buses to trains grace the mode of transportation. Energy management in these vehicles is highly sensitive for upcoming design of the EVs and advancement in cheap sensing and computation will be challenged to provide better efficiency systems that can be adapted to a wide variety of different types of batteries and vehicles with vastly diverse performance requirements. Multi-battery systems that combine a standard battery with Ultracapacitors (UC) are currently one of the most promising ways to increase battery lifespan and reduce operating costs. However, their performance crucially depends on how they are designed and operated. This performance implies improved battery thermal stability, efficiency, and endurance. In this chapter, the problem of optimizing real-time energy management of hybrid battery systems is discussed.

Keywords: Intelligent battery management system, hybrid energy storage system, electric vehicle, lithium-ion battery, ultracapacitor

10.1 Introduction

Electric vehicles, partially or fully powered by batteries, are one of the most promising directions towards a more sustainable transportation system. However, the high costs, limited capacities, and long recharge times of

*Corresponding author: wraziasultana@vit.ac.in

Chitra A, P. Sanjeevikumar, Jens Bo Holm-Nielsen and S. Himavathi (eds.) *Artificial Intelligent Techniques for Electric and Hybrid Electric Vehicles*, (179–206) © 2020 Scrivener Publishing LLC

batteries are the obstacles for their widespread adoption. EV battery packs are made up of multiple cell modules arranged in series and in parallel.

Since many researchers have proved that the characteristics of high energy and current density with long shelf life of lithium-ion batteries those are widely used in EVs [1]. Unluckily, lithium-ion batteries having less power density and it can be unsafe if they are not operated within their Safety Operation Area (SOA) [2]. Therefore, a Battery Management System (BMS) must be used in every lithium-ion battery, especially for those used in electric vehicles. Many lithium-ion combinations such as lithium ion phosphate, lithium manganese, and lithium-titanate are giving better performance with EVs. These are thermally stable and offer low Equivalent Series Resistance (ESR) to support high current and if managed properly it could last up to 10 to 15 years.

Although the rapid technology development of lithium ion battery increases the applications in EVs the main drawback of that causes the Supercapacitors (SC) which is known as Ultracapacitors (UC)/Electrical Double Layer Capacitor (EDLC) to fill the gap. The shortcomings of Lithium ion battery are overcome by the nature of high power density and high degree of recyclability of SCs. They have added advantages of low internal resistance, wide operating temperature window, and high efficiency, despite that they have relatively low energy density [3]. These conflicting characteristics of both lithium ion battery and SCs satisfying the requirements of EV when they are combined and operated as hybrid.

This chapter emphasizes on a complementary aspect of the problem that is optimizing the energy efficiency of batteries in electric vehicles. There are two main sources of inefficiencies in batteries.

- The first one is that due to internal resistance, battery energy is partially wasted as heat when it is charged and discharged.
- The second one is that due to Peukert's Law, the actual delivered capacity of a battery depends on the rate at which it is discharged.

Furthermore, current battery technology imposes relatively severe limits on the number of charge/recharge cycles a battery can handle, thus reducing their lifespan and increasing operating costs.

The combination of SCs and batteries i.e., a Hybrid Energy Storage System (HESS) has been intensively inspected by many researchers [4, 5]. To achieve a proper energy management between battery and SC several online and offline intelligent control strategies are used. The more innovative and active strategy is to optimize the power flow with intelligent algorithms. To afford real time energy management, the model predictive control strategy [6–9] is used which exhibit high speed computation capability and predict the future load conditions.

This chapter is organized in the following manner: Section 10.2 dictates the different energy storage technologies. Section 10.3 explains the Battery management system (BMS). Section 10.4 discusses the Intelligent techniques for BMS of HESS. Section 10.5 includes the conclusion and comparison.

10.2   Energy Storage System (ESS)

The Energy Storage Systems are the chemical technology in which electrical energy is stored and discharged when it is necessary into the circuit in which it is connected. The important criteria in the selection of proper energy storage systems based on application, size, lifetime, response time, capital, maintenance costs, energy density, specific energy, specific power, self-discharge and other important aspects. Figure 10.1 gives the details of different types of energy storage system.

For EVs Energy Storage System is the heart of the system, if ESS failed to operate the whole system would stop. The energy storage system usually consists of batteries and capacitors are necessary for PHEVs and EVs. Furthermore, in order to improve the power density and life cycle of the

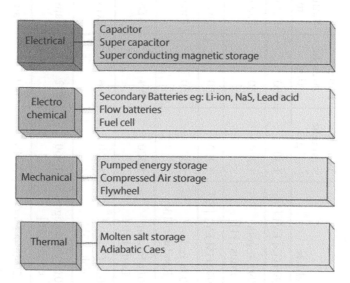

Figure 10.1 Types of energy storage system.

Table 10.1 Details of batteries for different set of vehicles.

Vehicle	Vehicle weight (kg)	Battery weight (kg)	Battery manufacturer	Chemistry	Rated energy (J)	Specific energy (Wh/Kg)	Cell/pack nominal voltage (v)
1996 GM EV1 [10]	1,400	500	Delphi	PbA	17	34	2/312
1997 Toyota Prius [11]	1,240	530	Panasonic	NiMH	18	34	1.2/274
1999 GM EV1 [12]	1,290	480	Ovonics	NiMH	29	60	1.2/343
2008 Tesla Roadster [13]	1,300	450	Panasonic	Li-ion	53	118	
2011 Nissan Leaf [14]	1,520	294	AESC	Li-ion	24	82	3.75/360
2011 Chevy Volt [15]	1,720	196	LG Chem	Li-ion	17	87	3.75/360
2015 Volkswagen e-Golf [16]	1,960	312	Sanyo	Li-ion	26.5		3.6/320
2020 Tesla Model S [17]	2,215	540	Panasonic	Li-ion	100	265	

battery, the SC has been proposed to hybridize with the battery to form hybrid energy storage system. Presently batteries have improved technologies based on the applications such as Lithium-ion, Nickel metal hydride, and Lead acid for EV applications. Table 10.1 states the different batteries for differerent EVs.

10.2.1   Lithium-Ion Batteries

Lithium has many advantages like largest energy density per weight and very light metal with high electrochemical potential of all metals. Due to this property it has many applications in battery variants to store electrical energy in which the anode is the lithium ion. The main drawback of it is unstable during charging and discharging which needs some safety measures by properly designing the battery.

The other major advantage of Li-ion battery is maintenance free which is the highlight when compared to other batteries. The self discharge rate of the Li-ion battery is very less compared to the other batteries like lead-acid and Ni-MH batteries. The other drawback of it is brittle in nature when the temperature limits exceeds. To get the safe and efficient operation of the Li-ion the best design of the battery management system is necessary which limits the voltage peak, temperature, and helps to operate within the specified current limit.

Despite the advantages of lithium-ion batteries, they also have certain drawbacks. Lithium ions are brittle. To maintain the safe operation of these batteries, they require a protective device to be built into each pack. This device, also referred to as the battery management system (BMS), limits the peak voltage of each cell during charging and prevents the cell voltage from dropping below a threshold during discharging.

10.2.1.1   Lithium Battery Challenges

Lithium-ion batteries are presently used in most transportable consumer electronics applications such as cell phones and laptops because of their higher energy density relative to other electrical energy storage systems. They also have a high power-to-weight ratio, high energy efficiency, good high-temperature performance, and low self-discharge. Most components of lithium-ion batteries can be recycled, but the cost of material recovery remains a challenge for the industry. Most of PHEVs and EVs use lithium-ion batteries, though the exact chemistry often varies from that of consumer electronics batteries. Research and development is ongoing to reduce cost and extend their useful life cycle.

Lithium-ion cells give a usual operating potential of 4 V at full charge and 2 V at full discharge. To reduce the level of current, which allows for lesser, lighter and less costly cables and motors, the EV battery pack is normally stacked as a group of 100 to 200 series-connected cells. Though the voltages are high, the peak charge and discharge currents of EV battery stacks can exceed 200 A.

Charging any Lithium-ion cell to 100% of its SOC or discharging to 0% SOC will disgrace its capacity. Therefore, only a portion of a cell's capacity can be used if the battery must have a long life. With very accurate control of the SOC of each Li-Ion cell, battery pack capacity can be maximized while its degradation is minimized. However, controlling hundreds of series-connected cells is quite tricky. Table 10.2 lists the properties of different Li-ion variants. Table 10.3 states the advantages and disadvantages of Li-ion variants.

The variants of Lithium-ion:

- Lithium iron phosphate (LFP)
- Lithium manganite (LMO)
- Lithium cobalt oxide (LCO)
- lithium-polymer (LP)
- lithium nickel–manganese–cobalt (LNMC) Batteries
- lithium titanate (LiT)

10.2.2   Lithium–Ion Cell Modeling

The ideal battery model provides the equal voltage at both input and output without any voltage drop i.e without any energy loss. But practically it has some energy loss due to its internal resistances as mentioned in the following figure. The batteries are modelled in different methods those

Table 10.2 Properties of various Li-ion batteries [18].

Type of battery	Energy density (Wh/kg)	Power density (W/kg)	Life cycle (100%DOD)	Estimated cost ($/KWh)
Li-titanate oxide	70	1,000	≥10,000	~860
LFP	120	200	≥2,500	~360
LMO	160	200	≥2,000	~360
LNMC	200	200	≥2,000	~360
Li-sulfur	500	–	~100	–

Table 10.3 Advantages and disadvantages of Li-ion variants.

Category of LiB	LFP	LMO	LiT	LCO	LP
Advantages	Long cycle life High safety Very fast charge times Excellent thermal stability	Enables fast charging High safety	Good thermal stability no lithium plating when fast charging and charging at low temperature Very high cycle life	Very high energy density	Improved safety Strong over charge abilities Long cycle life
Disadvantages	less energy for a given volume/weight Sensitive to temperature	Poor performance at high temperature Poor energy density	Low energy density High cost	Short lifespan High cost due to Cobalt Safety issues	Under research stage Low energy density and decreased cycle count No standard sizes High cost

are Equivalent Circuit Model, Lumped-Parameter Model, and Electro-chemical model. Among the all three the Electro-chemical model is the most efficient and most robust accurate model.

The electrical equivalent model has to be developed of any component to test and evaluate the real time performance of that. So to test the battery management algorithm and performance the Li-ion cell has to be mathematically modelled. The real time battery performance depends on many factors like loading condition, age of the battery, the operating temperature and many such conditions. It is very tedious to run the battery in all these conditions to test the battery management system performance. So the model of the battery is necessary for testing its performance.

Based on the accurate model of the battery the measurement of the battery parameters like SOC (state of charge) and SOH (state of health) will be accurate, hence it should always provide high fidelity and robustness. A typical usage of electrical equivalent battery model is shown in Figure 10.2.

The ideal battery model provides the equal voltage at both input and output without any voltage drop i.e without any energy loss. But practically it has some energy loss due to its internal resistances as mentioned in the following figure. The batteries are modelled in different methods those are Equivalent Circuit Model, Lumped-Parameter Model, and Electro-chemical model. Among the all three the Electro-chemical model is the most efficient and most robust accurate model.

10.2.3   Nickel-Metal Hydride Batteries

Nickel-metal hydride batteries used routinely in computer and medical equipment, offer reasonable specific energy and specific power capabilities. Nickel-metal hydride batteries have a much longer life cycle than lead-acid

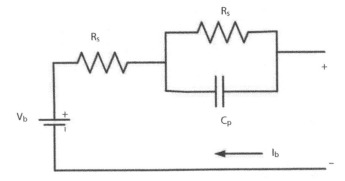

Figure 10.2 Li-ion cell equivalent circuit model.

batteries and are safe and abuse tolerant. These batteries have been widely used in hybrid electric vehicles. The main challenges with nickel-metal hydride batteries are their high cost, high self-discharge and heat generation at high temperatures, and the need to control hydrogen loss.

10.2.4   Lead-Acid Batteries

Lead-acid batteries can be designed to be high power and are inexpensive, safe, and reliable. However, low specific energy, poor cold-temperature performance, and short calendar and cycle life impede their use. Advanced high-power lead-acid batteries are being developed, but these batteries are only used in commercially available electric-drive vehicles for ancillary loads.

10.2.5   Ultracapacitors (UC)

Ultracapacitors store energy in a polarized liquid between an electrode and an electrolyte. Energy storage capacity increases as the liquid's surface area increases. UCs can provide vehicles additional power during acceleration and hill climbing and help recover braking energy. They may also be useful as secondary energy-storage devices in electric-drive vehicles because they help electrochemical batteries level load power.

The UC provides a higher specific power and lower specific energy than batteries. Its specific power ranges from few kilowatts per kilogram and its specific energy ranges from few watt-hour per kilogram. Since it is having low specific energy density and the dependence of terminal voltage on SOC, it is not suitable to use UCs alone in energy storage system of HEVs and EVs. So the UCs are best fit for using as auxiliary power source in HESS. Due to the load leveling effect of the UC, the high current discharging from the battery and the high current charging to the battery by regenerative braking are minimized so that available energy, endurance, and life of the battery can be significantly increased. Table 10.4 shows the merits and demerits of different models of UC.

10.2.5.1   *Ultracapacitor Equivalent Circuit*

The performance of an ultracapacitor may be represented by its terminal voltages during discharge and charge with different current rates. The equivalent circuit has three parameters in a capacitor: the capacitance itself (its electric potential V_C), the series resistance R_S, and the dielectric leakage resistance, R_L, as shown in Figures 10.3 and 10.4.

Table 10.4 Merits and demerits of different models of UC.

Models of UC	Merits	Demerits
Electrochemical models [3]	Description of inside physical-chemical reactions; High possible accuracy	Heavy computation Immeasurability of some parameters
Equivalent circuit models [3]	Moderate accuracy; Absence of physical meanings; susceptible to aging process, relatively easy implementation and model identification	Absence of physical meanings; susceptible to aging process
Intelligent models [3]	Good modeling capability; disclosure of the influencing factors to desirable model output	Sensitive to training data quality and quantity; poor robustness
Fractional-order models [3]	Better capability to fitting experimental data; few model parameters	Heavy computation

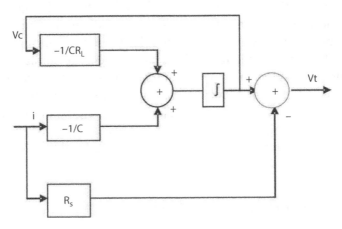

Figure 10.3 Block diagram representation of UC.

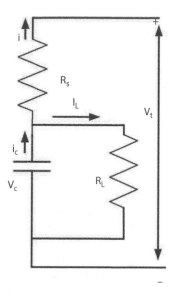

Figure 10.4 Equivalent circuit of UC.

The terminal voltage of the UC can be represented by the following equation,

$$Vc=[V\_co-\int\_0^t [\![i/C \ e^{\wedge}(t/(CR\_L" ")) \ dt]\!] \ ] \ e^{\wedge}(-(t/(CR\_L)))$$

The energy stored in an UC can be obtained through the energy needed to change it to a certain voltage level, that is

$$E\_C=1/2 \ CV\_C^{\wedge}2$$

The usable energy in an UC can also be expressed in State of Energy (SOE), which is defined as the ratio of the energy in the UC at a voltage of V_C to the energy at full charged voltage, V_{CR}, as expressed as

$$SOE=[V\_C/V\_CR]^{\wedge}2$$

10.2.6   Other Battery Technologies

Due to the lack of raw material and less safety other than Lithium ion batteries few battery technologies have been developed with different characteristics and improvements to make it suitable for EVs. Table 10.5 shows some other battery technologies.

Table 10.5 Other types of batteries under development.

S. no.	Type of battery	Advantages	Disadvantages
1	Sodium ion battery (SIB): battery that uses sodium ions as charge carriers [19]	cheap and abundant, can be completely drained without damaging, better columbic efficiency, stored and shipped safely.	poor power density
2	Potassium ion battery (KIB): uses potassium ions for charge transfer instead of lithium ions [20]	the cell design is simple, both the material and the fabrication procedure are cheaper, abundance and low cost, can be charged faster.	poor power and energy density.
3	Solid state battery (2017 by John Goodenough): battery technology that uses both solid electrodes and solid electrolytes [21]	higher energy density, safe, tolerance to high temperature, allows fast charging	expensive to make, low temperature operation may be challenging, may break due to mechanical stress.

10.3   Battery Management System

An efficient BMS is one of the primary component in EVs to guarantee the safe, reliable, efficient and long lasting operation of a Li-ion battery while dealing with the electric grid and challenging driving conditions not only that it also gives the information on the battery State Of Charge (SOC), State of Life (SOL), and State of Health (SOH). The BMS can sense the battery voltage, battery current and battery temperature to avoid over charge and over discharge conditions.

The crucial task of BMS is to rapidly and accurately measure the battery voltage and SOC. The BMS should include as many features like interfacing the data acquisition system which incorporate measurement of temperature and battery current and controllers used to maintain the cell balance. Cell balancing is a critical function for high-powered battery packs because it is vital that the charge level of all cells does not stray outside the recommended SOC range. BMS serves as the brain behind the battery packs to manage the output, charging and discharging and provide notifications on the status of the battery pack. They also afford significant control to protect the batteries from damage.

A simple and cost-effective technique for cell balancing, commonly used in EV/HEV designs today, is active and passive-balancing. With passive-balancing, a resistor is placed across a cell when its state of charge exceeds that of its neighbors. It should be noted that in passive-balancing wastes energy and can generate considerable heat. In active balancing the storage elements are used.

A BMS is an embedded system that is built and designed for the following purpose:

- ✓ Protects cells of battery from damage in abuse/failure cases.
- ✓ Prolongs life of battery.
- ✓ Maintains battery in a state in which it can fulfil its functional design requirements.
- ✓ Informs the application controller how to make the best use of the pack right now (e.g. Power limits, control charger, etc.)
- ✓ Inform the user about the status of the battery (e.g. SOC, SOH)

10.3.1   Need for BMS

The Lithium-ion batteries have proved to be the battery of interest for Electric Vehicle manufacturers because of its high charge density and low weight. Even though these batteries pack in a lot of punch for its size they are highly unstable in nature. It is very important that these batteries should never be over charged or under discharge at any circumstance which brings in the need to monitor its voltage and current. This process gets a bit tougher since there are a lot of cells put together to form a battery pack in EV and every cell should be individually monitored for its safety and efficient operation which requires a special dedicated system called the Battery Management System. Also to get the maximum efficiency from a battery pack, we should completely charge and discharge all the cells at the same time at the same voltage which again calls in for a BMS. Apart from this the BMS is held responsible for many other functions as,

- ✓ To reduce cost associated with battery—includes labor, maintenance, operation, and replacement costs.
- ✓ To increase lifetime of the battery.
- ✓ Proper thermal management
- ✓ Cell balancing
- ✓ To ensure that the energy of the battery is optimized to power the product.
- ✓ To monitor and control the charging and discharging process of the battery.
- ✓ To provide the present status of the battery
- ✓ Battery voltage/current, SOC, SOH, insulation resistance, etc.
- ✓ To enhance safety and protection of the battery unit
- ✓ To analyze fault and provide alarm.

10.3.2 BMS Components

The battery management system (BMS) is comprised of several components, including monitoring components close to the battery cells

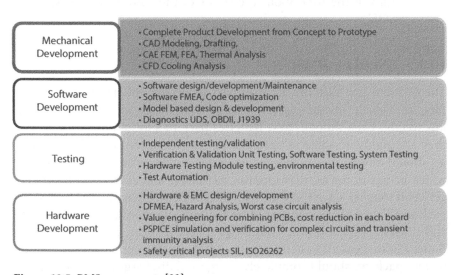

Mechanical Development	• Complete Product Development from Concept to Prototype • CAD Modeling, Drafting, • CAE FEM, FEA, Thermal Analysis • CFD Cooling Analysis
Software Development	• Software design/development/Maintenance • Software FMEA, Code optimization • Model based design & development • Diagnostics UDS, OBDII, J1939
Testing	• Independent testing/validation • Verification & Validation Unit Testing, Software Testing, System Testing • Hardware Testing Module testing, environmental testing • Test Automation
Hardware Development	• Hardware & EMC design/development • DFMEA, Hazard Analysis, Worst case circuit analysis • Value engineering for combining PCBs, cost reduction in each board • PSPICE simulation and verification for complex circuits and transient immunity analysis • Safety critical projects SIL, ISO26262

Figure 10.5 BMS components [22].

themselves, one or more power-conversion stages dictated by the needs of the vehicle, and intelligent controllers or embedded processors placed at strategic locations in the architecture to manage various aspects of the power subsystem. Figure 10.5 shows the components of BMS.

The following diagram depicts the different operating states of electric vehicle.

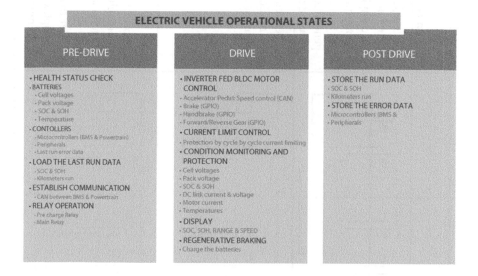

10.3.3   BMS Architecture/Topology

The BMS is broadly classified into three types as centralized, distributed, modular. The merits and demerits of these types are described in Table 10.6.

10.3.4   SOC/SOH Determination

One feature of the BMS is to keep track of the state of charge (SOC) of the battery. The SOC could signal the user and control the charging and discharging process. There are three methods of determining SOC: through direct measurement, through coulomb counting and through the combination of the two techniques.

To measure the SOC directly, one could simply use a voltmeter because the battery voltage decreases more or less linearly during the discharging cycle of the battery. In the coulomb-counting method, the current going into or coming out of a battery is integrated to produce the relative value of

Table 10.6 Types of BMS.

S. no.	Type of BMS	Description	Diagram	Pros and cons
1	Centralized [23]	a single controller is connected to the battery cells through a multitude of wires		Pros: Single installation point, one single controller, no complex inter-module communication. Cons: excess heat could be generated, complex wiring, reduced functional safety.
2	Distributed [23]	a BMS board is installed at each cell, with just a single communication cable between the battery and a controller		most expensive, simplest to install, and offer the cleanest assembly
3	Modular [23]	a few controllers, each handing a certain number of cells, with communication between the controllers		Pros: Supports plug and play, more reliable, improved functional safety. Cons: Costlier than centralized, complex inter module communication.

Table 10.7 Different SOC determination methods.

SOC method	Advantages	Disadvantages	Input
ECC [24]	• Easy to implement • Cheap • Computationally less intensive	• Accuracy depends on initial values and on precise measurement • Not suitable for batteries under heavy dynamic varying conditions • Needs some rest time for SOC correction	• Current, voltage • Initial SOC and SOH
OCV [24]	• Accurate • Easy to implement • Cheap • Computationally less intensive	• Needs large rest time, which may not be practically feasible in EVs • Can't be used to find SOH of batteries	• Rest time, voltage
EKF/DEKF/SKF [24]	• Accurate Insensitive to noise in measurement. • Doesn't depend on initial SOC • Can be used to compute SOH	• Lots of computation • Costly • Can lead to instability if not properly designed	• Current, voltage, temperature • battery model
ANN model [24]	• Suitable for all kinds of batteries • Comparatively less computations	• Needs large training data	• Current, voltage, temperature

Table 10.8 Cell balancing techniques.

S. no.	Type of balancing	Diagrammatic representation	Merits	Demerits
1	active cell balancing [25]		Relatively simple Good efficiency fast	Switch network Complex control
2	passive balancing [25]		Very simple Very cheap	0% efficiency Slow Can't charge cell
3	charge shunting [25]		Simple control	Complex connection, Requires (n-1) inductors and 2(n-1) switches

its charge. This is similar to counting the currency going into and out of a bank account to determine the relative amount in the account.

In addition, the two methods could be combined. The voltmeter could be used to monitor the battery voltage and calibrate the SOC when the actual charge approaches either end. Meanwhile, the battery current could be integrated to determine the relative charge going into and coming out of the battery.

The state of health (SOH) is a measurement that reflects the general condition of a battery and its ability to deliver the specified performance compared with a fresh battery. Any parameter such as cell impedance or conductance that changes significantly with age could be used to indicate the SOH of the cell. In practice, the SOH could be estimated from a single measurement of either the cell impedance or the cell conductance. Table 10.7 gives details of different SOC and SOH methods advantages and disadvantages.

10.3.5   Cell Balancing Algorithms

Cell balancing is a method of compensating weaker cells by equalizing the charge on all cells in the chain to extend the overall battery life. In chains of multi-cell batteries, small differences between the cells due to production tolerances or operating conditions tend to be magnified with each charge-discharge cycle. During charging, weak cells may be overstressed and become even weaker until they eventually fail, causing the battery to fail prematurely.

To provide a dynamic solution to this problem while taking into account the age and operating conditions of the cells, the BMS may incorporate one of the three cell balancing schemes to equalize the cells and prevent individual cells from becoming overstressed: the active balancing scheme, the passive balancing scheme and the charge shunting scheme. Table 10.8 depicts the different cell balancing techniques.

10.3.6   Data Communication

The communications function of a BMS may be provided though a data link used to monitor performance, log data, provide diagnostics or set system parameters. The function may also be provided by a communications channel carrying system control signals.

The choice of the communications protocol is not determined by the battery, it is determined by the application of the battery. The BMS used in electric vehicles must communicate with the upper vehicle controller and the motor controller to ensure the proper operation of the vehicle. There are two major protocols used by the BMS to communicate with the vehicle through the data bus or the controller area network (CAN) bus.

Data buses include the RS232 connection and EIA-485 (also called the RS485 connection). The industry standard for on-board vehicle communications is the CAN bus, which is more commonly used in vehicle applications proper operation of the vehicle.

10.3.7   The Logic and Safety Control

The various logic and safety control are:

1. Power up/down control
2. Charging and discharging control
3. Temperature/fault control

10.3.7.1   Power Up/Down Control

The control of power and voltage is one of the major factors for battery management. The following diagrams (Figure 10.6) depict the control of power and voltage constraints by using four relays that are named as positive relay, precharge relay, negative relay, and charger relay. As per the algorithm shown in the following flowchart (Figure 10.7) the power up/down control executes.

This control mainly to meet the voltage and power constraints under any fault conditions.

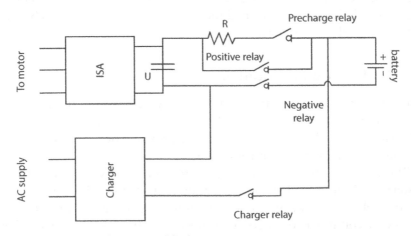

Figure 10.6 Power up/down control [26].

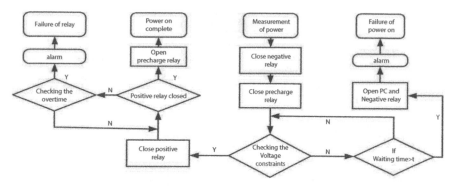

Figure 10.7 Power up/down control algorithm [26].

10.3.7.2   Charging and Discharging Control

Batteries are more frequently damaged by inappropriate charging than by any other cause. Therefore, charging control is an essential feature of the BMS. For lithium-ion batteries, a 2-stage charging method called the constant current–constant voltage (CC–CV) charging method is used.

During the first charging stage (the constant current stage), the charger produces a constant current that increases the battery voltage. When the battery voltage reaches a constant value, and the battery becomes nearly full, it enters the constant voltage (CV) stage. At this stage, the charger maintains the constant voltage as the battery current decays exponentially until the battery finishes charging. The primary goal of a BMS is to keep the battery from operating out of its safety zone. The BMS must protect the cell from any eventuality during discharging. Otherwise, the cell could operate outside of its limitations.

10.4   Intelligent Battery Management System

The control of BMS for the HESS can be done by using many intelligent techniques based on rules like Fuzzy, artificial intelligence like Artificial Neural Network, optimization techniques and traffic flow-based. Many algorithms are implemented based on these four types only. Each algorithm has its own merits and demerits. The following figure (Figure 10.8) shows the categories of intelligent BMS for HESS.

The common configuration of Intelligent BMS for HESS is denoted as the following figure (Figure 10.9). The battery and the UC are connected through the converter which controls the power flow between battery,

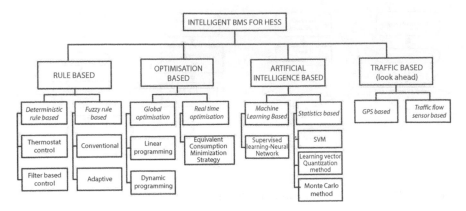

Figure 10.8 Categories of Intelligent BMS for HESS [27].

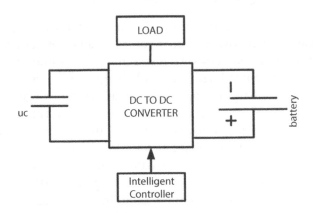

Figure 10.9 Configuration of Intelligent HESS BMS [28].

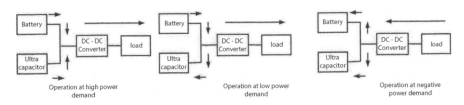

Figure 10.10 Power flow of HESS at different power demand conditions [28].

UC and load. The DC to DC converter may be either half-bridge topology, isolated dual active bridge, isolated half bridge topology, isolated full bridge topology. But the control of charging, discharging and power flow to load is controlled by the controller which may be rule-based, AI-based or optimization-based.

The main purpose of the energy management system is to manage the power from UC and battery according to the load power demand. Figure 10.10 shows the power split condition for different power demand condition. The UC act as the buffer device which supplies the power during the high power demand and during the lower power demand it stores the energy and during the negative power demand both battery and UC stores the energy. The main role of the UC power is to supply and absorb the relatively fast charging condition of the load power. The power flow control can be done by using any of the intelligent method.

10.4.1   Rule-Based Control

The rule based control is classified further as deterministic and Fuzzy based methods. Then the thermostat type is the typical deterministic method, which is designed based on if-then-else based. Designed the thermostat type control in which a threshold is set [29], beyond which the excess power is supplied by the UC. By using the another criteria as splitting the SOC of the battery and the SOC of the UC into different levels and organizing in a 2D map then by combining the rules based on the power demand better control had been achieved. The other method called as filter-based method is considering the frequency spectrum of the load profile [30, 31]. The low pass filter or band pass filters can be used to filter out the lower frequency of the load frequency spectrum and the battery power get supplied for that for that base load. But these typical methods has many uncertainties because of the nonlinearity in the load condition.

To overcome the non-linearity of the typical methods the fuzzy logic based method [32] is introduced for managing the power demand. By considering the SOC of both battery and UC, and the desired load power as inputs the power split ratio is set and based on that the power is supplied from either from battery or UC. For the Fuzzy adaptive strategy weight is assigned for all parameters based on the relative importance of that. By using the weighted sum approach the optimal operating points for each components of the HESS can be obtained to neutralize the conflicting objectives [33, 34].

10.4.2   Optimization-Based Control

The optimization-based control is divided into global optimization and real-time optimization method. The global optimization requires the knowledge of entire driving cycle and it is suitable only for the known routes. In this the linear programming uses many piecewise—linear approximations to optimize the HESS and the overall power train efficiency. In Hu *et al.* [35] performed simultaneous optimal sizing and energy management via convex programming. The major drawback of this is the approximation formulation of the problem and so it is restricted to uncomplicated HESS. At last the genetic algorithm is the option to solve the complex non-linear optimization problem [36, 37]. The major drawback of this is more time for computation and its black-box nature made it very difficult for the researcher to track the process.

The Equivalent consumption minimization strategy is a better concept to strategize EVs. For HESS applications in EVs the main objective is to obtain the highest possible efficiency at all times. The HESS components battery, UC, and DC to DC converter efficiencies are mapped under both charging and discharging condition then the optimization starts searching to get the optimized power split ratio value [38] implemented this fuel minimization problem by using the Pontryagin's minimum principle with Hamiltonian system.

10.4.3   AI-Based Control

The above mentioned rule-based and optimization methods focus on supply side of the plant. But the actual problem also depends on the load side. Thus, the conventional methods are not properly designed for uncertainties. The advanced computing techniques which is AI-based like [39, 40] supervised learning and machine learning are giving more efficient control by giving proper training to the data and generate the proper control output variables. Figure 10.11 is an example of NN control for 5 inputs single output.

For a large number of data to obtain the meaningful data, a statistical analysis is necessary. For this particular solution we need more data to analyze which leads to the statistical-based control methods. Liang *et al.* [41] introduced a technique called Support Vector Machine (SVM) by taking

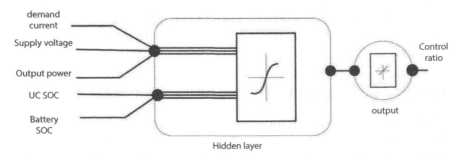

Figure 10.11 Model of 5 input single output neural network [42].

18 input variables to obtain the four driving pattern categories. Another method called Learning vector quantization network was applied for driving pattern classification. Monte Carlo approach was used on the historical data to get the useful data of load consumption. The main drawback of the AI approach is the probability of loss of information due to application of binary classification.

10.4.4   Traffic (Look Ahead Method)-Based Control

The above discussed methods are either present-based or past-based strategies. When the computation linked with past data obviously the time for computation become high. So only from the PID controller the derivative control made the sense to back looking nature. The feedforward network makes a strong compensation into the system [43, 44] found that the real-time GPS data processing is done to detect the presence and relative positions of the stop signs, any obstacles and traffic signals within the certain distance and the judgement can be drawn from this inferred solution.

10.5   Conclusion

The detailed discussion on BMS from basics to intelligent techniques to manage the HESS states that the current scenario is in need of hybrid battery system to satisfy the requirement of non-linear load demand. The load demand and the battery life has to be managed properly by adopting the proper intelligent control techniques. The main constraint in the battery management is that thebattery should operate in its SOA and then the life of the battery would not get affected. The integration of battery and UC has many challenges and issues to properly meet the load demand. Currently the EVs are built with UC as the major source and the battery is the buffer source to meet the current scenario.

References

1. Zaghib, K. *et al.*, Safe and fast-charging Li-ion battery with long shelf life for power applications. *J. Power Sources*, 196, 8, 3949–3954, 2011.
2. Vidal, C., Member, S., Gross, O., Gu, R., Kollmeyer, P., Emadi, A., xEV Li-Ion Battery Low-Temperature Effects—Review. *IEEE Transactions On Vehicular Technology*, vol. 68, no. 5, May 2019.

3. Zhang, L., Hu, X., Wang, Z., Sun, F., and Dorrell, D.G. A review of superca-pacitor modeling, estimation, and applications: A control/management per-spective. *Renew. Sustain. Energy Rev.*, 81, 1868–1878, 2018.

4. Lu, X., Member, S., Chen, Y., Fu, M., Wang, H., Member, S., Multi-Objective Optimization-Based Real-Time Control Strategy for Battery/Ultracapacitor Hybrid Energy Management Systems. *IEEE Access*, 7, 11640–11650, 2019.

5. Zhu, Y., Fan, Q., Xiong, L., Zhang, G., Qian, X., Coordination Control Strategy for Battery–Ultracapacitor Hybrid Energy Storage System in Microgrids with Unbalanced and Nonlinear Loads. XX, *IEEE Access*, vol 7, Aug 2019.

6. Uebel, S., Murgovski, N., Bernard, B., Sj, J., A Two-Level MPC for Energy Management Including Velocity Control of Hybrid Electric Vehicles. *IEEE Transactions On Vehicular Technology*, vol. 68, no. 6, June 2019.

7. Wu, J., Zou, Y., Zhang, X., Liu, T., Kong, Z., He, D., An Online Correction Predictive EMS for a Hybrid Electric Tracked Vehicle Based on Dynamic Programming and Reinforcement Learning. *IEEE Access*, vol 7, Aug 2019.

8. Ali, A.M., Shivapurkar, R., Dirk, S., Optimal situation-based power man-agement and application to state predictive models for multi-source elec-tric vehicles. *IEEE Transactions on Vehicular Technology*, vol. 68, no. 12, December 2019.

9. Rosewater, D., Baldick, R., Santoso, S., Transactions on Smart Grid Risk-Averse Model Predictive Control Design for, no. September. 1–9, 2019.

10. https://en.wikipedia.org/wiki/General_Motors_EV1

11. https://en.wikipedia.org/wiki/Toyota_Prius_(XW10)

12. https://en.wikipedia.org/wiki/General_Motors_EV1

13. https://en.wikipedia.org/wiki/Tesla_Roadster_(2008)

14. https://en.wikipedia.org/wiki/Nissan_Leaf

15. https://en.wikipedia.org/wiki/Chevrolet_Volt

16. https://en.wikipedia.org/wiki/Volkswagen_Golf_Mk7

17. https://en.wikipedia.org/wiki/Tesla_Model_S

18. Xiaosong Hu, Changfu Zou, Caiping Zhang, and Yang Li, Technological Developments in Batteries. *IEEE Power Energy Mag.*, 42–44, 2017.

19. Tian, W., Li, M., Niu, J., Li, W., Shi, J., The Research progress and compari-sons between Lithium-ion battery and Sodium ion battery, *Proc. IEEE Conf. Nanotechnol.*, vol. 2019-July, no. 2, pp. 313–318, 2019.

20. I. E. Agency and S. Komaba, "POTASSIUM BATTERIES," pp. 11–12, 2020.

21. Bindra, A., Electric Vehicle Batteries Eye Solid-State Technology: Prototypes Promise Lower Cost, Faster Charging, and Greater Safety, *IEEE Power Electron. Mag.*, vol. 7, no. 1, pp. 16–19, 2020.

22. Marques, J.M., *Battery Management System (BMS) for Lithium Ion batter-ies*, Electronic Theses and Dissertations, Coimbra: University of Coimbra, 2014.

23. Hu, R., "Battery Management System For Electric Vehicle Applications". Electronic Theses and Dissertations. University of Windsor, 2011.

24. Regtien, P.P.L., Notten, P.H.L., Pop, V., Bergveld, H.J., Danilov, D., *Battery Management Systems - Accurate State-of-Charge Indication for Battery-Powered Applications (Philips Research Book Series).*

25. Kelkar, A., Dasari, Y., Williamson, S.S., A Comprehensive Review of Power Electronics Enabled Active Battery Cell Balancing for Smart Energy Management, *2020 IEEE Int. Conf. Power Electron. Smart Grid Renew. Energy, PESGRE 2020*, pp. 1–6, 2020.

26. Huang, Y., *et al.*, A review of power management strategies and component sizing methods for hybrid vehicles, *Renew. Sustain. Energy Rev.*, 96, no. August, 132–144, 2018.

27. Kouchachvili, L., Yaïci, W., Entchev, E., Hybrid battery/supercapacitor energy storage system for the electric vehicles, *J. Power Sources*, 374, no. October 2017, 237–248, 2018.

28. Shen, J. and Khaligh, A., Design and Real-Time Controller Implementation for a Battery-Ultracapacitor Hybrid Energy Storage System, *IEEE Trans. Ind. Informatics*, 12, 5, 1910–1918, 2016.

29. Carter, R., Cruden, A., Hall, P.J., Optimizing for efficiency or battery life in a battery/supercapacitor electric vehicle. *IEEE Trans. Veh. Technol.*, 61, 4, 1526–1533, 2012.

30. Jaafar, A., Akli, C.R., Sareni, B., Roboam, X., Jeunesse, A., Sizing and energy management of a hybrid locomotive based on flywheel and accumulators. *IEEE Trans. Veh. Technol.*, 58, 8, 3947–3958, 2009.

31. Schaltz, E., Khaligh, A., Rasmussen, P.O., Influence of battery/ultracapacitor energy-storage sizing on battery lifetime in a fuel cell hybrid electric vehicle. *IEEE Trans. Veh. Technol.*, 58, 8, 3882–3891, 2009.

32. Chenghui, Z., Qingsheng, S., Naxin, C., Wuhua, L., Particle swarm optimization for energy management fuzzy controller design in dual-source electric vehicle. *PESC Rec.—IEEE Annu. Power Electron. Spec. Conf.*, 1405–1410, 2007.

33. Langari, R. and Won, J.S., Intelligent energy management agent for a parallel hybrid vehicle—Part I: System architecture and design of the driving situation identification process. *IEEE Trans. Veh. Technol.*, 54, 3, 925–934, 2005.

34. Won, J.S. and Langari, R., Intelligent energy management agent for a parallel hybrid vehicle—Part II: Torque distribution, charge sustenance strategies, and performance results. *IEEE Trans. Veh. Technol.*, 54, 3, 935–953, 2005.

35. Hu, X., Murgovski, N., Johannesson, L.M., Egardt, B., Comparison of three electrochemical energy buffers applied to a hybrid bus powertrain with simultaneous optimal sizing and energy management. *IEEE Trans. Intell. Transp. Syst.*, 15, 3, 1193–1205, 2014.

36. Adinolfi, G., Graditi, G., Siano, P., Piccolo, A., Multiobjective Optimal Design of Photovoltaic Synchronous Boost Converters Assessing Efficiency, Reliability, and Cost Savings. *IEEE Trans. Ind. Informatics*, 11, 5, 1038–1048, 2015.

37. Zhang, L. and Dorrell, D.G., Genetic Algorithm based optimal component sizing for an electric vehicle. in *Proc. 39th Annu. Conf. IEEE Ind. Electron. Soc.*, pp. 7331–7336, Vienna, Austria, 2013.

38. Malikopoulos, A.A., Supervisory power management control algorithms for hybrid electric vehicles: A survey. *IEEE Trans. Intell. Transp. Syst.*, 15, 5, 1869–1885, 2014.

39. Shen, J. and Khaligh, A., A supervisory energy management control strategy in a battery/ultracapacitor hybrid energy storage system. *IEEE Trans. Transp. Electrif.*, 1, 3, 223–231, 2015.

40. Moreno, J., Ortúzar, M.E., Dixon, J.W., Energy-management system for a hybrid electric vehicle, using ultracapacitors and neural networks. *IEEE Trans. Ind. Electron.*, 53, 2, 614–623, 2006.

41. Liang, Z., Xin, Z., Yi, T., Xinn, Z., Intelligent energy management based on the driving cycle sensitivity identification using SVM. *Isc. 2009—2009 Int. Symp. Comput. Intell. Des.*, 2, 513–516, 2009.

42. Reddy, N.P., Pasdeloup, D., Zadeh, M.K., Skjetne, R., An Intelligent Power and Energy Management System for Fuel Cell/Battery Hybrid Electric Vehicle Using Reinforcement Learning, *ITEC 2019 - 2019 IEEE Transp. Electrif. Conf. Expo*, 2019.

43. Gong, Q. and Li, Y., Trip based nearly global optimal power management of plug-in hybrid electric vehicles using gas-kine. *IFAC Proc. Vol.*, 17, 1 PART 1, 3225–3230, 2008.

44. Gong, Q., Li, Y., Peng, Z.R., Trip based optimal power management of plug-in hybrid electric vehicles using gas-kinetic traffic flow model. *Proc. Am. Control Conf.*, 57, 6, 3225–3230, 2008.

11

A Comprehensive Study on Various Topologies of Permanent Magnet Motor Drives for Electric Vehicles Application

Chiranjit Sain[1]*, Atanu Banerjee[1] and Pabitra Kumar Biswas[2]

[1]Department of Electrical Engineering, National Institute of Technology Meghalaya, Bijni Complex, Laitumukhrah, Shillong, Meghalaya, India
[2]Department of Electrical & Electronics Engineering, National Institute of Technology Mizoram, Aizawl, India

Abstract

To suppress the discharge of greenhouse gasses and to address the environmental sustainability electric vehicles impart a crucial role in the latest energy-efficient environment. To face this challenge, electric vehicles which take part the energy conversion mechanism, should not only demand exact demand in performance and efficiency while also vibration, cost, etc. This chapter significantly reports a comprehensive solution for permanent magnet motors employed in recent electric vehicles. Eventually, permanent magnet motors are openly employed in electric vehicles technology due to the quick advancements in permanent magnet materials and several advanced constructional requirements like high torque to volume ratio, large power density, lower excitation losses, lesser noise and vibration, etc. compared to an induction motor. Additionally, permanent magnet synchronous machines could be designed to employ over extensive torque-speed operating regions with improved torque density and power density. Moreover the drawbacks of this strategy are operating cost and obtainability of the rare earth magnet materials. Specifically the generation of acoustic as well as electromagnetic noise and the range of power factors may be the challenging issues in electric vehicle drive.

Keywords: Comprehensive study, electric vehicle, efficiency, induction motor, permanent magnet motor, noise and vibration

*Corresponding author: chiranjitsain@nitm.ac.in

Chitra A, P. Sanjeevikumar, Jens Bo Holm-Nielsen and S. Himavathi (eds.) Artificial Intelligent Techniques for Electric and Hybrid Electric Vehicles, (207–218) © 2020 Scrivener Publishing LLC

11.1   Introduction

Society and mankind have been promisingly aware regarding the destruction it is effecting to the atmosphere and the role of electric vehicles are distinguished to act as a vital role in retrieving the balance. Presently the green energy sources generate lowers than 10% of the energy utilized in the electric grid, since majority of the electrical energy utilized for charging electric vehicles shall be generated from burning fossil fuels, such as coal, gas and oil, at the various generating units [1]. The transformation in the global atmosphere is one of the major environmental concerns in present day's scenario. The only initiative to overcome this critical hazardous is to reduce the level of greenhouse gases. In many developing countries several measures have been adopted to maintain the emission of harmful gasses such as carbon dioxide, carbon monoxide, nitrous oxides to a sustainable limit. With the advancement of IoT (the internet of Things) technology, electric vehicles can be promisingly established as an advanced type of mobile intelligent power consumption device. In a typical smart grid technology, electric vehicles can be used as energy storage protocol. Smart grid technology can provide intelligent monitoring and a wide area communicating the network with greater control on all aspects of operations [2, 3]. As a result charging system, monitoring system, billing system, entire data collection technology of a typical electric vehicle can be transformed into a smart system. Hence, this robust and intelligent control technology using IoT tools can be incorporated in a solar-powered electric vehicle for enhancing the environmental sustainability and future demand in a smart city.

Artificial Intelligence was provided a fruitful opportunity and scope for electrical automation in recent days. With an introduction to AI, control of electric vehicles becomes sophisticated as well as smart control. Moreover monitoring of all activities such as infrastructure, charging system, communication system, security system of an electric vehicle will be highly benefitted through the adoption in AI. AI Management is not complicated, so the objects design not required to be controlled by the AI feature approximator [4]. Results can be improved rapidly by properly adjusting related parameters. For an example fuzzy adaptive controllers respond more quickly and the percentage overshoot can be minimized in a significant manner. In this manuscript, efficiency calculations at various torque-speed operating ranges are considered to justify the comparative assessment of such motor topologies for the hybrid as well as electric vehicles applications in a descriptive manner [5, 6].

This article is organized as follows: Section 11.2 reports the proposed design considerations of PMSM for electric vehicle, Section 11.3 describes the comparative assessment of the motor topologies, Section 11.4 represents the electric vehicle smart infrastructure, and Section 11.5 concludes the paper.

11.2   Proposed Design Considerations of PMSM for Electric Vehicle

With the advancement of permanent magnet materials such as samarium cobalt, alnico, rare earth magnets, economic construction, better dynamic response, improved speed range, high torque to weight ratio PMSM motors are vastly employed in modern electric vehicles.

Here we are optimizing the 45/70 kW drive motor for the medium size electric vehicle of the future. This incorporates improvements in basic working mechanisms while more attentions need to incorporate in material construction and construction technology. The technology of hybrid vehicles provides greater flexibility on the motor performance [7]. An electric vehicle establishes a discrete torque-speed characteristic with fixed power operation from reference speed to maximum speed. The current carrying capability by the stator and rotor winding will be lesser for overall shape of structure in operation. The most significant advancement presently for PMSM machines is the invention of the daido magnet tube in magnequench material. This magnetic material serves the advantage of the high-energy magnet and containment tube. The Surface mounted motors generally provide a containment sleeve to maintain the several millimeters of the air gap to the magnetic circuit [8]. The typical important specifications for the design of the magnetic circuit are weight and minimum core losses while lowering the slot leakage to reduce the winding inductance. The proposed design is assumed for the selection of high power drives. The rotor structure comprises of a steel sleeve where the magnets are mounted, and a containment band has been combined on the outside. Majority of industrial motors utilize samarium cobalt which has excellent mechanical properties. In general, alloys of magnesium oxide are in common use and the tendency to design rotors located on standard size blocks, $1 \times 0.5 \times 5.5$ in. thick. Vector control or field oriented control makes PMSM machine more sophisticated and flexibility for high-performance applications. A typical constructional requirement for the proposed PMSM machine has been represented in Figure 11.1. In this diagram the different parts of

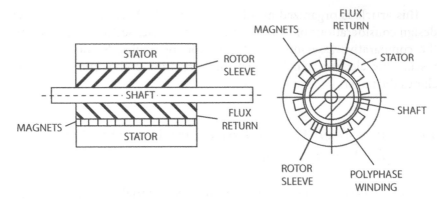

Figure 11.1 Typical constructional features of PMSM machine. Source: Permanent Magnet Motor Technology (Jacek F. Gieras, M. wing).

PMSM i.e. stator, rotor, position of magnets along with different paths for flux distribution has been demonstrated. Some practical economic design considerations for the high-speed heavy electric vehicles driven by PMSM are depicted in Table 11.1. This proposed technical specification for the designing of PMSM for electrical vehicles can be used by the designer or manufacturer in automobile industries [9, 10]. In the literature, a comprehensive discussion is established between an induction motor, PMSM motor and a switched reluctance motor for electric vehicle applications. A fast finite element analysis has adopted for such analytical design of IM. Finally various kinds of analysis such as noise and vibration, harness, etc. have been done and a suitable comparative performance analysis is achieved. Few authors proposed a solid rotor topology for high-speed interior PMSM constructed with a semi magnetic stainless steel. The proposed methodology has been validated using dynamic structural, static structural finite element method to meet the feasibility of the present design method. Some authors described a computational method for the design of an interior PMSM applicable for the traction systems [11]. Additionally by the introduction of FEM based technique saves the CPU time drastically without interrupting such accuracies. Few authors have addressed on multi objective optimal design procedure of IPMSM for high-performance applications. In this section, Taguchi method has been introduced while incorporating five multi-objective functions for a V shaped PMSM rotor.

Recently with the advancement of technology, energy-efficient motors are extensively used in electric vehicles technology as they operate at highest efficiency at some specified operating regions. In case of energy-efficient motor some characteristics like the power factor, efficiency, effect of noise

Table 11.1 Recent economic design of PMSM (35 KW is continuous rating, 70 KW is short time rating). Source: Electric Motor Drives, R. Krishnan.

Power (3.5:1 CPSR) (kW)	45	70	70	70	150
Speed max	12000	10 000	13 500	20 000	20 000
Stator OD (mm)	218	200	220	200	225
Rotor OD (mm)	141	113	141	113	145
Active length (mm)	80.5	190	97	110	160
Overall length (mm)	141	260	157	170	230
Stator voltage (V)	150	360	460	360	460
Max efficiency	96%	96%	98%	96.5%	98.6%
Winding L (mH)	0.1	1.78	1.37	0.85	0.28
Winding R (mV)	9.6	66	116	38	13.4
Poles	16	8	8	8	8
Stator/rotor mass (kg)	19	40	21	24	44

and vibration, temperature rise, dynamic behavior are the main considerations while designing the machine [12]. Production of noise and vibration in electric vehicles possess several inconveniences for high-performance applications. Therefore, reduction of acoustic noise and vibration in PMSM has a major concern in recent electric vehicles. During the designing of electric vehicles some important factors such as lamination structure, materials used for lamination, elimination of cogging torque, winding configuration, magnetic permeability, length of the air-gap, etc. are taken into consideration for such better performance of modern electric vehicles in an energy-efficient environment [13].

11.3   Impact of Digital Controllers

With the rapid advancement of discrete control theory, modern power electronics and the concept of signal conditioning and data acquisition systems ensure such sophisticated control techniques in motor drive applications [14]. Thus, there is a provision of Man to machine Interface (MMI) in order to enhance reliability, accuracy, flexibility of the system performance as compared to analog control implementation. The marvelous natures of analog controllers are due to the great advantages it possesses. Some of the best-known facts of analog controllers are for the user to comprehend easily due to its multirole features, high bandwidth and high-resolution. Like every device, the analog devices also possess limitations such as sensitivity to noise and temperature change. Digital controllers eradicate certain drawbacks of the analog controllers. However, to eradicate complete drawbacks, more advanced digital controllers such as the Digital signal processor and FPGA provide superior performance in industrial applications [15].

11.3.1   DSP-Based Digital Controller

Digital signal processor (DSP) controller is a state of the art system which has multi-fold advantages such as high-speed mathematical core and memory. Due to the controller's high pace and advantages, it is used to solve complex problems related to motor speed and servo control. Hence, due to the multi-fold advantages, the DSP controllers are able to produce high yields and better results [16]. Also, fixed point DSPs are preferred for motor control for most applications a dynamic range of 16 bits is enough.

11.3.2   FPGA-Based Digital Controller

FPGA is a state of the art controller which has multiple advantages such as it is fast pace in nature and the design cycle being extremely short. The gate array logic circuitry is followed in the FPGA controller [17]. FPGAs are slightly traditional in nature and follow more of the hardware connection in nature than software. FPGAs do not have an operating system for processing logic and hence use hardware methodology for logic processing. Though the connection and logic processing is hardware based, FPGA is an efficient and reliable technology [18].

11.4   Electric Vehicles Smart Infrastructure

With the rapid progress of Internet of Things (IoT) technology and the renewable energy integration electric vehicles play a significant role for the sustainable development in the environment [19]. The technology so called Self-Monitoring Analysis and Reporting Technology (Smart) has been an innovative interest in the industries as well in research institutions for such strong foundation and robust control. To meet the latest vision a huge change in the power supply infrastructure and traffic systems need to be incorporated. In fact drivers are supposed to get the reliability that they will be able to conveniently recharge their vehicle wherever they are [20]. The required closely meshed network of charging stations will only be obtained at sustainable cost with very smart and cost-effective electric charging systems that can be installed anywhere [21, 22]. Electricity is available everywhere, so that electric mobility can configure on a sound infrastructural basis. The charging stations are only energized after a registered user has activated the charging function. Thus, there is no danger of live cables being exposed even when a smart charging station is destroyed or knocked over in an accident. The proposed charging station can also be installed to display additional information such as road map, tourist guidance in nearby places, etc. [23, 24].

Recently SIEMENS Technology Solution has been proposed and designed smart technology based charging solution for a modern electric vehicle is shown in Figure 11.2. In Figure 11.3 a typical IoT based architecture for a smart electric vehicle has been represented [25]. Generally, the entire architecture comprises of several elements like different sensors (motion sensor, optical sensor, smart sensor), network having wireless connectivity for communication; cloud computing, data storage devices and some security as well as safety devices [26, 27].

Figure 11.2 Smart technology based charging solution for a modern electric vehicle. Source: SIEMENS Technology solution.

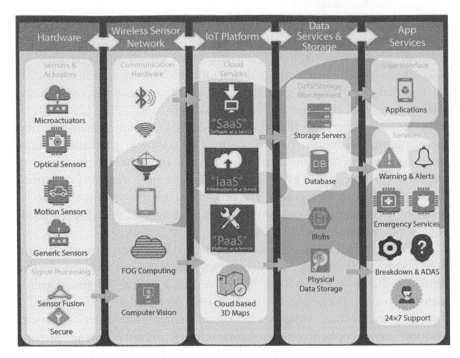

Figure 11.3 IoT based architecture for a smart electric vehicle. Source: Internet of Things for Smart Cities (Andrea Zanella, *et al.*, 2014).

11.5   Conclusion

This paper significantly describes the comprehensive review of different technologies for the development of electric vehicles. To protect the environment from the emission of greenhouse gasses and for the sustainable development, electric vehicles are the promising technology used in different developed countries. This proposed design analysis and various topologies considered for the benefit of an energy-efficient electric vehicle can be considered in recent automobile industries as well as in various research organizations to meet the future goal. Various kinds of PMSM drives such as interior PMSM, surface mounted PMSM, surface inset PMSM, line start PMSM, hybrid PMSM are categorized depending upon the rotor configuration and design methods. Interior PMSM machine takes the advantage of generating greater flux linkage, lesser armature current to attend the optimum torque. Surface mounted machines are generally not adopted for very high-speed propulsion applications. Moreover these machines possess quiet lesser mechanical robustness compared with surface inset

PMSM machines. On the other hand, interior PMSM is suited in high-speed applications and construction is mechanically sound. Furthermore, a line start PMSM with a cage-winding was employed in constant speed application and they are quiet efficient in comparison with conventional induction motor drives. Additionally, Hybrid PMSM machines may be constructed depending upon the arrangement of permanent magnets and the nature of air-gap flux distribution in various applications. Therefore, the various topologies of PMSM drives and the related comparative discussions could be helpful for the readers in the area of electric vehicles and sustainable development. Furthermore, this comprehensive report demonstrates such fruitful methodologies and associated advancements to meet with smart technologies. Applications of ICT-based IoT tools in electric vehicles would be an innovative and sophisticated technology in recent days in different smart cities for sustainable industrial developments. Comparison analysis involves performance, efficiency, and configuration. The outcome of the proposed study would be an extensive interest towards the researchers as well as professional engineers for the sustainable development in the environment.

References

1. Robinson, A.P., Blythe, P.T., Bell, M.C., Hübner, Y., Hill, G.A., Analysis of electric vehicle driver recharging demand profiles and subsequent impacts on the carbon content of electric vehicle trips. *Energy Policy*, 61, 337–348, 2013.
2. Richardson, D.B., Electric vehicles and the electric grid: A review of modeling approaches, impacts, and renewable energy integration. *Renew. Sustain. Energy. Rev.*, 19, 247–254, 2013.
3. Daziano, R.A. and Chiew, E., Electric vehicles rising from the dead: Data needs for forecasting consumer response toward sustainable energy sources in personal transportation. *Energy Policy*, 51, 876–894, 2012.
4. Ewing, G. and Sarigöllü, E., Assessing consumer preferences for clean-fuel vehicles: A discrete choice experiment. *J. Public Policy Mark*, 19, 106–118, 2000.
5. Taylor, J., Maitra, A., Alexander, M., Brooks, D., Duvall, M., Evaluation of the impact of plug-in electric vehicle loading on distribution system operations, in: *Power & Energy Society General Meeting, 2009. PES'09*, pp. 1–6, IEEE, 2000.
6. Galus, M.D. and Andersson, G., Integration of plug-in hybrid electric vehicles into energy networks, in: *Power Tech 2009*, pp. 1–8, IEEE Bucharest, 2009.

7. Bandhauer, T.M., Garimella, S., Fuller, T.F., Temperature-dependent electrochemical heat generation in a commercial lithium-ion battery. *J. Power Sources*, 247, 618–628, 2014.

8. *On-site electric vehicle fire investigation*, US Department of Transportation—National Highway Traffic Safety Administration, 2013.

9. IEC 62133-2, Secondary cells and batteries containing alkaline or other non-acid electrolytes—Safety requirements for portable sealed secondary cells, and for batteries made from them, for use in portable applications—Part 2: in: *Lithium systems*, 2017.

10. *Accident assistance and recovery of vehicles with high-voltage systems*, German Association of the Automotive Industry (VDA), Berlin, 2013.

11. Karan, K., Pandey Krishan, K., Jain, A.K., Ashish, N., Evolution of solar energy in India: A review. *Renew. Sustain. Energy Rev.*, 40, 475–87, 2014.

12. Glerum, A., Frejinger, E., Karlström, A., Beser Hugosson, M., Bierlaire, M., Modeling car ownership and usage: A dynamic discrete-continuous choice modeling approach, in: *Presented at the International Choice Modelling Conference*, Sydney, Australia, 2013.

13. Parks, K., Denholm, P., Markel, T., Costs and emissions associated with plug-in hybrid electric vehicle charging in the Xcel energy Colorado service territory. *NREL Report*, No. TP-640-41410, pp. 1–29, 2007.

14. Soares, F.J., Pecas Lopes, J.A., Rocha Almeida, P.M., Moreira, C.L., Seca, L., A stochastic model to simulate electric vehicles motion and quantify the energy required from the grid, in: *Presented at the Power Systems Computation Conference (PSCC)*, Stockholm, Sweden, 2011.

15. Taylor, J., Maitra, A., Alexander, M., Brooks, D., Duvall, M., Evaluation of the impact of plug-in electric vehicle loading on distribution system operations, in: *Power & Energy Society General Meeting, 2009. PES'09*, pp. 1–6, IEEE, Canada, 2009.

16. Chiba, A., Takeno, M., Hoshi, N., Takemoto, M., Ogasawara, S., Rahman, M.A., Consideration of number of series turns in switched reluctance traction motor competitive to HEV IPMSM. *IEEE Trans. Ind. Appl.*, 48, 6, 2333–2340, 2012.

17. Mille, J.M., *Propulsion Systems for Hybrid Vehicles*, IET, Stevenage, U.K., 2010.

18. Boesing, M. and De Doncker, R.W., Exploring a vibration synthesis process for the acoustic characterization of electric drives. *IEEE Trans. Ind. Appl.*, 48, 1, 70–78, 2012.

19. Arata, M., Takahashi, N., Fujita, M., Mochizuki, M., Araki, T., Hanai, T., Noise lowering for a large variable speed range use permanent magnet motor by frequency shift and structural response evaluation of electromagnetic forces. *J. Power Electron.*, 12, 1, 67–74, 2012.

20. Goss, J. and Popescu, M.A., comparison of an interior permanent magnet and copper rotor induction motor in a hybrid electric vehicle application. *Proc. IEEE Elect. Mach. Drives Conf. (IEMDC)*, 220–225, 2013.

21. Neudorfer, H. and Wicker, N., Comparison of three different electric power-trains for the use in hybrid electric vehicles. *Proc. IET Conf. Power Electron. Mach. Drives*, 510–514, 2008.

22. Yang, Z., Krishnamurthy, M., Brown, I.P., Electromagnetic and vibrational characteristic of IPM over full torque-speed range. *Proc. IEEE Elect. Mach. Drives Conf. (IEMDC)*, 295–302, 2013.

23. Blomqvist, E. and Thollander, P., An integrated dataset of energy efficiency measures published as linked open data. *Energy Efficiency*, 8, 6, 1125–1147, 2015.

24. Zeraoulia, M., Benbouzid, M., Diallo, D., Electric motor drive selection issues for HEV propulsion systems: A comparative study. *IEEE Trans. Veh. Technol.*, 1756–1764, 2006.

25. Sain, C., Banerjee, A., Biswasm, P.K., *Modelling and Comparative Dynamic Analysis due to Demagnetization of a Torque Controlled Permanent Magnet Synchronous Motor Drive for Energy-Efficient Electric Vehicle*, ISA Transactions, Elsevier, Aug 2019.

26. Sain, C., Biswas, P.K., Banerjee, A., Padmanaban, S., An Efficient Flux Weakening Control Strategy of a Speed Controlled Permanent Magnet Synchronous Motor Drive for Light Electric Vehicle Applications. *IEEE-CALCON Conf.*, 1–5, 2017.

27. Chakravarthi, M.K. and Venkatesan, N., Adaptive type-2 fuzzy controller for nonlinear delay dominant MIMO systems: An experimental paradigm in LabVIEW. *Int. J. Adv. Intel. Paradigms*, 10, 4, 354–373, 2018.

12

A New Approach for Flux Computation Using Intelligent Technique for Direct Flux Oriented Control of Asynchronous Motor

A. Venkadesan[1]*, K. Sedhuraman[2], S. Himavathi[3] and A. Chitra[4]

[1]NIT Puducherry, Karaikal, India
[2]MVIT Puducherry, Puducherry, India
[3]Pondicherry Engineering College, Puducherry, India
[4]EPE Department, SELECT, VIT, Vellore, India

Abstract

The accurate estimation of magnitude and angle of flux is vital for good performance of Direct Flux/Field Oriented Control (DFOC) of Asynchronous Motor (AM)/Induction Motor (IM). For this control, accurate value of flux plays a major role. The current equations (CE) of the motor estimate flux with stator current and rotor speed as the inputs without the need of difficult stator voltage PWM voltage measurement. Hence CE can be comfortably used for flux estimation. But CE majorly depends on the rotor resistance (R_r) and varies during motor operation. This leads to significant error in the flux estimation. To address this problem, an intelligent approach namely neural network is employed. A novel Neural Network (NN) approach for flux estimation is proposed in this paper. The proposed approach uses stator current and rotor speed as the inputs similar to CE. The proposed NN based estimator is shown to handle rotor resistance variation problem as compared to current model-based flux estimator through MATLAB simulation.

Keywords: Flux estimator, current model, intelligent technique, neural network, induction motor, direct field oriented control

*Corresponding author: venkadesan@nitpy.ac.in

Chitra A, P. Sanjeevikumar, Jens Bo Holm-Nielsen and S. Himavathi (eds.) Artificial Intelligent Techniques for Electric and Hybrid Electric Vehicles, (219–232) © 2020 Scrivener Publishing LLC

12.1   Introduction

For high performance requirements in industries, Field Oriented Control (FOC) approach for induction motor is employed [1]. The torque and flux component can be independently controlled similar to the separately excited conduction motor which results in better dynamic response. For effective and efficient control, knowledge of magnitude and angle of motor flux is highly important which depends on the motor flux. The voltage equations (VE) and current equations (CE) can be used to compute flux. The low speed problems namely integrator drift and stator resistance variation are the two vital problems in VE [2, 3]. The VE also need complex Pulse Width Modulated (PWM) stator voltage measurement. The current model is free from one major problem that is drift and noise problems and compute rotor fluxes with only stator current and rotor speed and avoids stator voltage measurement. Hence CE can be used to compute rotor fluxes. The CE depends on R_r which varies during motor operation majorly due to temperature change and variation can be go upto 100% [4–6]. This leads to significant error in the flux and in turn in flux angle and magnitude estimation. This will affect the performance of the drive system. Numerous rotor resistance estimation methods in on-line are dealt in the literature [4, 5, 7, 8] to compute the change in the R_r. These methods require separate rotor resistance estimator. Because of this, the complexity of the drive system is increased.

An alternate solution using NN can be used for flux estimation. It offers better robustness as compared to conventional estimators. It involves only the computation of algebraic equations and does not have integral equations as compared to current model equations. Many NN model trained using data is proposed in the literature. The single hidden-layer feed-forward back-propagation neural network (SHLFFBP-NN) is proposed for flux computation [9]. The Multi-hidden layer feed-forward back-propagation neural network (MHLFFBP-NN) is proposed to estimate flux [10, 11]. The cascade forward back-propagation neural network (CFBP-NN) is used to compute rotor flux. The architecture is shown to provide needed accuracy with reduced number of neurons with ease in design as compared to (FFBP-NN) [13–16]. The flux estimator designed using CFBP-NN is used for speed estimation in sensorless indirect FOC of IM [14, 16, 17]. The same neural model is used for flux angle and magnitude computation for DFOC of IM [18]. The inputs to the flux estimator are chosen as direct (d) and quadrature (q) axis stator voltages and currents and the outputs are kept as d and q axis rotor fluxes. It is stated in [9] that it is not easy to measure high frequency stator PWM voltage of the motor. Hence, in this proposed paper, the same neural architecture is used to compute rotor fluxes. But the NN model is designed to compute rotor fluxes without the knowledge of motor stator voltage which is major novelty in this paper.

12.2 Direct Field-Oriented Control of IM Drive

Figure 12.1 shows the schematic diagram for the DFOC. The motor speed is compared with reference speed. The speed error is given as input to the proportional-integral (PI) controller. The PI controller gives torque command as the output. The reference torque producing component of stator current is computed with the help of torque command. Similarly, the reference flux producing component of stator current is generated. The actual torque producing component is compared with reference torque producing component. The error is processed through the PI controller and corresponding reference d-axis voltage is generated. Similarly, q-axis voltage is generated.

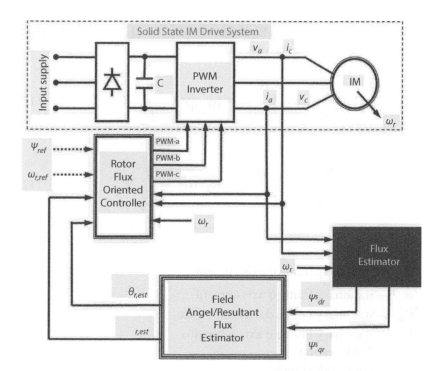

Figure 12.1 DFOC with flux estimator.

The d and q-axis reference voltage are transformed to 3 phase reference voltage using the field angle (1). The 3 phase reference voltage is compared with triangular wave. The pulses are generated to trigger the 3 phase inverter. The drive receives the inputs from the inverter. It is observed that the accuracy of flux estimation is very important for good performance of DFOC.

$$\theta_{r,est} = \tan^{-1}\left(\frac{\psi_{qr}^s}{\psi_{dr}^s}\right) \tag{12.1}$$

$$\Psi_{r,est} = \sqrt{\left(\psi_{dr}^s\right)^2 + \left(\psi_{qr}^s\right)^2} \tag{12.2}$$

12.3   Conventional Flux Estimator

The CE which is presented in Equations (12.3) and (12.4) can be employed to compute the d and q-axis rotor fluxes.

$$\frac{\Psi_{dr}^s}{dt} = \frac{L_m R_r}{L_r} i_{ds}^s - \omega_r \Psi_{qr}^s - \frac{R_r}{L_r} \Psi_{dr}^s \tag{12.3}$$

$$\frac{\Psi_{qr}^s}{dt} = \frac{L_m R_r}{L_r} i_{qs}^s + \omega_r \Psi_{dr}^s - \frac{R_r}{L_r} \Psi_{qr}^s \tag{12.4}$$

Where,

i_{ds}^s —Stationary frame d axis current
i_{qs}^s —Stationary frame q axis current
Ψ_{dr}^s —Stationary Frame d axis rotor flux
Ψ_{qr}^s —Stationary Frame q axis rotor flux
R_r —Rotor resistance
L_r —Rotor inductance
L_m —Magnetizing inductance

The advantage of using CE is that the DFOC operation can be brought down to zero speed. It is free from drift and noise problem as compared to voltage model equations. From the equations, it is understood that CE require only stator side currents and rotor side speed as inputs for flux computation and the model is independent of stator voltage. However, note that the estimation accuracy is affected by the rotor resistance variation. If the rotor resistance value in the CE is not matched with the actual motor rotor resistance, the CE fails to compute correct value of the flux.

12.4   Rotor Flux Estimator Using CFBP-NN

To overcome the drawback of CE, estimator is designed using neural network. The flux estimator is modeled using 6 inputs with only stator current and rotor speed without the stator voltage as inputs. This is shown in Figure 12.2. This avoids the requirement of stator voltage measurement. Generally, voltage measurement is not required for DFOC. Only current and speed measurement are unavoidable requirements for DFOC and will serve as the inputs to the NN based flux estimator also. This eliminates the measurement of complex high frequency PWM stator motor voltage. The MATLAB/SIMULINK tool is used to simulate DFOC. 11,244 data were collected for various operating conditions. A three phase 1.1KW, 415 V, 50 Hz, 4 poles, 7.5 Nm IM is used for study. The detailed parameter is given in [6]. For hidden layers, the tan-sigmoid function is chosen. For output layer, pure-linear function is chosen. The Levenberg Marquardt algorithm (LM) is used to train CFBP-NN. The Average Square Error (ASE) achieved is 5.61×10^{-6} with 13 hidden layers. The NN-Model has

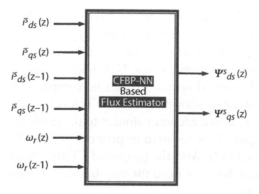

Figure 12.2 The flux estimator using CFBP-NN showing inputs and outputs.

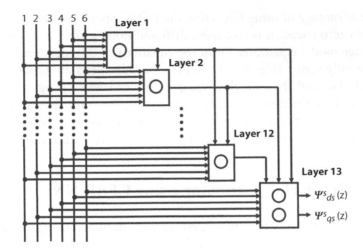

$1\text{-}i^s_{ds}(z),\ 2\text{-}i^s_{qs}(z),\ 3\text{-}i^s_{ds}(z-1),\ 4\text{-}i^s_{qs}(z-1),\ 5\text{-}\omega_r(z),\ 6\text{-}\omega_r(z-1)$

Figure 12.3 Flux Estimation using CFBP-NN Architecture.

the structure as 6-13(h)-2. The architecture of CFBP-NN for flux estimation is shown in Figure 12.3. The architecture has multiple hidden layers
with 1 neuron in each hidden layer. The layer receives inputs from all
previous layers.

12.5   Comparison of Proposed CFBP-NN With Existing CFBP-NN for Flux Estimation

The proposed CFBP-NN is compared with existing CFBP-NN [18] in terms
of accuracy, computational complexity and type of inputs. The number of
additions, multiplications and non-linear activation functions determines
the computational complexity of the NN model based flux estimator. The
number of mathematical operations can be computed using the formula
[17]. The comparison is shown in Table 12.1. It is found that the proposed
model gives the required accuracy similar to the existing model. The additions and multiplications required in proposed CFBP-NN model is lesser
than in the model [18]. Also the proposed CFBP-NN model is free from
stator voltage and does not need the requirement of tedious voltage measurement process.

Table 12.1 Comparison of proposed CFBP-NN with the model proposed in [18].

Flux estimator	CFBP-NN structure	MSE	Type of inputs	Adders	Multipliers	Tan-Sigmoid functions
Proposed CFBP-NN Model	6-13(h)-2	5.61×10^{-6}	Current and speed	194	194	13
CFBP-NN Model Proposed in [18]	8-13(h)-2	1.88×10^{-6}	Current and voltage	224	224	13

12.6 Performance Study of Proposed CFBP-NN Using MATLAB/SIMULINK

The performance of CFBP-NN and current model is investigated for R_r variation problem. The drive is operating at 75 rad/s under 100% rated load. To study R_r variation problem in MATLAB, dq-stationary frame model for induction motor is developed and the variation is created. The R_r is varied in a step fashion at 3 s. 50% change is created. The rotor flux (d-axis) estimated using CE and CFBP-NN are presented in Figure 12.4(a) and Figure 12.4(b) respectively. The rotor flux (q-axis) estimated using CE and CFBP-NN are presented in Figure 12.5(a) and Figure 12.5(b) respectively. Even in the presence of rotor resistance variation, the estimated flux using CFBP-NN tracks the actual flux of the machine. But flux estimated using CE deviates from the actual flux when the step change in R_r is effected at 3 s. For more clarity, the rotor flux locus diagram estimated using CE and CFBP-NN model is also shown in Figure 12.6(a) and Figure 12.6(b)

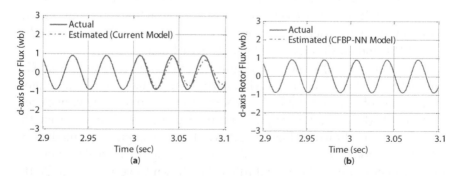

Figure 12.4 d-axis Flux: (a) CE and (b) CFBP-NN.

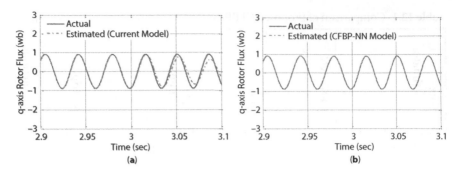

Figure 12.5 q-axis Flux: (a) CE and (b) CFBP-NN.

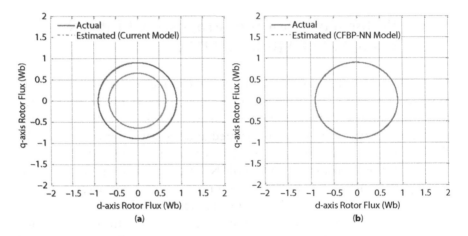

Figure 12.6 Locus Diagram (rotor flux): (a) CE (b) CFBP-NN.

respectively. The radius of the actual flux locus is 0.9006 Wb. It is centered on the zero co-ordinates. The radius of the locus of the flux estimated using the CFBP-NN is found to be 0.8998 Wb. The locus of the flux estimated using the CFBP-NN is also centered similar to the actual flux locus. But the radius of the locus diagram of rotor flux estimated using CE is decreased to 0.6522 Wb and fails to track the locus of actual flux.

The Figure 12.7(a) shows the magnitude of the flux estimated from CE. The magnitude of rotor flux deviates from the actual value. The magnitude of flux obtained using CFBP-NN tracks the actual value very closely (Figure 12.7(b)). The flux angle computed using CE deviates from the actual value as shown in Figure 12.8(a). The flux angle computed using CFBP-NN model tracks the actual very well (Figure 12.8(b)). Thus, the flux estimator designed using CFBP-NN is shown to very well handle the rotor resistance variation problem as compared to CE. The MSE is used as

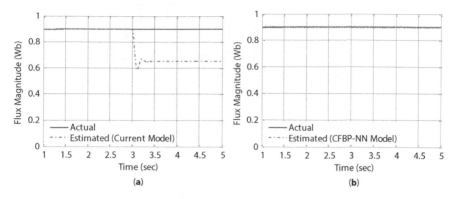

Figure 12.7 Flux Magnitude: (a) CE and (b) CFBP-NN.

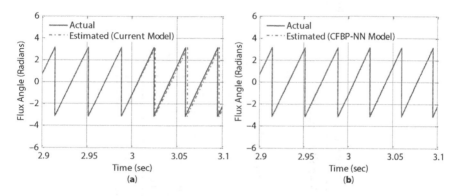

Figure 12.8 Flux angle: (a) CE and (b) CFBP-NN.

Table 12.2 Comparison of the CFBP-NN with CE to estimate flux for various % Rotor Resistance Variation.

%R_r change	d-axis rotor flux (MSE)		q-axis rotor flux (MSE)	
	Current model	CFBP-NN model	Current model	CFBP-NN model
10	0.0025	2.6572×10^{-5}	0.0026	2.7610×10^{-5}
20	0.0090	2.7590×10^{-5}	0.0088	2.8721×10^{-5}
30	0.0176	2.8281×10^{-5}	0.0177	3.0260×10^{-5}
40	0.0277	2.9541×10^{-5}	0.0277	3.1242×10^{-5}
50	0.0382	3.0438×10^{-5}	0.0388	3.2765×10^{-5}

Table 12.3 Comparison of the CFBP-NN with CE to estimate flux angle and magnitude for various % Rotor Resistance Variation.

%R_r Change	MSE for flux angle		Magnitude of Flux					
	Estimated using current model	Estimated using CFBP-NN model	Actual (Wb)	Estimated using current model (Wb)	%Error	Estimated using CFBP-NN model (Wb)	%Error
10	0.2628	0.0642	0.8996	0.8381	6.836	0.8998	−0.0222
20	0.4803	0.0571	0.9003	0.7839	12.9290	0.9002	0.0111
30	0.7023	0.0642	0.8999	0.7347	18.3575	0.9020	−0.2333
40	0.8669	0.0642	0.8997	0.6908	23.2188	0.9001	−0.0444
50	0.9555	0.0642	0.9006	0.6522	27.5816	0.8998	0.0888

the performance index for flux and field angle as it is instantaneous varying quantity. The % error is used as the performance index for resultant flux as it is constant with respect to time and not the instantaneous varying quantity. The computed MSE and %error is shown in Tables 12.2 and 12.3.

It is seen clearly that MSE of CE flux keeps on increases as the rotor resistance increases. But MSE of CFBP-NN flux shows good accuracy and tracks the actual flux very well. In the case of flux angle and magnitude, similar performance is observed.

12.7   Practical Implementation Aspects of CFBP-NN-Based Flux Estimator

To implement flux estimator designed using CFBP-NN in real time hardware, analog implementation technique with the use of operational amplifiers can be employed. But the digital technique to implement CFBP-NN based flux estimator has low noise sensitivity as compared to analog method of implementation. Also the development in the digital technology has made the NN estimator implementable on digital processors. The field programmable gate array (FPGA) preserves parallel operation and computes at high speed in real time as compared to sequential processor namely digital signal processor. To implement flux estimator designed using CFBP-NN in real time, the FPGA is found to be more suitable. This is because faster estimation of rotor flux is necessary to compute flux angle and magnitude for effective and efficient speed control. The major challenging issue in implementing CFBP-NN-based flux estimator on FPGA processor is to optimize execution time and resource. The execution time of CFBP-NN based estimator to a large extends depends on the computation of tan-sigmoid function. The tan-sigmoid function (5) contains non-linear exponent function. The series expansion method can be used but it gives large truncation error. The truncation error can be overcome by increasing the non-linear terms but it increases the computation time and also the resource. The LUT method can be used to reduce the computation time but higher accuracy requires more resource on FPGA. Hence Elliott function (6) is simple and does not contain any exponent function but it preserves non-linear nature similar to tan-sigmoid function. The plot of tan-sigmoid function and Elliott function is shown in Figure 12.9. The Elliott function contains only adder and divider function and provides faster rotor flux execution

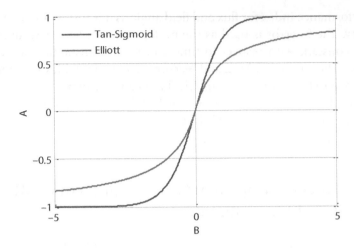

Figure 12.9 Plot of Tan-Sigmoid and Elliott function.

time with required accuracy on FPGA. Hence Elliott function is a good alternate for tan-sigmoid function.

The Layer Multiplexing Technique (LMT) is proposed to realize reduced cost FPGA-based NN [16]. The same concept can be used to realize reduced cost NN-flux estimator. One neuron with maximum number of inputs is implemented. The same neuron is repeatedly used to realize complete CFBP-NN-based flux estimator. The appropriate weights and biases for each neuron are correctly placed using the proper control logic. Using this method, the flux estimator using CFBP-NN is realized with the single neuron with 19 inputs. This method requires only 19 additions, 19 multiplications and 1 Elliott function. But without LMT, the implementation of CFBP-NN based flux estimator requires 194 additions, 194 multiplications, 13 Elliott functions which will increase the resource utilization in FPGA. Hence, using FPGA processor, the CFBP-NN can be implemented with Elliott function using LMT.

$$A = \frac{e^{B} - e^{-B}}{e^{B} + e^{-B}} \tag{12.5}$$

$$A = \frac{B}{1 + |B|} \tag{12.6}$$

12.8 Conclusion

In this chapter, a novel NN-flux estimator is proposed to compute flux angle and magnitude in DFOC OF IM. The NN model is designed using cascade forward back propagation neural network. The Proposed CFBP-NN Model compute rotor fluxes without the knowledge of stator voltage of the motor drive and eliminates the need of cumbersome high frequency PWM voltage measurement process. The CFBP-NN based flux estimator uses current and rotor speed as the inputs which is harmonics free as compared to stator PWM voltage. The current and speed can be easily measured without much difficulty as compared to PWM stator voltage measurement. The proposed CFBP-NN based flux estimator is compared with CE for rotor resistance variation. The CFBP-NN model performs similar to CE with the drive operating with nominal rotor resistance value and outperforms when the drive operating with change in the rotor resistance. The practical implementation aspects of CFBP-NN based flux estimator are also comprehensively presented in this paper. Hence it can be concluded that the proposed CFBP-NN for flux computation is found to be promising for DFOC of IM.

References

1. Venkadesan, A. and Sedhuraman, K., *Novel neural network based speed estimator for multilevel inverter fed sensorless field oriented controlled IM drive*, Springer Journal-Energy Systems, 2019.
2. Bose, B.K., *Modern Power Electronics and AC Drives*, Prentice-Hall, Inc, USA, 2002.
3. Himavathi, S. and Venkadesan, A., Flux Estimation Methods for High Performance Induction Motor Drives-A Survey. *Electric. India Magazine*, 54, 4, 116–126, April 2011.
4. Karanayil, B., Rahman, M.F., Grantham, C., Online Stator and Rotor Resistance Estimation Scheme Using Artificial Neural Networks for Vector Controlled Speed Sensorless Induction Motor Drive. *IEEE Trans. Ind. Electron.*, 54, 1, 167–176, February 2007.
5. Karanayil, B., Rahman, M.F., Grantham, C., Stator and Rotor Resistnace Observers for Induction Motor Drive Using Fuzzy Logic and Artificial Neural Networks. *IEEE T. Energy Conver.*, 20, 4, 771–780, December 2005.
6. Venkadesan, A., Himavathi, S., Muthuramalingam, A., A Novel NN Based Rotor Flux MRAS to overcome Low Speed Problems for Rotor Resistance

Estimation in Vector Controlled IM Drives. *Front. Energy-Springer*, 10, 4, 382–392, 2016.

7. Chitra, A. and Himavathi, S., A modified neural learning algorithm for online rotor resistance estimation in vector controlled induction motor drives. *Front. Energy*, 9, 22–30, 2015.

8. Venkadesan, A., Carrier Based PWM Technique and adaptive Neural Network Based Rotor Resistance Estimator for the Performance Enhancement of Vector Controlled Induction Motor Drives. *J. Eng. Res.*, 16, 1, 63–76, 2019.

9. Gadoue, S.M., Giaouris, D., Finch, J.W., Sensor-less Control of Induction Motor Drives at very Low and Zero Speeds Using Neural Network Flux Observer. *IEEE T. Ind. Electron.*, 56, 8, 3029–3039, August 2009.

10. Grzesiak, L.M. and Kazmierkowski, M.P., Improving Flux and Speed Estimators for Sensorless AC Drives. *IEEE Ind. Electron. M.*, 7, 8–19, Fall 2007.

11. Venkadesan, A., Himavathi, S., Muthuramalingam, A., Design of Feed-Forward Neural Network Based On-line Flux Estimator for Sensor-less Vector Controlled Induction Motor Drives. *Int. J. Recent Trends Eng Technol.*, 4, 3, 110–114, Nov 2010.

12. Himavathi, S., Anitha, D., Muthuramalingam, A., Feed-forward Neural Network Implementation in FPGA Using Layer Multiplexing for Effective Resource Utilization. *IEEE T. Neural Networ.*, 18, 3, 880–888, 2007.

13. Muthuramalingam, A., Venkadesan, A., Himavathi, S., On-Line Flux Estimator using Single Neuron Cascaded Neural Network Model for Sensor-less Vector Controlled Induction Motor Drives, in: *Proc. International Conference on System Dynamics and Control (ICSDC-2010)*, pp. 96–100, Manipal Insititute of Technology, Manipal, India, 2010.

14. Venkadesan, A., Himavathi, S., Muthuramalingam, A., A Novel SNC-NN-MRAS Based Speed Estimator for Sensorless Vector Controlled IM Drives. *Inter. J. Electric. Electron. Eng.*, 5, 2, 73–78, 2011.

15. Himavathi, S., Venkadesan, A., Muthuramalingam, A., Sedhuraman, K., Nonlinear System Modeling Using Single Neuron Cascaded Neural Network For Real-Time Applications. *ICTACT J. Soft Comput.*, 2, 3, 309–318, April 2012.

16. Venkadesan, A., Himavathi, S., Sedhuraman, K., Muthuramalingam, A., Design and field programmable gate array implementation of cascade neural network based flux estimator for speed estimation in induction motor drives. *IET Electr. Power Appl.*, 11, 1, 121–131, 2017.

17. Venkadesan, A., Himavathi, S., Muthuramalingam, A., Performance Comparison of Neural Architectures for On-Line Flux Estimation in Sensor-Less Vector Controlled IM Drives. *Springer J. Neural Comput. Appl.*, 22, 1735–1744, 2013.

18. Venkadesan, A., Himavathi, S., Muthuramalingam, A., A Simple Cascade NN based Flux Estimator to overcome Low Speed Problems in Sensor-less Direct Vector Controlled IM Drives. *Lecture Notes Electric. Eng.*, 326, 1593–1602, 2014.

13

A Review on Isolated DC–DC Converters Used in Renewable Power Generation Applications

Ingilala Jagadeesh and V. Indragandhi*

School of Electrical Engineering, Tamilnadu, India

Abstract

In this paper, we reported isolated DC–DC converters. Based on the review, the performances of isolated converters are evaluated. DC–DC CLCC and Dual active bridge (DAB) converters can attain bidirectional power flow, wide gain range, galvanic isolation, high power density and high energy efficiency for bidirectional electric vehicle charging systems. Gallium Nitride (GaN) devices have zero reverse recovery losses, very low gate drive losses and low output charge compared to a silicon MOSFET, which makes GaN devices relevant for high-efficiency power converters.

Keywords: Solar PV, isolated converters, electric vehicles (EV), bi-directional converters

13.1 Introduction

The maximum voltage gain of the cascaded boost converter, switched-capacitor converter and switched inductor converter are limited because of the high duty cycle. To overcome this problem, forward converter, bridge converter, fly-back and push-pull converter type isolated converters used to step-up the voltage [1]. Another common DC–DC isolated converter is the resonant converter, which can be used for the soft switching in the whole load spectrum. The full-bridge DC–DC current fed converter is

Corresponding author: indragandhi.v@vit.ac.in

Chitra A, P. Sanjeevikumar, Jens Bo Holm-Nielsen and S. Himavathi (eds.) Artificial Intelligent Techniques for Electric and Hybrid Electric Vehicles, (233–240) © 2020 Scrivener Publishing LLC

used to reduce the input current ripple. To attain smooth switching conditions and to transfer energy the transformer parasitic elements are worked as resonant elements [2, 3]. An isolated auxiliary current pump module is operated as a generic supporting module for step-down/step-up DC–DC converters [4]. The three-port bidirectional isolated converter is designed for concurrent power managing of a rechargeable battery, PV panel, and load [5]. The current mode control system is designed and implemented in conjunction with an isolated auxiliary current pump module for interleaved boost converters [6]. The isolated power converter contains three-winding transformer, two full-bridge rectifiers and a half-bridge inverter. The switching circuit is connected in parallel or series can be applied to isolated power converters to regulate the voltages [7]. The Isolated modular DC–DC converters need to be worked by an extreme ac-link frequency in order to decrease the size of the network, but this will result in boosted switching losses and reduced efficiency [8].

13.2   Isolated DC–DC Converter for Electric Vehicle Applications

DC–DC isolated converters are widely applied in battery chargers for EVs. These isolated converters interface between energy storage unit along with DC voltage connection. DAB and CLLC DC–DC converters can achieve galvanic isolation, wide gain range, high energy efficiency, bidirectional power flow, high power density and therefore have potential applications [9].

During the charging condition, the highest efficiency of the HBCLLC circuit is 96.5% and FBCLLC circuit is 95.0% in the discharging mode 97.4% and 96.1% respectively shown in Figures 13.1a and b. For the HBDAB and FBDAB circuits during the charging mode, the highest efficiencies are 93.9% and 95.1% in the discharging mode 94.3% and 93.5% (Figure 13.2a). At light load conditions the DAB switches lose ZVS and the single-phase shift control technique generates huge reactive power which decreases the efficiency in Bidirectional HBCLLC resonant converter circuit. Based on the high-frequency a DAB-BDC control strategy is derived from the conventional buck and boost DC–DC converter technique. The converter strategy ensures that buffering inductor current is controlled in BCM or DCM which outcomes in high efficiency (Figure 13.2b).

The DAB DC–DC converter is presented in Figure 13.3. The current fed hybrid DC–DC DAB converter is used to decrease the high-frequency input ripple current. All the power MOSFETs switches using the ZVS

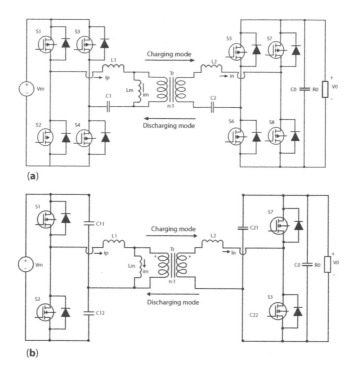

Figure 13.1 (a) Bidirectional FBCLLC resonant converter [9] (b) Bidirectional HBCLLC resonant converter [9].

technique. The DAB converter is designed for low-voltage FC power conditioning systems. The input side consists of two inductors and four power MOSFETs. The output side consists of four MOSFETs.

The auxiliary half-bridge contains two power MOSFETs and two capacitors. The input and output sides are linked by the transformer T. Here, the transformer turns ratio is 1: n.

The maximum conversion efficiency is more than 95%. With increasing output power, the efficiency increases until the efficiency reach its maximum value.

An interleaved bidirectional DC–DC isolated converter as shown in Figure 13.4. Switching losses are fairly decreased due to soft switching of semi-conductor switches that is ZVS of secondary switches and ZCS of primary switches. The converter operates in the reverse mode as a conventional full-bridge DC–DC voltage-fed converter by a load side filter. To attain ZCS of the low voltage side and ZVS of the high voltage side, normal phase modification modulation can be hired [11]. The efficiency comparison presented in Figure 13.5.

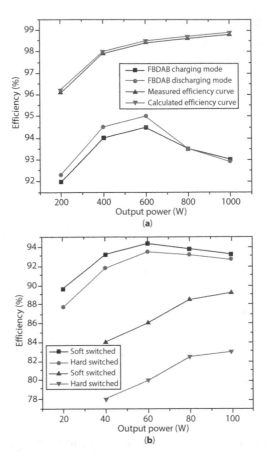

Figure 13.2 (a) Calculated and measured efficiency curves used for the DC–DC isolated DC–DC GaN converter and FBDAB converter [9, 13]. (b) Comparison of soft switched converter versus hard switched converter [5, 16].

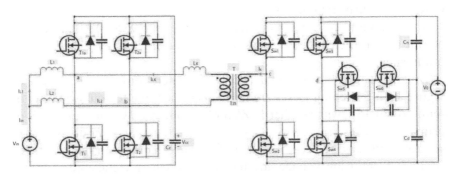

Figure 13.3 DAB DC–DC converter [10].

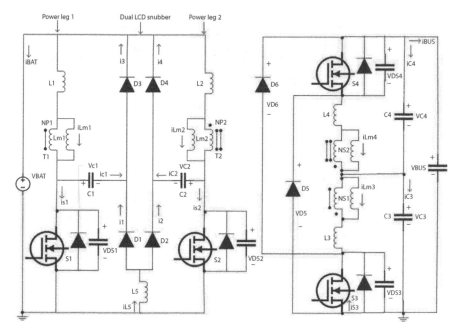

Figure 13.4 Interleaved bidirectional DC–DC Isolated converter circuit.

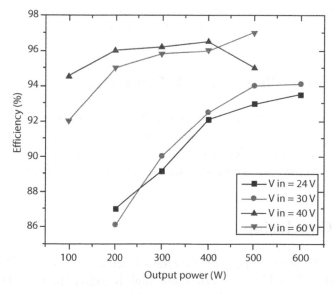

Figure 13.5 Graph between Efficiency versus output power [10, 23].

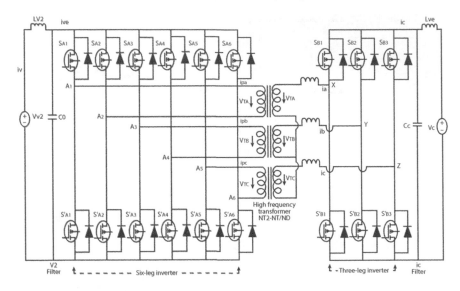

Figure 13.6 Three phase DC-DC converter.

The DC/DC bidirectional Three phase converter technique combines the six-leg converter and three-phase DAB converters. The topology can increase the power capability and withstand high currents of the DAB converter, preserving related modulation technique without changing its main features. Compared to conventional current fed 3-Φ bidirectional DC-DC converters this converter has additional switches (Figure 13.6).

13.3   Three-Phase DC–DC Converter

A three-phase DC–DC converter used as bidirectional converter in between the source and battery of the vehicle. The proposed 3-Φ DC–DC bidirectional converter with six leg inverter have more current capability compared to 3-Φ DAB converter. This converter is relevant for EV charging.

13.4   Conclusion

The DC–DC isolated power converters extensively used in EV and dc microgrids. The CLLC converters are slightly better than the DAB converters for comprehensive bidirectional EV charge systems. The voltage stress and di/dt value of the isolated three-port DC–DC bidirectional converter main switch have been decreased compared to the equivalent hard-switched converter. The converter peak efficiency is 94.5%. The LLC can achieve an efficiency of 98.39% undercharging condition and 97.80% in discharged condition. The GaN converter achieved 98.8% efficiency at 50% of the full load.

References

1. Li, R. and Shi, F., Control and Optimization of Residential Photovoltaic Power Generation System With High Efficiency Isolated Bidirectional DC–DC Converter. *IEEE Access*, 7, 116107–116122, 2019.
2. Wang, L., Zhu, Q., Yu, W., Huang, A.Q., A medium-voltage medium-frequency isolated DC–DC converter based on 15-kV SiC MOSFETs. *IEEE J. Emerg. Sel. Topics Power Electron.*, 5, 1, 100–109, 2016.
3. Emrani, A., Adib, E., Farzanehfard, H., Single-switch soft-switched isolated DC–DC converter. *IEEE Trans. Power Electronics*, 27, 4, 1952–1957, 2011.
4. Modepalli, K., Ali, M., Tao, L., Leila, P., Three-phase current-fed isolated DC–DC converter with zero-current switching. *IEEE Trans. Ind. Appl.*, 53, 1, 242–250, 2016.
5. Zeng, J., Qiao, W., Qu, L., An isolated three-port bidirectional DC–DC converter for photovoltaic systems with energy storage. *IEEE Trans. Ind. Appl.*, 51, 4, 3493–3503, 2015.
6. Kolluri, S. and Lakshmi Narasamma, N., A new isolated auxiliary current pump module for load transient mitigation of isolated/nonisolated step-up/step-down DC–DC converter. *IEEE T. Power Electron.*, 30, 10, 5991–6000, 2015.
7. Jou, H.-L., Huang, J.-J., Wu, J.-C., Wu, K.-D., Novel isolated multilevel DC–DC power converter. *IEEE T. Power Electron.*, 31, 4, 2690–2694, 2015.
8. Xing, Z., Ruan, X., You, H., Yang, X., Yao, D., Yuan, C., Soft-switching operation of isolated modular DC/DC converters for application in HVDC grids. *IEEE T. Power Electron.*, 31, 4, 2753–2766, 2015.
9. He, P. and Khaligh, A., Comprehensive analyses and comparison of 1 kW isolated DC–DC converters for bidirectional EV charging systems. *IEEE T. Trans. Elect.*, 3, 1, 147–156, 2016.
10. Sha, D., Xu, Y., Zhang, J., Yan, Y., Current-fed hybrid dual active bridge DC–DC converter for a fuel cell power conditioning system with reduced input current ripple. *IEEE T. Ind. Electron.*, 64, 8, 6628–6638, 2017.
11. Xuewei, P. and Rathore, A.K., Novel bidirectional snubberless naturally commutated soft-switching current-fed full-bridge isolated DC/DC converter for fuel cell vehicles. *IEEE T. Ind. Electron.*, 61, 5, 2307–2315, 2013.
12. Waltrich, G., Hendrix, M.A.M., Duarte, J.L., Three-phase bidirectional DC/DC converter with six inverter legs in parallel for EV applications. *IEEE T. Ind. Electron.*, 63, 3, 1372–1384, 2015.

13. Ramachandran, R. and Nymand, M., Experimental demonstration of a 98.8% efficient isolated DC–DC GaN converter. *IEEE T. Ind. Electron.*, 64, 11, 9104–9113, 2016.

14. Chen, Y., Zhao, S., Li, Z., Wei, X., Kang, Y., Modeling and control of the isolated DC–DC modular multilevel converter for electric ship medium voltage direct current power system. *IEEE J. Emerg. Select. Topics Power Electron.*, 5, 1, 124–139, 2016.

15. Cong, L. and Lee, H., A 1–2-MHz 150–400-V GaN-based isolated DC–DC bus converter with monolithic slope-sensing ZVS detection. *IEEE J. Solid-State Circuits*, 53, 12, 3434–3445, 2018.

16. Yeşilyurt, H. and Bodur, H., New active snubber cell for high power isolated PWM DC–DC converters. *IET Circ. Device. Syst.*, 13, 6, 822–829, 2019.

17. Liu, C., Mandal, D., Yao, Z., Sun, M., Todsen, J., Johnson, B., Kiaei, S., Bakkaloglu, B. A 50-V Isolation, 100-MHz, 50-mW Single-Chip Junction Isolated DC-DC Converter With Self-Tuned Maximum Power Transfer Frequency. *IEEE Trans. Circuits Systems II: Express Briefs*, 66, 6, 1003–1007, 2018.

18. Huang, R. and Mazumder, S.K., A soft-switching scheme for an isolated dc/dc converter with pulsating dc output for a three-phase high-frequency-link PWM converter. *IEEE T. Power Electron.*, 24, 10, 2276–2288, 2009.

19. Kan, J., Wu, Y., Tang, Y., Zhang, B., Zhang, Z., Dual active full-bridge bidirectional converter for V2G charger based on high-frequency AC buck-boost control strategy, in: *2016 IEEE Transportation Electrification Conference and Expo, Asia-Pacific (ITEC Asia-Pacific)*, Busan, Korea, pp. 046–050, IEEE, 2016.

20. Xuewei, P. and Rathore, A.K., Comparison of bi-directional voltage-fed and current-fed dual active bridge isolated dc/dc converters low voltage high current applications, in: *2014 IEEE 23rd International Symposium on Industrial Electronics (ISIE)*, Istanbul, Turkey, pp. 2566–2571, IEEE, 2014.

21. Sha, D. and Xu, G., *High-Frequency Isolated Bidirectional Dual Active Bridge DC–DC Converters with Wide Voltage Gain.*, Springer, United States, 2018.

22. Zhan, Y., Guo, Y., Zhu, J., Li, L., Input current ripple reduction and high efficiency for PEM fuel cell power conditioning system, in: *In 2017 20th International Conference on Electrical Machines and Systems (ICEMS)*, Sydney, Australia, pp. 1–6, IEEE, 2017.

23. Wu, H., Mu, T., Ge, H., Xing, Y., Full-range soft-switching-isolated buck-boost converters with integrated interleaved boost converter and phase-shifted control. *IEEE T. Power Electron.*, 31, 2, 987–999, 2015.

14

Basics of Vector Control of Asynchronous Induction Motor and Introduction to Fuzzy Controller

S.S. Biswas

M. Tech (PED), Engineer In Charge (R&D), BHAVINI, Kalpakkam, India

Abstract

From early 1900s when the speed control of the prime mover was concerned, separately excited DC machine were dominating in the field control of any electrical machine. A separately excited DC machine can be controlled in a decoupled manner but for combustion engines, the torque and speed are highly coupled in nature. In V/F control to change the frequency we need to change the voltage to maintain the flux. But the problem is the transfer function of the system is of higher order, may be of 5th order transfer function. Due to this higher order system effect, the flux response becomes sluggish and it takes quite more time to settle down to the desired value. To improve the performance, vector control method of squirrel cage asynchronous induction machine is evolved which is nothing but to operate squirrel cage asynchronous induction machine analogous to a separately excited DC machine to obtain a better dynamic response. A complete analysis and simulation of Indirect Field Oriented (IDFOC) control of asynchronous squirrel cage induction motor (ASCIM) and circuit concept is included in this chapter.

Keywords: Separately excited DC machine, squirrel cage asynchronous induction machine, PID controller, fuzzy logic, vector control

14.1 Introduction

In rotating electrical machine, electrical energy converted from electrical domain to mechanical domain in terms of torque and speed in rpm. In separately excited DC machine, the unique advantage is that machine can

Email: sitangshu_sekharbiswas@srmuniv.edu.in

Chitra A, P. Sanjeevikumar, Jens Bo Holm-Nielsen and S. Himavathi (eds.) *Artificial Intelligent Techniques for Electric and Hybrid Electric Vehicles*, (241–258) © 2020 Scrivener Publishing LLC

be controlled in a decoupled manner even though the torque and speed are highly coupled in nature for mechanical prime movers. For an example, we can say when we are riding our bike in a plane road, we can go to fifth gear to raise the speed but if suddenly inclined road is there or it is rough or the torque requirement is high, we cannot operate our bike in fifth gear. Definitely we have to come down to third or second because torque requirement is high, so these are the basic issue with internal combustion engines. Due to this coupled nature, torque and speed cannot be controlled in an isolated manner but same thing is possible in separately excited DC machine because the torque and flux circuit those are electrically isolated. So the torque and flux can be control in an isolated manner in electrical prime mover. But the problem in the DC machine is, it's not maintenance free and it cannot operate in hazardous environment like refineries or pharmaceuticals or any petrochemicals industries where the hazard free operation is desirable. So to avoid those kinds of things, squirrel cage asynchronous induction machine was evolved.

These machines are very robust, rugged and it can operate in hazardous environment also. Due to these advantages, today if we take statistics of total prime mover of any process and power or any kind of industries, we can see more than 95% of prime movers are asynchronous induction motor. Here by the virtue of its construction, it is obvious that the rotor is getting magnetized due to stator field and as this is happening so definitely the rotor flux will be always lagged from the stator flux. That's why the rotor will never able to catch the speed of the synchronous rotating speed of the stator flux. As it is always being lagging and it is not synchronous with stator flux speed, that's why it is called asynchronous induction machine. These things make the task of control engineer very difficult when high performance dynamic response of the machine is concerned in connection with the decoupled control of it.

We know in V/F control, to change the frequency, we need also to change the voltage to maintain the flux but the problem is the transfer function of the system is a higher order may be it is 5th order transfer function. Due to this higher order system effect, the flux response is become sluggish, so it is taking quite more time to settle down to the desired value. We can take an example that we change the flux by changing the frequency to change the torque, because for an induction machine, torque is controlled by slip. So suddenly our requirement is to increase torque hence definitely we have to change the frequency, so we are changing the frequency, torque is getting changed but to maintain the flux, our voltage need to be changed. In this operation to maintain the flux, the asynchronous squirrel cage induction machine can be operated analogous to a separately excited machine using Vector control method.

So Vector control method of squirrel cage asynchronous induction machine is nothing but to operate squirrel cage asynchronous induction machine analogous to a separately excited DC machine by positioning the instantaneous rotor flux with the direct axis of synchronous rotating reference frame. If we are doing so, the torque equation of the asynchronous induction machine will be converted as separately excited DC machine which is nothing but called vector control or field oriented control.

14.2   Dynamics of Separately Excited DC Machine

By nature of construction in Figure 14.1, the armature circuit and field circuit is isolated. There is no electrical connection in between, only some magnetically coupling exists. So in armature side, the armature current and in field side, the field current can be controlled separately. Which is not possible is induction machine. In above phasor diagram it is clear that rotor flux will be always lagged from the stator flux by a quadrature and it is not influenced by each other.

Torque equation of separately excited DC machine is

$$T = K \Psi_f I_a \qquad (14.1)$$

Where, K = constant
Ψ_f = field flux
I_a = Armature current

Back EMF equation of separately excited DC machine is

$$E_b = K\omega\Psi \qquad (14.2)$$

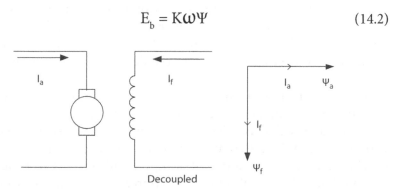

Figure 14.1 Equivalent circuit of separately excited DC machine and phasor diagram of armature flux versus field flux.

Where, K = constant
 ω = rpm
 Ψ = flux

From both the Equations (14.1) and (14.2), there is no relationship between torque and rpm and back EMF is totally independent of armature current. Both the armature flux (Ψ_a) and field flux (Ψ_f) are perpendicular to each other. So field flux is not getting interfered by armature flux and *via* versa. To change the torque we need to change the armature current by keeping field current constant.

14.3   Clarke and Park Transforms

Clarke and Park transforms methods are normally fit in field-oriented control of three-phase AC machines. The Clarke transform transfer the time domain components of a three-phase system (in abc frame) to two components in an orthogonal stationary frame (αβ). The Park transform transfer the components in the αβ frame to an orthogonal rotating reference frame (dq). Utilizing such transforms in a consecutive way simplifies computations by transferring AC voltage and current waveform into DC signals.

The DQZ transform is made of the Park and Clarke transformation matrices. The Clarke transforms converts vectors in the *ABC* reference frame to the *αβγ* reference frame. The primary value of the Clarke transform is isolating that part of the *ABC*-referenced vector which is common to all three components of the vector; it isolates the common-mode component (i.e., the Z component).

The Park transform converts vectors in the *XYZ* reference frame to the *DQZ* reference frame. The primary value of the Park transform is to rotate the reference frame of a vector at an arbitrary frequency. The Park transform shifts the frequency spectrum of the signal such that the arbitrary frequency now appears as dc and the old dc appears as the negative of the arbitrary frequency.

In phasor diagram (Figure 14.2) consider stator α axis as a reference axis, this axis is perpendicular with stator β axis. Similarly q axis is perpendicular with d axis. The entire d and q axis is rotating with synchronous speed. By differentiating Θs with respect to time, it will give synchronous speed. By differentiating Θr with respect to time, it will give mechanical speed of rotor. The difference between d axis and rotor α axis gives slip frequency.

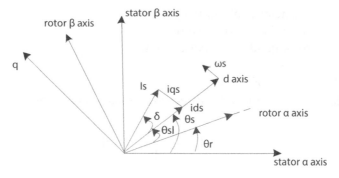

Figure 14.2 Phasor diagram.

In phasor diagram

Let,

α_s = stator phase A axis
α_r = stator phase A axis
α–β = stator fixed reference frame
d–q = synchronous rotating reference frame

Let

V_{sd} = stator voltage component on direct axis of synchronous rotating reference frame.

I_{sd} = stator current component on direct axis of synchronous rotating reference frame.

Rs = stator resistance.

ω_s = synchronous frequency.

V_{sq} = stator voltage component on quadrature axis of synchronous rotating reference frame.

Ψ_{sq} = stator flux on quadrature axis of synchronous rotating reference frame.

Ψ_{rq} = rotor flux on quadrature axis of synchronous rotating reference frame.

Ψ_{sd} = stator flux on direct axis of synchronous rotating reference frame

I_{sq} = stator current component on quadrature axis of synchronous rotating reference frame.

P (rot) = total rotational power.

L_{ss} = total stator inductance (leakage + mutual)

L_{rr} = total rotor inductance (leakage + mutual)

L_m = inductance of mutual part.
I_{rd} = rotor direct axis current.
I_{rq} = rotor quadrature axis current.
Γ = torque
P = number of poles

Standard equation for stator direct axis voltage is given by

$$V_{sd} = R_S I_{sd} + \frac{d\Psi sd}{dt} - \omega_s \Psi_{sq} \qquad (14.3)$$

$$\text{Let } V_{sd}(rot) = -\omega_s \Psi_{sq} \qquad (14.4)$$

Similarly Standard equation for stator direct axis voltage is given by

$$V_{sq} = R_S I_{sq} + \frac{d\Psi sq}{dt} + \omega_s \Psi_{sd} \qquad (14.5)$$

$$\text{Let } V_{sq}(rot) = \omega_s \Psi_{sd} \qquad (14.6)$$

Total rotational power is given by

$$P(rot) = V_{sd}(rot) * I_{sd} + V_{sq}(rot) I_{sq} \qquad (14.7)$$

Substitute Equations (14.4) and (14.6) in Equation (14.7)

$$P(rot) = -\omega_s \Psi_{sq} I_{sd} + \omega_s \Psi_{sd} I_{sq} \qquad (14.8)$$

$$\text{Let } \Psi_{sd} = L_{ss} I_{sd} + L_m I_{rd} \qquad (14.9)$$

$$\Psi_{sq} = L_{ss} I_{sq} + L_m I_{rq} \qquad (14.10)$$

Equations (14.9) and (14.10) in Equation (14.8)

$$
\begin{aligned}
P(rot) &= -\omega_s (L_{ss} I_{sq} + L_m I_{rq}) I_{sd} + \omega_s (L_{ss} I_{sd} + L_m I_{rd}) I_{sq} \\
&= \omega_s [-(L_{ss} I_{sq} + L_m I_{rq}) I_{sd} + (L_{ss} I_{sd} + L_m I_{rd}) I_{sq}] \\
&= \omega_s [-L_{ss} I_{sq} I_{sd} - L_m I_{rq} I_{sd} + L_{ss} I_{sd} I_{sq} + L_m I_{rd} I_{sq}] \\
&= \omega_s [L_m I_{rd} I_{sq} - L_m I_{rq} I_{sd}] \\
&= \omega_s L_m [I_{rd} I_{sq} - I_{rq} I_{sd}] \qquad (14.11)
\end{aligned}
$$

$$\text{Let } \Psi_{rd} = L_{rr}I_{rd} + L_m I_{sd} \tag{14.12}$$

$$I_{rd} = \frac{\Psi rd - Lm\, Isd}{Lrr}$$

$$\Psi_{rq} = L_{rr}I_{rq} + L_m I_{sq} \tag{14.13}$$

$$I_{rq} = +\frac{\Psi rq - Lm\, Isq}{Lrr}$$

Substituting back in equation (14.11)

$$P(\text{rot}) = \omega_s L_m\Big[\frac{\Psi rd - Lm\, Isd}{Lrr}I_{sq} - \frac{\Psi rq - Lm\, Isq}{Lrr}I_{sd}\Big]$$

$$P(\text{rot}) = \frac{Lm\;\omega s}{Lrr}\Big[\Psi_{rd}I_{sq} - L_m I_{sq}I_{sd} - \Psi_{rq}I_{sd} + L_m I_{sq}I_{sd}\Big]$$

$$P(\text{rot}) = \frac{Lm\;\omega s}{Lrr}\Big[\Psi_{rd}I_{sq} - \Psi_{rq}I_{sd}\Big] \tag{14.14}$$

We know that

$$P(\text{rot}) = \Gamma * \omega_s\,(\text{mech}) \tag{14.15}$$

In order to get mechanical speed, the synchronous speed will be divided by $\dfrac{P}{2}$

Equating Equations (14.14) and (14.15)

$$\Gamma * \frac{\omega s}{p/2} = \frac{Lm\;\omega s}{Lrr}\Big[\Psi_{rd}I_{sq} - \Psi_{rq}I_{sd}\Big]$$

Torque is given by,

$$\Gamma = \frac{p/2}{\omega s}\Big[\frac{Lm\;\omega s}{Lrr}\big(\Psi_{rd}I_{sq} - \Psi_{rq}I_{sd}\big)\Big]$$

$$\Gamma = \frac{P}{2}\left[\frac{Lm}{Lrr}\left(\Psi_{rd}I_{sq} - \Psi_{rq}I_{sd}\right)\right] \tag{14.16}$$

As 3 phases is converted to 2 phase, then for power balance, 3/2 is multiplied and torque Equation (14.16) is converted as

$$\Gamma = \frac{3}{2}\frac{P}{2}\left[\frac{Lm}{Lrr}\left(\Psi_{rd}I_{sq} - \Psi_{rq}I_{sd}\right)\right] \tag{14.17}$$

Now let us assume $\dfrac{3}{2}\dfrac{P}{2}\dfrac{Lm}{lrr} = K$

We know vector control is nothing but to align instantaneous rotor flux with the direct axis of synchronous rotating reference frame which makes rotor quadrature axis flux to zero.

$$\Psi_{rq} = 0$$

So that $\Gamma = k\left(\Psi_{rd}I_{sq}\right)$
Let us assume $\Psi_{rd} = \Psi_f$ and $I_{sq} = I_a$

$\Gamma = k\left(\Psi_f I_a\right)$ which is analogous to Equation (14.1)

Rotor voltage on direct axis of synchronous reference frame is given by,

$$V_{rd} = R_r I_{rd} + \frac{d\,\Psi rd}{dt} - (\omega s - \omega r)\Psi rq \tag{14.18}$$

In the Figure 14.3, reference flux and i_{sd} is compared to obtain v_{sd}. To establish vector control, we need to make Ψrq is equal to zero. In rotor construction of synchronous induction machine, the rotor bars are short circuited through short circuit ring at both the end. So as it is short circuited, voltage Vrd should be zero.

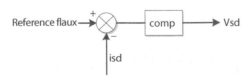

Figure 14.3 Flux loop.

Therefore,

$$R_r I_{rd} + \frac{d\,\Psi rd}{dt} = 0 \tag{14.19}$$

Assuming $\dfrac{d\left(Lm\,imr \right)}{dt} + R_r L_{rd} = 0$ (14.20)

(Rotor getting magnetized by mutual part)

$$\Psi rd = L_{rr}\,I_{rd} + Lm\,i_{sd} = L_m\,i_{mr}$$

$$\text{Let } I_{rd} = \frac{Lm}{Lrr}\,(i_{mr} - i_{sd}) \tag{14.21}$$

Using Equation (14.21) in Equation (14.20)

$$\frac{d\left(Lm\,imr \right)}{dt} + R_r \frac{Lm}{Lrr}(i_{mr} - i_{sd}) = 0$$

$$\frac{d\,imr}{dt} + \frac{1}{\Gamma r}(i_{mr} - i_{sd}) = 0 \tag{14.22}$$

Where Γr = rotor time constant.
In Laplace domain

$$\left(s + \frac{1}{\Gamma r} \right) i_{mr} = \frac{isd}{\Gamma r} \tag{14.23}$$

So in steady state $i_{mr} = i_{sd}$

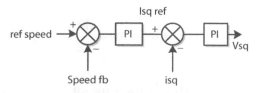

Figure 14.4 Speed loop and torque loop.

Figure 14.4, consist of two loops namely speed loop and torque loop. The speed loops produces torque components i.e. I_{sq} reference that will be compared with the actual i_{sq}. When reference speed is compared with speed feedback an error signal is generated. This error signal is compensated using PI regulator and it's producing I_{sq} reference current. This I_{sq} reference current again is compared with actual machine isq which is again regulated through PI regulator and then it produces V_{sq}.

$$\text{Let } V_{rq} = R_r i_{rq} + \frac{d\Psi rq}{dt} + (\omega s - \omega r)\,\Psi rd \tag{14.24}$$

$$\omega_{sl} = -\frac{Rr\ irq}{\Psi rd} \tag{14.25}$$

Where ω_{sl} = slip speed.
$\Psi rq = 0 = L_{rr} i_{rq} + Lm\ i_{sq}$ (as it is aligned with direct axis of syn. Rotating reference frame)

$$\text{Let } i_{rq} = -\frac{Lm}{Lrr}\ i_{sq} \tag{14.26}$$

Equation (14.26) in Equation (14.25)

$$\omega sl = -\frac{Rr * - \dfrac{Lm}{Lrr}\ isq}{\Psi rd}$$

$$= \frac{Rr\ isq}{Lrr\ Imr}$$

$$\text{Slip speed }(\omega_{sl}) = \frac{1}{\Gamma r}\frac{isq}{isd} \tag{14.27}$$

$$\omega_{sl} + \omega r = \omega s = \frac{d\theta s}{dt}$$

$$\theta s = \int (\omega sl + \omega r)\,dt \tag{14.28}$$

14.4   Model Explanation

In Figure 14.5, simulation circuit mainly consists of inverter, current feed-back loop, first order low pass filter, rpm sensor and ABC to DQ transformation where Θ_s is required to be estimated and which gives out I_d and I_q components. A constant torque of 0.02 Nm is applied to the induction motor. For direct axis loop, the set magnetization current is compared with actual I_d. The output from PI regulator consisting of corresponding gain and time constant is feed to the limiter. The limiter is always better, which will not allow the loop to shot up and used for anti-wind up protection. The output from this limiter is feed to the ABC to DQ transformation. The sensed speed compared with set speed, after compensator, feed to the lim-iter, so the torque reference current may not shoot up more than 40 amp and then it's again compared with I_q to generate quadrature voltage com-ponent Once the modulating signal i.e. V_a, V_b, and V_c is generated from ABC to DQ transformation is compared with comparator to generate the switching pulses. Q_1, Q_3 and Q_5 are the generated pulse form comparator which is given to the inverter IGBTs.

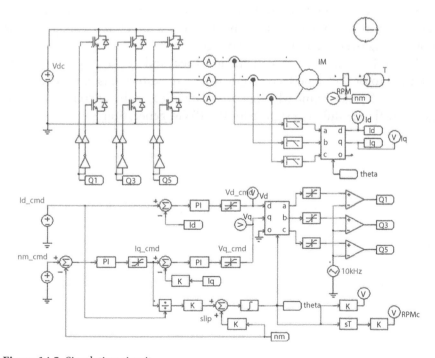

Figure 14.5 Simulation circuit.

Inverse rotor time constant is required for Θ_s estimation

Inverse rotor time constant = rotor resistances/(leakage + mutual) inductance

$$= 0.156/(0.00074 + 0.041)$$

Inverse rotor time constant $= 3.73$

14.5   Motor Parameters

Figure 14.6, is a plot of direct axis current (I_d) and quadrature axis current (I_q) with X axis in time domain in s. In this figure the direct axis current (I_d) is dominating over quadrature axis current (I_q). Immediately after the start, the direct axis current get settled very fast but for quadrature current takes slightly more time to settle down, at around 0.6 s.

Figure 14.7 is a plot of three phase sequence current I_{Sa}, I_{Sb} and I_{Sc} in time domain in s which infer that the inrush current is well restricted to occur the soft start of the machine.

Figure 14.8 is a plot of speed in rpm verse time in s. In this plot, at beginning the speed increases and becomes constant at set value which shows an improved dynamic response.

Figure 14.6 is a plot of direct axis voltage (V_d) and quadrature axis voltage (V_q) in time domain in s. In this figure the direct axis voltage (V_d) is dominating over quadrature axis voltage (V_q).

Figure 14.9 shows the instantaneous direct and quadrature axis voltage after the rotor flux is perfectly aligned with the direct axis of synchronous rotating reference frame which in turn converted to abc reference frame to generate the modulating signals for the PWM generation.

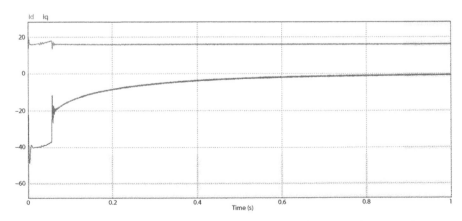

Figure 14.6 Plot of direct axis current (I_d) and quadrature axis current (I_q).

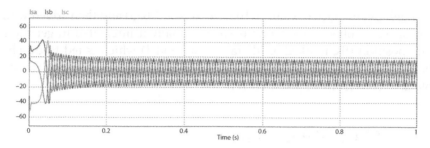

Figure 14.7 Phase currents plot.

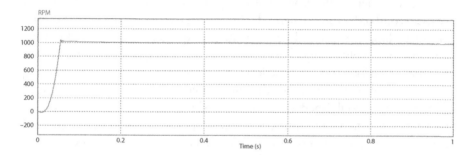

Figure 14.8 Speed plot.

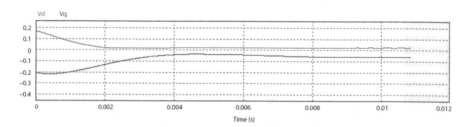

Figure 14.9 Plot of direct axis voltage (V_d) and quadrature axis voltage (V_q).

We know from Equation (14.27), to obtain the slip speed, i_{sq} and i_{sd} will be divided and should be multiplied with inverse rotor time constant. In the model, the bottom most theta estimation loop, there is a gain block of value 3.73 (Inverse rotor time constant) just after the division. Now the slip speed is to be added with rotor speed to get synchronous speed. Entire control is established in stator side, hence the rotor speed is to be taken in stator side and then is to be added with sleep speed. Hence the RPM is converted to radian/s by multiplying ($\pi/30$) and then by (P/2 for this model it is 3) to take it in stator side. In the model, RPM (marked as nm) is passed through a gain block of value $\pi/10$ (which is$(\pi/30)*3$) and then added with slip speed to obtain synchronous speed. Finally it integrated to get rotor flux position (θs, marked as 'theta' in the model) which is fed to dq-abc block to generate modulating signal for inverter switching and to abc-dq block to convert three phase current to i_d and i_q.

14.6   PI Regulators Tuning

PI regulator tuning is mostly done by trial and error method but it needs more practical experience and proper knowledge of process control. In this model, we use second order tuning method. Three loops namely torque loop, flux loop and speed loop which has different natural frequencies but we need to tune both together to obtain high performance dynamic response from the motor. In tuning, each loop transfer function is simplified to a first order system using some fair approximation. After that the closed loop transfer function with compensator is established which consist of motor passive parameters like inductance, resistance and time constants, proportional gain (k_p) and integral gain (k_i) of the compensator. Then denominator is simplified and compared with standard second order control system equation ($s^2 + 2\xi\omega_n s + \omega_n^2$).

For better dynamic response and stable performance, all the loops are considered as critically damped with $\zeta = 1$, please refer Figure 14.10, how

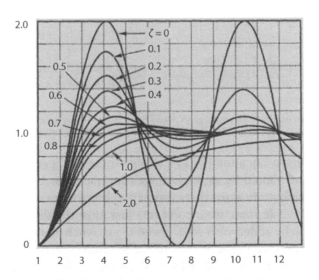

Figure 14.10 Second order response with respect to damping ratio.

Table 14.1 Motor specification values.

Name	Values
Rated frequency	50 Hz
No. of poles	6
Rated speed	1,000 rpm
Rotor resistance	0.156 Ω
Stator resistance	0.294 Ω
Stator inductance	0.00139 H
Rotor inductance	0.00074 H
Magnetizing inductance	0.041 H
Inertia	0.002 H
Viscous friction	0.001 Nm/(rad/s)

Table 14.2 Values different loops of PI controller.

PI controller	K_p	K_i
Speed controller	0.13	0.4242
Flux controller	4.65	8.94
Torque controller	13.4	197.45

the response varied with ζ. Form the practical experience, if a motor used in fan or pump application, the natural frequencies of torque, flux and speed loops are considered 100, 10 and 1 Hz respectively. After the tuning with simulation and lab module, the results obtained are tabulated in Tables 14.1 and 14.2. The performance again can be enhanced if PI regulator is replaced with fuzzy controller.

Figure 14.11 presents the laboratory setup for rapid prototyping of the concept where semikron IGBTs are used and skyper32 driver circuit is installed to generate complementary switching pulses. This setup has been used to soft-start a 30kW asynchronous induction motor and all the performance parameters are validated w.r.t. to the concept mentioned in this chapter.

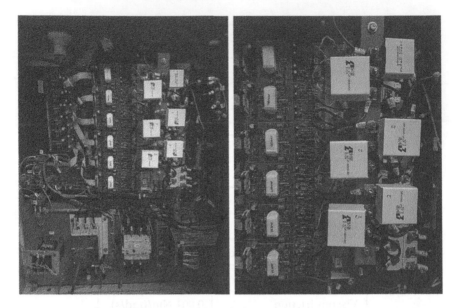

Figure 14.11 Laboratory setup to benchmark the model.

14.7   Future Scope to Include Fuzzy Control in Place of PI Controller

Fuzzy logic control is a special class of artificial intelligent. Normally when we need very tight control over the output, we need to introduce one compensator, basically it will take the error signal which is nothing but the differences between the desired set point and actual output obtained from the plant. Then it is transferred in very loop interval and producing controlled exaction to the plant so that it can maintain the output at the desired level. Conventionally we use PI regulator because it is very simple to implement but the thing is, to get very accurate high performance dynamic response, the tuning of the controller is very essential. Eventually the PI controller only can take linear gains but some time due to some transient or due to nonlinearity of the plant if compensator required nonlinear gains, that time the PI regulator is not able to cater the requirement and we need to introduce a model free adaptive controller. The dynamic response of fuzzy controller is much better than the PI regulator and also fuzzy controller is a semi model free adaptive controller which can take non-linear gain factors.

In Figure 14.12, basic construction of fuzzy controller is shown which can be used in torque, flux and speed loop as a compensator for better dynamic response. The top model in Figure 14.12 is a classical PI controller

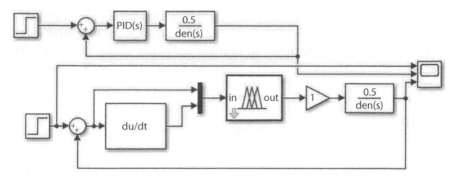

Figure 14.12 Fuzzy PI controller.

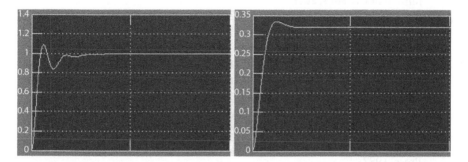

Figure 14.13 Output response of PI regulator (Left), Output response of Fuzzy regulator (Right).

and bottom one is the fuzzy compensator. A second order plant transfer function is considered to establish the output response of both the cases with a unit step input. Figure 14.13 shows the comparison of PI and fuzzy controller where it exhibits better dynamic response.

For the above figure, it is obvious that PI regulator exhibits with over-shoot whereas fuzzy controller provides better output response. Hence it is being proposed to replace the PI regulators in vector control by fuzzy controller as future work to improve the control.

14.8   Conclusion

In process and power industries, speed control is very much concerned, that time we need to use some electrical prime movers through which we can vary the speed. But the problem somewhere arises that the torque and speed is needed to be controlled in an isolated manner. For that purpose this method is more useful. Conventionally the use of PI regulator it is very simple to imple-ment but to get very accurate high performance dynamic response the tuning of the controller is very essential. Perfect tuning is impossible unless each loop is linearized properly. In order to overcome this limitation the fuzzy controller can be used. The dynamic response of fuzzy controller is much better the PI regulator and also fuzzy controller is and semi model free adaptive control.

References

1. Vaez-Zadeh, S., and Reicy, S.H., Sensorless vector control of single-phase induction motor drives. In *2005 International Conference on Electrical Machines and Systems*, vol. 3, pp. 1838–1842, IEEE, 2005.
2. Bose, B.K., *Power Electronics in Renewable Energy Systems and Smart Grid*, John Wiley & Sons, 2019.
3. Bose, B.K., *Power Electronics and Motor Drives-Advances and Trends*, Elsevier/Academic Press, 2010.
4. Bose, B.K., *Modern Power Electronics and AC Drives*, Prentice-Hall, 416, 1986.
5. Bose, B.K., *Power Electronics and AC Drives*, vol. 5, Prentice-Hall, Bose, 416, 1986.
6. Bose, Bimal K., and Bimal K. Bose, eds. *Power Electronics and Variable Frequency Drives*, Vol. 996. Piscataway, NJ: IEEE Press, 1997.
7. Bose, Bimal K., *Modern Power Electronics*, IEEE Transactions on Power Electronics 7, no. 1, 2–16, 1992.
8. Bose, B.K., *Microcomputer Control of Power Electronics and Drives*, IEEE Press, 1987.
9. Bose, B.K., *Adjustable Speed AC Drive Systems*, IEEE Press Selected Reprint Series, New York: IEEE Press, 1981, edited by Bose, Bimal K. 1981.
10. Rashid, M.H., *Power Electronics: Devices, Circuits and Applications*. Elsevier, 2010.
11. Rashid, M.H. and Rashid, H.M., *SPICE for Power Electronics and Electric Power, Second Edition*, Electrical and Computer Engineering.
12. Rashid, M.H., *Power Electronics: Circuits, Devices, and Applications: International Edition*. In University of West Florida. Pearson Prentice Hall, 2004.
13. Liu, Shuxi, Shan Li, and Huihui Xiao. Vector control system of induction machine supplied by three-level inverter based on a fast svpwm algorithm. In *2010 International Conference on Intelligent System Design and Engineering Application*, vol. 2, pp. 810–813, IEEE, 2010.
14. Reddy, Siddavatam Ravi Prakash, and Umanand Loganathan. Improving the Dynamic Response of Scalar Control of Induction Machine Drive Using Phase Angle Control. In *IECON 2018-44th Annual Conference of the IEEE Industrial Electronics Society*, pp. 541–546, IEEE, 2018.
15. Wang, Ding. Hybrid fuzzy vector control for single phase induction motor. In *2010 International Conference on Computing, Control and Industrial Engineering*, vol. 2, pp. 122–125, IEEE, 2010.
16. Hybrid Fuzzy Vector Control for Single Phase Induction Motor, ieeexplore. ieee.org/document/5491982/

Index

Printed and bound by CPI Group (UK) Ltd, Croydon, CR0 4YY

27/10/2024

14580471-0001